Leadership for a Better World

Leadership for a Better World

Understanding the Social Change Model of Leadership Development

Susan R. Komives, Wendy Wagner, and Associates

JOSSEY-BASS
A Wiley Imprint
www.josseybass.com

Published by Jossey-Bass
A Wiley Imprint
989 Market Street, San Francisco, CA 94103-1741—www.josseybass.com

Readers should be aware that Internet Web sites offered as citations and/or sources for further information may have changed or disappeared between the time this was written and when it is read.

Jossey-Bass books and products are available through most bookstores. To contact Jossey-Bass directly call our Customer Care Department within the U.S. at 800-956-7739, outside the U.S. at 317-572-3986, or fax 317-572-4002.

Jossey-Bass also publishes its books in a variety of electronic formats. Some content that appears in print may not be available in electronic books.

Credits appear on page 451.

Library of Congress Cataloging-in-Publication Data

Komives, Susan R., 1946-
    Leadership for a better world : understanding the social change model of leadership
    development / Susan R. Komives, Wendy Wagner, and Associates.
        p. cm.
    Includes bibliographical references and index.
    ISBN 978-0-470-44949-3 (pbk.)
        1. Universities and colleges—Administration. 2. College administrators—Professional
    relationships. 3. Educational leadership. 4. Social change. I. Wagner, Wendy (Wendy
    Elizabeth) II. Title.
    LB2341.K66 2009
    378.1'01—dc22   2009004209

Printed in the United States of America
FIRST EDITION
PB Printing   10 9 8 7 6 5 4 3 2 1

CONTENTS

PART 5   CHANGE AGENTS   392

ABOUT THE NATIONAL CLEARINGHOUSE
FOR LEADERSHIP PROGRAMS

The National Clearinghouse for Leadership Programs (NCLP) provides a central clearinghouse of leadership materials, resources, and assistance to leadership educators. NCLP members receive publications, Web access to resources, consultation assistance, and networking opportunities with other professionals engaged in leadership education with a focus on college students.

The NCLP supports cutting-edge research on leadership development, and the dissemination of knowledge through a member listserv, Web site, institutes, symposia, and high-quality publications.

The diversity of leadership programs in higher education and the dynamic nature of the subject challenge student affairs educators and faculty continually to create and refine programs, training techniques, and contemporary models to fit the changing context of leadership education. The NCLP exists to help meet that challenge.

The NCLP is proud of this publication, *Leadership for a Better World: Understanding the Social Change Model of Leadership Development*, as it complements other NCLP resources related to the Social Change Model of Leadership Development (SCM). These resources include the Socially Responsible Leadership Scale (SRLS), an instrument designed to measure students' leadership capacities. NCLP also sponsors the Multi-Institutional Study of Leadership, an international research project measuring college students' leadership development using the SRLS.

Visit http://www.nclp.umd.edu for more information on the NCLP and other educational material on the Social Change Model.

NCLP Director
Craig Slack
NCLP Research and Scholarship Editor
Susan R. Komives

PREFACE

Leadership is much more an art, a belief, a condition of the heart, than a set of things to do. The visible signs of artful leadership are expressed, ultimately, in its practice.
MAX DE PREE

Welcome to a challenging and wonderful journey—a journey about the commitments needed to make this world a better place; a journey exploring how you and the people in the groups you belong to can work together for meaningful change; and ultimately, a journey into yourself. Dennis Roberts (2007), a member of the team that developed the Social Change Model of Leadership Development (SCM) presented in this book and author of *Deeper Learning in Leadership,* calls this the "Journey of Deeper Leadership" (p. 203).

THE SOCIAL CHANGE MODEL OF LEADERSHIP DEVELOPMENT

Contemporary times require a collaborative approach to leadership that can bring the talent of all members of a group to their shared purposes. The Social Change Model of Leadership

Development (Higher Education Research Institute [HERI], 1996) approaches leadership as a purposeful, collaborative, values-based process that results in positive social change.

ASSUMPTIONS ABOUT THIS APPROACH TO LEADERSHIP

This approach to leadership is built on several key assumptions:

- "Leadership" is concerned with effecting change on behalf of others and society.
- Leadership is **collaborative.**
- Leadership is a **process** rather than a position.
- Leadership should be **value-based**.
- **All students** (not just those who hold formal leadership positions) are potential leaders.
- **Service** is a powerful vehicle for developing students' leadership skills.

In short, the approach proposed here differs in certain basic ways from traditional approaches that view "leaders" only as those who happen to hold formal leadership positions and that regard leadership as a value-neutral process involving positional "leaders" and "followers." (HERI, 1996, p. 10)

Goals of the Social Change Model

The SCM focuses on two primary goals:

1. To enhance student learning and development; more spe-
    cifically, to develop in each student participant greater:

    +   **Self-knowledge:** understanding one's talents, values,
        and interests, especially as these relate to the student's
        capacity to provide effective leadership.

    +   **Leadership competence:** the capacity to mobilize one-
        self and others to serve and work collaboratively.

2. To facilitate positive social change at the institution or in
    the community. That is, undertake actions which will help
    the institution/community to function more effectively
    and humanely. (HERI, 1996, p. 19)

Introducing the Seven C's

The SCM includes seven dimensions or values, referred
to throughout the book as the "Seven C's," that synergisti-
cally become leadership for social change. These values are
Citizenship, Collaboration, Common Purpose, Controversy
with Civility, Consciousness of Self, Congruence, and Commitment. All seven values work together to accomplish the
transcendent C of Change. These values are grouped into
three interacting clusters or dimensions: societal/community,
group, and individual. The *societal* or *community dimension* is
presented as Citizenship. *Group values* include Collaboration,

Common Purpose, and Controversy with Civility. *Individual values* include Consciousness of Self, Congruence, and Commitment.

The Ensemble

The Social Change Model was developed by a team of leadership educators and scholars who have worked extensively with college students. Funded by an Eisenhower Grant from the U.S. Office of Education in 1993–1996, the team realized early in the process that, like a good jazz ensemble, every member's contributions were essential, energy could flow among members of the group, and the whole was greater than the sum of its parts. They named themselves "The Working Ensemble" to reinforce the value of the whole.

The ensemble was concerned that college students needed to value collective action for social change and to learn to work with others in socially responsible ways. The ensemble was further concerned that old paradigms of leadership emphasized only the role of the positional leader and not the process of leadership among participants. Grounded in the belief that leadership capacity can be developed by anyone, the ensemble developed this values-based model that focused on how individuals can work effectively with others toward shared social concerns.

The model developed during a two-year process, including a weekend retreat with students from a diverse range of colleges and universities.

THE SCM BOOK PROJECT

The primary publication of the ensemble was a guidebook (Higher Education Research Institute [HERI], 1996) designed for the use of leadership educators. This guidebook is available from the National Clearinghouse for Leadership Programs (NCLP; www.nclp.umd.edu). The guidebook was often used as a textbook for students but needed to be updated and reframed for undergraduate college students who might be studying leadership and seeking to develop their own effective leadership perspective and practices. Professor Susan R. Komives, a member of the original ensemble and scholarship editor for the National Clearinghouse for Leadership Programs, challenged her graduate class of leadership educators in the College Student Personnel Program at the University of Maryland to research what college students needed to learn abut leadership and to design and write a book that could be used as a text to teach about the Social Change Model. Leadership educator and former coordinator of the NCLP, Wendy Wagner joined Komives to write and edit this book.

Purpose of the SCM Book

Nearly every college or university acknowledges that its graduates *can, will,* and, indeed, *must* be active leaders in their professions, their communities, and their world. Colleges expect their graduates to make this a better world. College students consistently affirm that they want their lives to matter and to make a difference (Komives, Lucas, & McMahon, 2007). College seniors seek jobs in which they can do well *and* do good (Levine & Cureton, 1998).

This book is both a call to action and a framework for developing your capacity to work with other people as you engage in leadership to address shared purposes. The book encourages raising awareness of social issues that need attention and ways of being with each other that promote effectively addressing those issues.

Alexander Astin (2001), co-facilitator of the ensemble who developed the Social Change Model of Leadership, observes that

> American higher education has traditionally defined
> a "student leader" either as someone who occupies a
> formal student office (e.g., student body vice-president
> or editor of the student paper) or as someone who has
> achieved visibility on the campus by virtue of athletic
> or some other form of achievement. This rather narrow
> approach not only relegates most students to the role
> of "non-leader," but also creates an implicit "leader-fol-
> lower" hierarchy, which, in the minds of most students,
> greatly limits their notions of who can or should "lead."
> The great power of the non-hierarchical approach to
> student leadership that characterizes this book is that
> it expands the number of potential "student leader"
> to include virtually all students, while simultaneously
> transforming the *process* by means of which leadership
> is exercised on campus. (p. x)

 In this book, the term *leader* is used without regard to a specific role in a group—whether as a positional leader or a participant engaging in the leadership process as a group member.

We believe—and research supports—that leadership can be learned and that the capacity to engage in leadership with others can be developed (Dugan & Komives, 2007). This journey into deeper leadership is facilitated by action (practicing leadership and engaging with others) and by reflection (thinking about your experiences and making meaning about your observations). This action and reflection cycle is the heart of experiential learning (Dewey, 1923; Kolb, 1981). This cycle expands the individual's capacity to learn more effective ways of thinking about and engaging in leadership.

An old Hindu proverb says, "There is nothing noble about being superior to some other (person). The true nobility is in being superior to your previous self." Psychologist Carl Rogers' (1961) concept of *On Becoming a Person* validates the exploration of one's own experiences as the most potent source of knowledge for personal development.

> Experience is, for me, the highest authority. The touchstone of validity is my own experience. No other person's ideas, and none of my own ideas, are as authoritative as my experience. It is to experience

that I must return again and again, to discover a closer approximation to truth as it is in the process of becoming in me. Neither the Bible nor the prophets— neither Freud nor research—neither the revelations of God nor man—can take precedence over my own direct experience. (p. 23)

The processes *of becoming* something—becoming collaborative, becoming congruent, becoming a change agent—move one from an uninformed consciousness about that awareness to a more informed consciousness able to examine the previous way of being in this *process of becoming* (Kegan, 1994).

In *On Becoming a Leader,* former university president and noted leadership scholar Warren Bennis (1989) wrote, "To become a leader, then you must become yourself, become the maker of your own life" (p. 40). Each of the chapters of this book asks you to reflect on how you are becoming the specific leadership dimension being presented. Think about the journey toward becoming more conscious of your effectiveness with that leadership value. Indeed, developing each of these leadership values, attitudes, and skills is a journey—the "becoming" process.

Focus of the Book

The ensemble and authors of this book focus on social change and socially responsible actions that readers can take to make the world a better place for everyone. The book is comprised of five parts. Part One sets the foundation by exploring what social change means and presents the SCM. Parts Two through Four present the three key dimensions of the model and the values they contain. Part Five challenges you to think about yourself as a change agent.

Part One includes Chapters One through Four. Chapter One explores the common social problems that people share and some of the processes used to address them. We encourage the reader to think deeply and personally about issues that need shared attention and how people can work collaboratively toward those changes. Chapter Two describes and provides an overview of the Social Change Model of Leadership Development. Chapter Three introduces three case studies of college students who are facing shared challenges and demonstrates how the elements of the model inform effective ways to accomplish change in each of those cases. Two of the cases are then continued in each of the rest of the chapters of the book, so readers can apply the content of that chapter to the evolving cases. The SCM is all about change; Chapter Four looks at change as a concept, how individuals and groups can lead for change, and why change may be resisted.

We encourage all readers to read the four chapters in Part One of the book in sequence, from understanding of the need for social change, to how the SCM proposed addressing this change, to what change is about.

Parts Two through Four delve into the seven values (the Seven C's) of the model grouped into three dimensions.

Although these values can be examined in any order, we encourage reading them in the order presented. In Part Two, the dimension of societal/community explores the value of citizenship along with how communities work for change. Part Three focuses on the group dimension of social change, specifically Collaboration (Chapter Six), Common Purpose (Chapter Seven), and Controversy with Civility (Chapter Eight). Finally, Part Four presents the values on the individual level, which include the importance of having Consciousness of Self (Chapter Nine), Congruence (Chapter Ten), and Commitment (Chapter Eleven) in order to be effective in working with others to make change happen.

Part Five puts all this together; Chapter Twelve discusses becoming a change agent. The Epilogue ends the book by encouraging the reader to become a person who will have the courage to make this a better world. Additional resources on the SCM are also included at the end of the book.

Personal Reflection

Encouraging personal reflection is an essential aspect of this book. As Carl Rogers (1961) affirmed, one is always "becoming," and the journey into effective leadership is a process of enhancing, improving, informing, and becoming. Deeper learning in leadership (Roberts, 2007) only happens through experiential learning and personal reflection. Each chapter in the book encourages the reader to reflect on the material through discussion questions and journal probes. The discussion questions focus your thinking on how the material relates to your experience and may be used in a class conversation to explore those topics. The journal probes relate to the process of becoming more competent with the material in the chapter. Kolb's (1981) model of experiential learning also frames the journal probe questions in each chapter. Readers are encouraged to think about Kolb's cyclical model of *concrete experience* (engaging with others or doing something), followed by *reflective observation* (thinking about what happened and why it happened—trying to make meaning from the experience). That reflection is followed by *abstract conceptualization* (creating a general principle, theory, or hypothesis based on the experience), then *active* experimentation (using this theory in new situations and seeing if it explains what is happening or helps things improve). Intentionally engaging in these reflections should enrich each reader's experience with becoming a more effective leader for social change.

Our Collaborative Process

The chapters in this book were a true collaborative process between and among authors and editors. Most chapters contain some material or ideas collaboratively generated by other team members. The lead author for each chapter deserves authorship credit for the chapter and gratefully acknowledges how the team enriched and improved the concepts and material throughout the book.

References

Astin, A. A. (2001). Foreword. In C. L. Outcalt, S. K. Faris, & K. N. McMahon (Eds.), *Developing non-hierarchical leadership on campus: Case studies and best practices in higher education* (p. x). Westport, CT: Greenwood.

Bennis, W. G. (1989). *On becoming a leader.* Reading, MA: Addison-Wesley.

Dewey, J. (1923). *Democracy and education.* New York: Macmillan.

Dugan, J. P., & Komives, S. R. (2007). *Developing leadership capacity in college students: Findings from a national study.* College Park, MD: National Clearinghouse for Leadership Programs.

Higher Education Research Institute. (1996). *A social change model of leadership development* (Version III). Los Angeles: University of California Los Angeles Higher Education Research Institute.

Kegan, R. (1994). *In over our heads: The mental demands of modern life.* Cambridge, MA: Harvard University Press.

Kolb, D. A. (1981). Learning styles and disciplinary differences. In A. W. Chickering & Associates (Eds.), *The modern American college: Responding to the new realities of diverse students and a changing society* (pp. 232–255). San Francisco: Jossey Bass.

Komives, S. R., Lucas, N., & McMahon, T. R. (2007). *Exploring leadership: For college students who want to make a difference* (2nd ed.). San Francisco: Jossey-Bass.

Levine, A., & Cureton, J. S. (1998). *When hope and fear collide: A portrait of today's college student.* San Francisco: Jossey-Bass.

Roberts, D. R. (2007). *Deeper learning in leadership: Helping college students find the potential within.* San Francisco: Jossey-Bass.

Rogers, C. R. (1961). *On becoming a person: A therapist's view of psychotherapy.* Boston: Houghton Mifflin

ACKNOWLEDGMENTS

Great admiration, gratitude, and credit go to the members of the original "ensemble" who developed the Social Change Model (SCM) of Leadership Development and the guidebook that was the primary document for presenting this model for nearly fifteen years. The commitment to social change, the passion for collaboration, belief in service as a pedagogy, and wisdom of these scholars and leadership educators lives in this new book. The book is a tribute to their experience and ideas that have transcended time and context. Special thanks to co-principal investigators of the project, Helen S. Astin (Professor Emeritus, University of California, Los Angeles) and Alexander Astin (Professor Emeritus, University of California, Los Angeles), and ensemble members Dr. Marguerite Bonous-Hammarth (Director, Office of Admissions, University of California, Irvine), Dr. Tony Chambers (Associate Vice Provost, Students, and Assistant Professor, University of Toronto), Dr. Len Goldberg (Retired Vice President for Student Affairs, University of Richmond), Dr. Cynthia S. Johnson (Professor Emeritus, California State University-Long Beach), Dr. Susan R. Komives (Professor, University of Maryland), Dr. Emily Langdon formerly of St. Norbert College, Dr. Carole Leland (Center for Creative Leadership, San Diego), Dr. Nance Lucas (Associate Dean and Associate Professor, New Century College, George Mason University), Dr. Raechele L. Pope (Associate Professor, University of Buffalo), Dr. Dennis Roberts (Assistant Vice President for Education Faculty and Student Services, Qatar Foundation, Education City), and Dr. Kathy M. Shellogg (Associate Vice President for Student Affairs, Nebraska Wesleyan University). Their affiliations at the time of developing the SCM appear in the 1996 guidebook. Hosted by the National Clearinghouse for Leadership Programs, most of this group convened for a reunion of the ensemble in the summer of 2007 and affirmed the promise and role of this model in student leadership development.

In the summer of 2007 we invited volunteers from the National Leadership Symposium to review a draft of this manuscript. With no advance notice, we sent the manuscript to these volunteers in the summer of 2008, and all readily agreed to review this work. Our sincere thanks to Dr. David Rosch (University of Illinois), Kim Northrup (University of Tampa), Christen Vannelli Christopherson (University of Minnesota), Dr. Suzanne Martin (Stamford University), along with treasured colleague, Dr. Julie Owen (George Mason University), and longtime friend and leadership scholar, Dr. Denny Roberts with the Qatar Foundation in Education City, along with new leadership educator, Darbi Roberts with Carnegie-Mellon University at Education City in Doha, for their superb comments that shaped the final version of this document.

Special thanks to the NCLP, which has promoted best practices in college student leadership development for twenty years. Check out this fine organization at www.nclp.umd.edu. We appreciate the support of longtime NCLP Director, Craig

Slack. Special thanks to the NCLP coordinator, Kristan Cilente, for her work on the stories that appear throughout the manuscript. NCLP intern Carla Christensen (Loyola University Chicago) and Maryland PhD student, Matt Johnson, assisted with production of the book. We also thank Dr. Laura Osteen for her fine research on the process of students becoming change agents that is used in Chapter Twelve.

Wendy and Susan also thank the researchers on the Multi-Institutional Study of Leadership team (especially co-PI Dr. John Dugan) for the research on the SCM that is advancing the practice and teaching of leadership for college students. Check out that study at www.nclp.umd.edu or www.leadershipstudy.net.

Thanks also to the team at Jossey-Bass, particularly David Brightman and Erin Null, whose unwavering support and encouragement to bring the SCM to a broader audience made this project possible.

Wendy thanks Parker and Anicka, who already make her world a better place. She also thanks her parents, Wendell and Cathy Wagner, for their lifelong example of community involvement and leadership. Susan is always grateful to Ralph, who makes everything possible. Special thanks also to Ralph for rendering the SCM graphics.

Susan R. Komives
Wendy Wagner
University of Maryland, College Park
January 2009

ABOUT THE AUTHORS AND EDITORS

Cecilio Alvarez is an academic advisor in the Center for Advising and Student Achievement at Colorado State University. Formerly he was the coordinator of the National Clearinghouse for Leadership Programs and was engaged with research as a member of the Multi-Institutional Study of Leadership research team. He has served as an associate at the National Leadership Symposium, has taught undergraduate leadership courses, and has presented on leadership at the ACPA College Student Educators International. He earned a Master of Education in College Student Personnel at the University of Maryland.

Jennifer Bonnet is a graduate candidate in the University of Michigan's Master of Science in Information program. Formerly she was the coordinator of the National Clearinghouse for Commuter Programs and worked with the Leadership, Community Service-Learning, and Student Involvement team in the Office of Campus Programs at the University of Maryland. She has presented on cocurricular leadership programs at the Maryland College Personnel Association conference and the ACPA-College Student Educators International convention, and she has been an associate at the National Leadership Symposium. While studying at the University of Maryland, she was a member of two research teams examining college student leadership development and cocurricular leadership programs. Her thesis research examined community service participation and citizenship among undergraduate students. In 2008, she earned a Master of Arts degree in College Student Personnel at the University of Maryland.

Kristan Cilente is a leadership educator who has worked at Georgetown University, the University of Arizona, and the University of Maryland, College Park. Kristan is a lead facilitator with the LeaderShape Institute, has taught numerous leadership courses, has presented at dozens of national and international conferences, and is a member of the Multi-Institutional Study of Leadership Research Team. She has served on the executive council of ACPA-College Student Educators International, has been an associate at the National Leadership Symposium, and is the coordinator for the National Clearinghouse for Leadership Programs. She is currently the coordinator of the National Clearinghouse for Leadership Programs and a doctoral student in College Student Personnel at the University of Maryland.

Marybeth J. Drechsler is a staff member in the College Park Scholars living-learning program at the University of

Maryland, where she works with student leadership development and service learning initiatives. She was a residence hall coordinator at the University of Missouri and the University of Central Missouri. Marybeth has worked with the National Study of Living-Learning Programs and served as an executive board member for the Missouri College Personnel Association. She also has conducted research and presented on topics of leadership self-efficacy, student engagement in living-learning environments, and dimensions of identity development. She is a doctoral student in College Student Personnel at the University of Maryland.

Jordan England is a student conflict resolution coordinator at the University of Michigan. She has facilitated courses on leadership at the University of Maryland and the University of Michigan and has coordinated the development of social justice and diversity-oriented leadership retreats for students and staff at the University of California, Santa Cruz. Jordan is a member of the directorate body for ACPA's Commission for Social Justice Educators and has presented locally, regionally, and nationally on topics including leadership development and social identities, collaborative leadership, and the relationship among service, leadership, and civic engagement. She earned a Master of Education in College Student Personnel at the University of Maryland.

Justin Fincher is the associate director for Student and Young Alumni Programs at Johns Hopkins University. He has taught introductory and advanced undergraduate leadership courses. He is a member of the ACPA Commission Directorate for Student Involvement, and he has presented at national, state, and numerous regional conferences. Additionally, Justin is a member of a few research teams, including the Multi-Institutional Study of Leadership research team. He earned a Master of Arts in College Student Personnel at the University of Maryland, where his thesis research examined leadership self-efficacy for college students with learning disabilities.

William A. Jones Jr. serves as the special assistant to the executive director for Leadership, Marketing and Assessment in the University Career Center and the President's Promise office at the University of Maryland. One of Wil's various roles within the University Career Center is to help student leaders transform their leadership experience into the world of work by helping them to understand and recognize their own transferable skills. Wil has taught various courses relating to career and leadership development and has most recently coinstructed a Leadership in Groups and Organization course. Wil is also serving a three-year term on ACPA's Commission for Career Development. His research interests include the career decision-making self-efficacy of student leaders. He earned a Master of Education in College Student Personnel at the University of Maryland.

Ashlee M. Kerkhoff is the program assistant for the Denton Community Initiative in the Department of Resident Life at the University of Maryland. One of her main roles is to provide coordination, planning, and support in the development of a residential program aiming to engage students in the academic community and prepare for living and working in a global society. She has taught leadership and resident assistant training courses and has research interests focusing on social class and student involvement. Ashlee also has a strong interest in sexual assault initiatives on campus and has done research, programming and policy development, and training on the issue. She is completing a Master of Education in College Student Personnel at the University of Maryland.

Susan R. Komives is a professor of College Student Personnel at the University of Maryland. She is cofounder of the National Clearinghouse for Leadership Programs (NCLP) and serves as research and scholarship editor of the NCLP publication, *Concepts & Connections.* She is co-author of *Exploring Leadership: For College Students Who Want to Make a Difference* (Jossey-Bass, 1998, 2007), *Management and Leadership Issues for a New Century* (Jossey-Bass, 2000), co-editor of *Student Services: A Handbook for the Profession* (Jossey-Bass, 1996, 2003), and was a member of the ensemble that developed the Social Change Model of Leadership Development. She is editor of the NCLP *Insights & Applications* leadership monograph series and co-editor of the *Handbook for Student Leadership Programs* (2006). Her recent leadership research includes serving as principle investigator for a grounded theory on leadership identity development (*Journal of College Student Development*, 2005, 2006) and is co-principal investigator for the Multi-Institutional Study of Leadership examining the Social Change Model of Leadership Development (see www.leadershipstudy.net). She is the president of the Council for the Advancement of Standards in Higher Education (CAS). She is a senior scholar with the James MacGregor Burns Academy of Leadership. In addition to receiving local and national teaching and mentoring awards, in 2006 Susan was honored with both the ACPA: College Educators International's Contribution to Knowledge Award and the National Association of Student Personnel Administrators' Outstanding Contribution to Literature or Research Award.

Daniel T. Ostick is the coordinator for Leadership Curriculum Development and Academic Partnerships for the Adele H. Stamp Student Union-Center for Campus Life including serving on the team coordinating the Counseling and Personnel Services Department's Leadership Studies Minor at the University of Maryland.

Previously he served as coordinator for training and development/coordinator for human resources in the Department of Resident Life at the University of Maryland. He was a member of the Association of College and University Housing Officers–International delegation to South Africa in 2007. He is the author of "Leadership and Diversity" in the *Handbook for Student Leadership Programs* (2006). He was the 2007 recipient of the University of Maryland Division of Student

Affairs Outstanding Service Award. Daniel is currently a doctoral candidate in the College Student Personnel Program.

José-Luis Riera has presented on leadership throughout his career and has taught about issues of organizational behavior, most recently a master's capstone seminar for College Student Personnel students focusing on leadership and organizational dimensions of student affairs. He most recently served as the director of residential living at Drexel University in Philadelphia. He currently serves as the coordinator of the student honor council with the Office of Student Conduct at the University of Maryland. His dissertation research concerns the intersection of spirituality/ethics with leadership among higher education administrators.

Tricia R. Shalka is assistant director/hall director at Drexel University. She previously worked with the Office of Fraternity and Sorority Life at the University of Maryland and was formerly a community director at Dartmouth College. She has taught learning strategies classes and is a member of two research teams that examine aspects of student leadership development and cocurricular leadership programs. Her thesis examined dimensions of self-awareness in fraternity men. She earned a Master of Arts in College Student Personnel at the University of Maryland.

Alex Teh is the coordinator for Facilities and Sport Clubs in Campus Recreation Services at the University of Maryland.

He has taught leadership and university orientation courses and advised a tobacco awareness student coalition at Anne Arundel Community College in Maryland. Alex was formerly the coordinator of the America Reads mentoring program and has previously done extensive work in recruitment and training with Teach for America. He earned a Master of Education in College Student Personnel at the University of Maryland.

Wendy Wagner is a co-editor of *Handbook for Student Leadership Programs* (2006). She has both served as a consultant and published on the Social Change Model. She is the former coordinator of the National Clearinghouse for Leadership Programs and former coordinator of the University of Maryland America Reads*America Counts program. She is currently a doctoral candidate in the College Student Personnel Program and is a staff member at the American Association of Colleges and Universities on the Liberal Education and America's Promise project. She has taught numerous undergraduate and graduate-level leadership courses. She has been a member of the Multi-Institutional Study of Leadership research team for the 2006 and 2009 studies. Her own research involves the measurement of leadership identity development.

Nurredina Workman is a leadership development program coordinator at University of California, Berkeley and is a former coordinator of the Intercultural Connections Community at Colorado State University. She has taught courses on leadership, diversity, and freshman orientation and is currently designing a course on multicultural leadership. She serves as scholarship coordinator for the ACPA Commission for Social Justice Educators and has presented regionally and nationally on topics such as developing a personal and community practice for deepening dialogue across difference; creating intercultural resident communities; and understanding the relationship among service, civic engagement, and leadership.

Leadership for a Better World

PART 1

Social Change and the Social Change Model of Leadership Development

*We must not, in trying to think about how we can make
a big difference, ignore the small daily differences we can
make which, over time, add up to the big differences that
we often cannot foresee*
MARIAN WRIGHT EDELMAN

The Social Change Model of Leadership Development
(SCM) is all about positive, social change. As identified
in Chapter One, social change often includes acts that aim to
improve the human condition or care for the environment. It
may also be revealed in the more purposeful ways people work
together because they value socially responsible leadership. The
SCM embraces both modal and end values (Burns, 1978). *How
people engage with each other matters, along with the outcomes and
purposes of their change activity.*

Change is a dynamic constant in people's lives. Heracli-
tus wrote, "Nothing endures but change." Change comes at us
all the time. It is the intersection of the way things are with the
way they will be. Leadership for social change is the opportunity people have to direct change toward a future we desire.
Futurist Alvin Toffler observed that "change is the way the
future invades our lives" (p. 00). Extending Toffler's observation, Komives (2005) asserts that "leadership is the way we
invade the future" (p. 157). *Leadership means responsibly choosing courses of action toward a desirable future.*

Leadership and change are inexorably intertwined. After
developing the SCM, several ensemble members went on to

develop *Leadership Reconsidered* (Astin & Astin, 2000), which captured this important relationship:

> We believe that leadership is a process that is ultimately concerned with fostering **change**. In contrast to the notion of "management," which suggests preservation or maintenance, "leadership" implies a process where there is movement—from wherever we are now to some future place or condition that is different. Leadership also implies **intentionality**, in the sense that the implied change is not random—"change for change's sake"—but is rather directed toward some future end or condition which is desired and valued. Accordingly, leadership is a purposive process which is inherently **value-based**. (p. 8)

The leadership values of the SCM could guide this purposive process. Chapter Two presents an overview of the Social Change Model and a summary of its key values. Chapter Three introduces case studies so the reader can apply the dimensions and values of the model to social change scenarios. Chapter Four, on Change, unpacks the complexities with how change occurs and how people engage with change.

References

Astin, A. W., & Astin, H. S. (2000). *Leadership reconsidered: Engaging higher education in social change*. Battle Creek, MI: W. K. Kellogg Foundation.

Burns, J. M. (1978). *Leadership*. New York: Harper & Row.

Komives, S. R. (2005). It's all about relationships. In A. B. Harvey-Smith (Ed.), *The seventh learning college principle: A framework for transformational change in learning organizations* (pp. 157–164). Washington, DC: National Association of Student Personnel Administrators.

Toffler, A. (1970). *Future shock*. New York: Bantam.

WHAT IS SOCIAL CHANGE?

Wendy Wagner

> *How wonderful it is that nobody need wait a single*
> *moment before starting to improve the world.*
> ANNE FRANK

College students across the country are finding many ways to make a positive difference on their campuses, in their communities, and even in the world. Consider the experiences of these students:

+ Monica Cevallos coordinated a project to improve the literacy rates in the struggling elementary schools near her campus. Working with local teachers, she and other students presented workshops for parents on activities to do at home to help their children learn to read.
+ Altmann Pannell and other members of the Black Student Union coordinated a student response to a threatening hate crime that occurred near the student union. More than 250 students attended their speak-out rally, voicing concerns and considering creative ways to convey a message of

campus unity against acts of race-based hatred (Hernandez, 2007).

+ Kim Singleton, an architecture major, working with students majoring in engineering, construction management, and other fields, was able to raise awareness of environmentally friendly housing options by designing and constructing a house powered entirely by the sun. Participating in the U.S. Department of Energy's annual Solar Decathlon, Kim acted as one of the Team Leaders, seeing the project from hypothetical ideas to the built product. The house was showcased on Washington, D.C.'s National Mall for one week; the students provided tours to thousands of people. Kim particularly enjoyed the opportunity to research and implement solar and sustainable technologies that made the solar-powered house possible, as well as the chance to share those aspects of the house with the public.

+ Students Against Sweatshops is a group operating through local chapters at hundreds of college campuses. These students have influenced their college administrators to approve policies that require clothing bearing the official college logos to be manufactured under fair and ethical conditions for the workers.

These are true stories of students who are acting to create positive changes in their community—through service, community building, raising awareness, educating the public about issues, or advocating for policy change. Some of these students identified themselves as "leaders" and found worthwhile places to invest their time and skills. Others had a passion about a certain issue but would not necessarily have thought, "I am a leader."

Regardless of whether one comes to social change through leadership, or whether one comes to leadership through an interest in social change, the Social Change Model of Leadership Development (SCM), the leadership model on which this book is based, identifies the two as having a powerful influence on each other.

> The ensemble that developed the Social Change Model wrote:
>
> "Leadership is ultimately about change, and ... effective leaders are those who are able to effect positive change on behalf of others and society." (Higher Education Research Institute [HERI], 1996, p. 10)
>
> "Change ... is the ultimate goal of the creative process of leadership—to make a better world and a better society for self and others." (HERI, p. 21)

CHAPTER OVERVIEW

While many of the leadership concepts in this book can be applied to a variety of contexts, such as leadership in corporate business, politics, team sports, a worksite, a student organization, or even a small group class assignment, this book was written for college students who want to work with others to create social change. Chapter One explores issues related to the concept of social change itself. These include motivations to get involved in social change, faith in one person's ability to make a real impact, and potential pitfalls of doing work that is intended for the public good. Additionally, socially responsible leadership is discussed as an application of the SCM in contexts other than social change.

WHAT IS MEANT BY SOCIAL CHANGE?

Every society in history has had public problems. Today, U.S. citizens in the early 21st century face a widening gap between the rich and poor, an education system that is failing children who live in less than affluent school districts, concerns about whether the planet can continue to sustain our modern lifestyle, deep divisions within governing bodies at all levels, and many other public challenges. Sometimes, these kinds of social problems appear to affect only the well-being of "other people," but upon closer study, they reveal themselves to have direct or indirect affects on us all. Working for social change is one approach to solving these problems. Social change addresses each person's sense of responsibility to others and the realization that making things better for one pocket of society makes things better for the society as a whole.

One way to describe the concept of social change has been to contrast it with charity and sporadic volunteerism

(Morton, 1995). While these latter approaches often provide needed services and create opportunities for members of communities to engage with each other at a personal level, they run the risk of creating dependencies, and ultimately the community problem continues. The two criteria that distinguish social change from charity are giving attention to the root causes of problems and collaboration with others (Morton; Strain, 2006).

Social Change Addresses the Root Causes of Problems

An important aspect of working for social change is focusing one's attention on the *root causes* of problems rather than the *surface-level* issues they create. When a person gets recurrent headaches, an aspirin can be relied upon to dull the pain. However, since the cause of the headaches goes unaddressed, the person will continue to get them. By thinking about the problem more thoroughly, one might realize that by reducing stress, getting enough sleep, and eating more healthfully, the underlying causes of the headaches would be addressed, and they would go away, as would the dependency on aspirins. What differentiates social change from charity is the examination of social problems to determine what their root causes are and how to address them (Morton, 1995).

Many students have experienced volunteering at a homeless shelter by serving food or handing out warm clothing. This service, which many would call charity, addresses two symptoms of the problem of homelessness: the needs for food and for warmth. While it cannot be stressed enough that this work is invaluable and critical for meeting people's immediate needs, acts like these will not eliminate homelessness. Social change efforts, in contrast, involve becoming educated about *why* people are homeless. How do our economic, political, and social systems and cultural values allow the problem to continue? Through volunteering, participants can get to know homeless individuals and shelter staff personally. They might learn more about the complex web of circumstances that result in homelessness. Maybe the community has unreasonable eviction laws, a minimum wage that does not cover the increasing cost of housing, or a lack of resources for individuals struggling with substance abuse. It is likely all three issues, and others, contribute to the problem. Working for social change could include writing to politicians about raising the minimum wage, circulating a petition to change eviction laws, participating in "Walk for the Homeless" events aimed at both fundraising and raising public awareness of the issues, and ongoing volunteering to provide regularly scheduled substance abuse support groups through the shelter.

Social Change Is Collaborative

Western movies portray the heroic cowboy: the stranger who comes to town, fixes all the problems, and then leaves with the admiration of the townsfolk (Bellah, Madsen, Sullivan, Swidler, & Tipton, 1985). Unfortunately, some people doing volunteerism or community improvement projects approach their work in the same way. These individuals do service *to* others rather than *with* them. Social change, in sharp contrast to the "cowboy" approach, requires building relationships with others and taking action together. Social change agents see themselves not as outsiders who help or fix others, but as fellow members of a community working to make it better.

An important issue related to social change is the question of how "positive" change is defined. Who decides whether the change being sought is a good thing or not? When working for the common good, who retains the power to decide what "good" is? What if the community does not want the change? Consider the historical example of the mandate to convert American Indian children to Christianity in 1609. The governor of the Virginia colony was instructed to take children from their parents, if necessary, in order to save them from the misery of their parents' "ignorance" (Takaki, 1993; quotation marks added). The mandate stemmed from the assumption that the colonists' faith was more legitimate than that of the American Indians they encountered. Surely many volunteers at the time thought they were making a positive change, helping people they perceived to be "uncivilized" become more like themselves. But forcing one's own belief system, be it religious, political, or ideological, onto others is clearly not an acceptable way to achieve social change.

Building relationships in the community and collaborating with others is the key to avoiding the imposition of one person's point of view onto others. Working *with* others and not *unto* others ensures that those most affected by the change have a say in what the change should be. Collaboration means the people in a community decide on a vision for change together and then work together to devise the means to achieve it.

Social Change Is Not Simple

Working for the common good is a concept that is immediately appealing to many people. Stories of people giving their time to help others, finding ways to contribute their expertise or skills to benefit their communities can be quite inspirational. However, sometimes stories and quotes about making a difference imply that because these ideas are so appealing at such a basic level, the efforts themselves must also be fairly basic, simple, and uncomplicated. They imply that the right action to take will be clear, and as long as people have good intentions the community will experience good results.

Charles Strain, a professor at DePaul University, illustrates the complexity of social change by examining the well-known proverb, "Give a man a fish and you feed him for a day. Teach a man to fish and you feed him for a lifetime." This proverb makes a nice point about the importance of building capacity and not just providing handouts. However, working for social change in real situations is rarely that straightforward. As Strain (2006) points out, if people are starving, they will need to have something to eat while they try to learn to fish. Going even further, he argues that "teaching someone to fish presumes that the person a) has access to a lake, b) that a corporate conglomerate has not fished out that lake and c) that our industrial waste has not poisoned all of the fish" (p. 6).

Efforts for social change involve coordinated work with many people on many fronts and often a sustained effort before any tangible results are achieved. Maintaining hope and commitment can be hard when visible signs of success are not immediate and when the role one plays in the greater effort seems small in comparison to the problem. This is a very real challenge of leadership for social change and is addressed in several later chapters of this book. Despite these challenges, many students choose to be involved, continually finding opportunities to work with others to make life better for people in their neighborhoods, on their campuses, or on their residence hall floors.

 Think of a time when you were involved in creating change for common good. How did you and others decide the change needed to be made? Did you collaborate with others involved with the issue or community? What were the root causes of the issue? Did your efforts address them?

WHY GET INVOLVED IN SOCIAL CHANGE?

In 1996, a study of social change agents identified several reasons people did not get involved in their communities (Parks Daloz, Keen, Keen, & Daloz Parks, 1996). People were busier than ever, not taking time to engage with neighbors long enough to identify ways in which coming together might benefit them all. Cynicism and a general belief in the futility of trying to make things better was prevalent, as was an individualistic outlook, a belief that each person should just look out for his or her own needs (Parks Daloz et al.). Many public problems just seemed so complex and far-reaching that it seemed like a waste of time even to try to solve them.

A recent study highlights the contrasts between college students in the 1990s and students today (Kiesa, Orlowski, Levine, Both, Kirby, Lopez, & Marcelo, 2007). While students in the 1990s volunteered, they did so individually rather than with an organized effort or with a larger institution. They were generally cynical about the usefulness of political institutions or the relevance of politics in their lives. In 2000, only 28 percent of college freshmen thought it was important to keep up with public affairs. Voter turnout among college students from 1997 to 2001 was the lowest in decades (Kiesa et al.).

In contrast, current college students, for the most part, believe it is important to be informed and engaged in politics and policymaking, and they are optimistic about the impact that collective action can have for the public good. In fact, 92 percent of current college students said they believed that people working together as a group can make some or a lot of difference in solving the problems they see in their community (Kiesa et al., 2007).

College students' specific reasons for getting involved in efforts for social change represent many motivations. A few explored here include:

+ Having a personal connection to the social issue or problem being addressed
+ Enjoying a connection with others that emerges from
working together on social problems
+ Having a sense of the interconnectedness of community
issues
+ Recognizing that helping others ultimately helps oneself
+ Experiencing a deep satisfaction from being involved in
making a difference for something that truly matters

People may get involved in social change work for several of
these reasons. Sometimes one's reasons change over time or
from project to project.

A Personal Connection to the Problem

Motivations about what social change one is called to engage
in often have very personal connections.

Being Directly Affected by the Problem

Some people find themselves involved in making a difference
around issues with which they have a personal connection.
Perhaps they, a family member, or friend have experienced
challenges for which they seek solutions that would make
things better not just for them, but for everyone who faces
that challenge. The ranks of those who raise funding and
public awareness by walking for breast cancer are full of people with personal connections to the disease. Fraternity and

sorority members who work together to create campuswide policies against hazing are often students who have seen firsthand how destructive the practice is to individual members and chapter unity. Newscaster Katie Couric worked publicly for colon cancer awareness following the untimely death of her husband to the disease.

Marginality

Some social change efforts, such as working for equal opportunity based on gender, race, sexual orientation, or disability, may come from a personal connection to feelings of marginality and a desire for equity, justice, and fairness. *Marginality* is a term used to describe the sense that one's presence in a group or community is not valued or that one's experiences or perspectives are not normal. The term refers to existing on the margins of one's community. The benefits of belonging, like being included, being heard, and having one's opinions given serious consideration, do not apply to the marginalized. While feeling marginal to one's community is painful, the experience builds personal strength and character. Marginal people often benefit from having "greater self-knowledge, greater awareness of others, and a kind of comfort with life at the edge" (Parks Daloz et al., 1996, p. 76). Having had feelings of marginality develops the awareness that everyone should count, not just those in the "in" crowd. It can be a powerful motivator to becoming an agent of social change.

A Connection to Others

From an outsider's perspective, acts to help others rather than attending to one's own needs are often seen as being "selfless." However, for many who get involved to benefit others, this kind of involvement actually feeds their need to matter to others. "... [W]e do not sacrifice for others at the expense of the self, but we give to others because love and compassion are essential to the self" (Rhoads, 1997, p. 87). Particularly when acts to benefit others involve building strong relationships with others, those involved discover that the roles they play in these relationships become a deeply important aspect of how they see themselves.

Non-Western cultures have long recognized that one finds the self through connections with others. Archbishop Desmond Tutu (2000) describes a South African concept, *ubuntu*, that illustrates this belief:

> Ubuntu is very difficult to render in a Western language. It speaks of the very essence of being human. . . . It is to say, "My humanity is caught up, is inextricably bound up, in yours." We belong in a bundle of life. We say, "A person is a person through other persons." A person with ubuntu . . . has a proper self-assurance that comes from knowing that he or she belongs in a greater whole and is diminished when others are humiliated or diminished. (p. 31)

Historically, mainstream American culture highly values individualism, each person's freedom to live how he or she chooses. We admire self-reliance and the ability to take care of one's own problems without burdening others. How is the value of individualism to be reconciled with having a sense of responsibility to the community and the welfare of those around us? The answer lies in reframing the issue. Rather than being competing opposites, the individual and the community reinforce each other. While it seems paradoxical, each person's ability to be a self-reliant individual is bolstered by having a strong, supportive community. Likewise, communities are strong when the individuals in them are free to think for themselves and act on their consciences.

Juana Bordas (2007), founder and chief executive officer of Mestiza and author of several leadership books, observes:

> I and we are not a dichotomy. The *I* is intrinsic to the *We* orientation—individuals must be strong for the collective to thrive. . . . The challenge is to balance communal good with individual gain—to reach the higher ground of interdependence. This implies a social imperative whereby personal gain cannot be shouldered at the expense of the common good. (p. 54)

This concept of interdependence with others is frequently reflected in nature. For example, while California redwood trees are the tallest living things in the world, reaching as high as 300 feet, they have astonishingly shallow root systems. Redwoods are able to survive strong winds and storms without toppling over because they always grow together in groves, with their roots intertwining together in a way that supports each tree.

Interconnectedness of Community Problems

Some people are involved in social change because they have come to realize that issues that seem like "somebody else's problem" do come back to affect them in the long run. The environment provides many clear examples of how other people's decisions affect everyone. For example, it may not be readily apparent why the workers in the Chesapeake Bay crab industry would be interested in the state of Maryland's farming policies. But when economic realities push farmers to increase their annual yields by using chemical fertilizers and pesticides, those toxins eventually run off into the bay, devastating the quantity of blue crabs (Stanford University, 2005).

Interconnections like these are found in social issues as well. Quality education is one example. A good education clearly benefits individuals, but it benefits the whole community as well. Individuals learn to read, calculate, and solve problems, all fundamental life and workplace skills. The whole community also benefits from having an educated populace. Economists have shown links between education disparity and increased crime, ethnic divisions, and income inequality (Fajnzylber, Lederman, & Loayza, 2000). Quality schools are also generally known to increase the value of homes. Although keeping real estate taxes low is an important consideration for individual families, in the long term, even people without children benefit from investing in quality schools. In his *I Have a Dream* speech, Dr. Martin Luther King Jr. conveyed his understanding of the connectedness of social issues this way:

> For many of our white brothers, as evidenced by their presence here today, have come to realize that their destiny is tied up with our destiny. And they have come to realize that their freedom is inextricably bound to our freedom.

Many community problems on campus have interconnections that may not be apparent at first glance. Consider a campus that has a moderately popular men's rugby team, but no women's rugby. Some of the players on the men's team may not see this lack of opportunity for female players as any of their concern. Why should they care? In fact, they might be hostile to women who approach them about playing on the men's team since they don't have a women's team to play on. Other members of the men's team might see the situation differently. They might see the opportunity to help their sport gain more visibility and popularity by the addition of a women's league. Having two campus rugby teams might eventually convince the institution to provide more space for practice fields. The men might even push for a coed league as well, which would increase the opportunity to play on a team for both men and women. By joining with interested women players to pressure the athletic department to give women the opportunity to play, the men's rugby team benefits as well.

While some are satisfied with only looking out for their own interests, activist and commentator Paul Loeb (1999) contrasts that sentiment with what he calls "a more hopeful way to live" (p. 2):

> The walls we're building around ourselves ... may provide a temporary feeling of security. But they can't prevent the world from affecting us. Quite the opposite. The more we construct such barriers, the more private life, for most of us, will grow steadily more insecure. (p. 7)

Satisfaction Derived from Making a Difference

In the late 1990s, a team of researchers interviewed 100 individuals who were identified as committed to working on behalf of the common good. Although many of these individuals had given significant time and energy to help others, there was "very little sense of sacrifice. . . . On the contrary most spoke of the 'deep gladness' they felt in their work" (Parks Daloz et al., 1996, p. 196). One interviewee commented, "This is what I love, what my purpose is, what drives me, and makes me happy" (p. 197). Participants reported that their efforts made their lives feel purposeful, and they enjoyed the process of meeting challenges and working with others to find solutions (Parks Daloz et al.). For a similar study during the civil rights movement, Robert Coles (1993) met an African American college student who was in prison for protesting segregation by attempting to have lunch in a "white restaurant." Coles asked the student why he was involved in the civil rights movement, considering the risks and obstacles to success. The student answered, "The satisfaction, man" (p. 69). He described meeting inspiring people and feeling part of something important: "There may be a sheriff out there waiting for me with a gun, but if he gets me, I'll die thinking: Dion, you actually *did* something" (p. 69).

What drives you to work for social change? How can you expand on this drive to move you from beliefs to action?

BUT I'M NOT A HERO, I'M JUST A REGULAR PERSON

There are many people whose efforts to make a positive difference led to their being well-known historical figures (for example, Harriet Tubman, Abraham Lincoln, Susan B. Anthony, Martin Luther King Jr., Mother Teresa). However, there is a danger that one might imagine that the kind of people who get involved to make a difference must be fundamentally different from "normal" people. Being committed to the common good does not mean becoming a saint, nor does it mean sacrificing one's other life goals. In his years of observing people doing community work, Loeb (1999) recognized:

The main distinction between those who participate
fully in their communities and those who withdraw in
private life doesn't rest in the active citizens' grasp of
complex issues, or their innate moral strength. . . . They
have learned specific lessons about approaching social
change: that they don't need to wait for the perfect
circumstances, the perfect cause, or the perfect level of
knowledge to take a stand; that they can proceed step
by step, so that they don't get overwhelmed before they
start. They savor the journey of engagement and draw
strength from its challenges. Taking the long view, they
come to trust that the fruits of their efforts will ripple
outward, in ways they can rarely anticipate. (pp. 8–9)

History is full of examples of tentative first steps leading to
lives of commitment. The people we now see as heroes were
once just getting started, learning as they went, just like everyone else does.

+ While she was still in college, Marion Wright Edelman
joined her professor Howard Zinn and other black students to challenge segregation by sitting in the "Whites
only" section of the state legislature. This and other early
experiences through which she observed how the legal and
political systems favored whites motivated her to become a
civil rights attorney (the first black woman admitted to the
Mississippi bar). She eventually became a critical figure in
the civil rights movement and later went on to form the
Children's Defense Fund (Edelman, 1999).

+ Eleanor Roosevelt's family hoped only for her to marry well. However, she did not find meaning in the lifestyle of the wealthy socialite and instead decided to join a group of women who were activists for women's equality and rights for the working poor (Gerber, 2002). Despite her concerns about having no experience or qualifications for this kind of work, she decided to accept a position on the board of directors of the New York League of Women Voters. She would later call this period "the intensive education of Eleanor Roosevelt" (Roosevelt as cited in Gerber, p. 87).

+ César Chávez, well-known activist for farm workers and labor unions, also began his journey with simple small steps. He accepting a job with a Latino civil rights group in which he traveled across California, encouraging Mexican Americans to register and vote (Ross, 1989).

For Chávez, just like for anyone else, the courage to get out there and try opened the doors to the opportunities that followed. "Each step, no matter how awkward or hesitant, prepares us for the next" (Loeb, p. 62).

The lesson from these stories is that one does not become an expert on social issues before getting involved; one becomes an expert through involvement and learning from experience. Of course a person should try to be informed about the issues, but the need to be informed should not forever serve as a barrier to action. Social change agents must be willing to learn as they go; to listen to those around them and those most directly affected, and be open to learning where they were wrong. Community service experiences can be a great place to start out on the hesitant and awkward first steps to which Loeb refers. Service provides opportunities to learn firsthand about social problems and possible solutions (HERI, 1996).

When people begin to feel that the world's problems are too big for them as individuals to make a difference, Beverly Tatum (1997), former dean of the college at Wellesley and president of Spelman College, responds this way: "While many people experience themselves as powerless, everyone has some sphere of influence in which they can work for change, even if it is just in their own personal network of family and friends" (p. 204). The more a person gets involved in the ways that they can, the more experience they will gain and the more influential relationships they will form. One's sphere of influence grows as one uses it.

Eli Winkelman was a student at Scripps College with a popular recipe for challah bread. Her friends could not get enough of it and even asked her to teach them how to make it for themselves. She recognized the demand for a product and wondered if she could take advantage of it for a good cause. Meanwhile, her friend Melinda Koster at nearby Pomona College was deeply concerned about the genocide in the Darfur region of Sudan. Although unsure of what she could do from her residence hall in Claremont, California, she was determined to get involved somehow. One day, Melinda's concern met Eli's fundraising idea and they decided to give it a try. With some initial success, Eli began asking questions of people within her sphere of influence. Would other students help her with the baking to have more to sell? Yes. Would the college dining hall let them use the kitchen equipment after hours in order to produce even more? Yes. Would the on-campus café sell them in the shop for her? No, but she kept asking questions. If they could not sell through the campus café, could they set up a sales table every week? Yes, and after a year of success, the campus café came around and began featuring challah in its pastry case every day. Today, Challah for Hunger is a quickly growing nonprofit organization. Eli has managed to help students at ten additional colleges around the country start chapters, and she is working with students at many more. She uses the project not only to raise money for hunger and disaster relief (more than $55,000 at the time of this writing) but to also raise awareness about these problems and about her beliefs regarding each person's responsibility to address them (personal communication, 2008).

 Who is in your sphere of influence? In what arenas do you have the power to make something better? How could you use it? In what arenas would you like things to be better? How could you utilize your current sphere of influence to create change there?

POSSIBLE PITFALLS IN SOCIAL CHANGE

Even with the best of intentions of working to benefit others, sometimes, without meaning to, it is possible to act in ways that are hurtful or insulting. The following is a short list of pitfalls to avoid when working for social change.

Paternalism

This pitfall is considered to be the underlying cause of many problems in community service (Morton, 1995). The term implies a "father knows best" analogy, reducing recipients of service to a childlike status, not having input on what service will be done to them because they do not know what is best for them. Paternalism maintains unequal relationships between the "helpers" and the "helped" (Rhoads, 1997). When "helpers" assume they have expertise that the "helped" do not, they keep decision-making power to themselves rather than empowering people to create their own solutions.

Assimilation

This approach assumes that the way one's own community or culture addresses an issue is the best way. In this pitfall, people attempt to "fix" another community by helping it become more like their own. This ignores the differences among communities and the expertise that exists outside of one's own. Efforts to build relationships with others should not assume that commonality is the only way to find a sense of connection (Rhoads, 1997).

A Deficit-Based Perspective of the Community

A deficit-based perspective sees only the problems in a community: poverty, poor schools, teen pregnancy. Deficit-based models tend to focus on how others can solve problems for a community, rather than on how the community can use its assets to create its own solutions (Kretzmann & McKnight, 1993). An asset-based view of the community starts by identifying all the resources the community has to build upon to make it stronger, and then think creatively about how these assets can be applied in new ways. For example, imagine a student organization that is seeking a community service project; it identifies a community neighborhood to work in based on its identified deficits: poor schools and an aging population that needs some assistance with household tasks and opportunities to socialize. The organization might decide either to offer a tutoring program in the schools or visit aging shut-ins to rake leaves and shovel snowy sidewalks. But consider how differently the student organization would approach their service project if the neighborhood was identified by its assets: the aging population has lived in this neighborhood for decades, they all know each other, and there is a strong sense of community history and pride. All of the sudden, the aging population is perceived as an asset, not a service recipient. Many of the seniors are likely to be proud alumni of the same neighborhood schools that are now struggling. If they could be provided rides, they might enjoy volunteering in these schools themselves. Likewise, in communities where neighbors have known each other for years, creating incentives for local school children to rake leaves and shovel snow for their aging neighbors might be a more sustainable service project than for the university students to do these things themselves.

Seeking a Magic Bullet

Social problems involve a complex web of issues. Poverty, illiteracy, poor schools, and racism are all interwoven problems. Complex problems require multiple solutions, not just one quick fix. More funding is often considered a solution, but it is rarely all that is needed. Other solutions are often needed to work along with funding, such as building stronger community relationships, changing policies, providing education or training, and changing public attitudes about the issue. Very often, those most affected by the problem will have the best idea of the systems and structures to be addressed.

Ignoring Cultural Differences

When Malcolm X was a child, a neighbor provided a butchered pig to his family so they would not go hungry. Because of religious-based diet restrictions, his mother would not serve it to the children. (If it is hard to imagine choosing hunger over a religious dietary restriction, imagine an American food bank serving dog meat to the poor, claiming that it is acceptable in other cultures.) His mother's decision was among a chain of events that led to the state taking the children out of her custody, claiming she was not taking proper care of them (Haley & Malcolm X, 1964). It is important not to let attempts to form a connection with others be confused with thinking everyone is the same.

Avoiding the Potential Pitfalls

One key to avoiding many of these pitfalls is to replace notions of "helping others" or "fixing others" with a sense of being *in community* with others. Rather than serving others, we work together toward solutions to problems we hold in common (Kendall in Jacoby, 1996, p. 13). The very act of distinguishing between "helper" and "recipient" can lead to many of the pitfalls noted.

> It is dangerous to our conception of democracy for us to think of service as the rich helping the poor or students paying a debt to their society in exchange for tuition breaks, as if the community building aspect of "community" service only applies to those "doing" service. . . . The language of charity drives a wedge between self-interest and altruism, leading students to believe that service is a matter of sacrificing private interests to moral virtue. The language of citizenship suggests that self-interests are always embedded in communities of action and that in serving neighbors one also serves oneself. (Barber, as quoted in Rhoads, 1997, p. 171)

 Can you think of a time when you were involved in a community effort that experienced one of these potential pitfalls? What might the project have looked like in order to avoid that pitfall?

SOCIALLY RESPONSIBLE LEADERSHIP

The Social Change Model of Leadership Development was created for those who want to learn how to work effectively with others for the public good. However, its values are useful even for an organization whose mission is not related to serving the public good. It is an approach to leadership that is collaborative rather than coercive, civil and respectful rather than defensive, open to different perspectives rather than controlling and single-minded, and clear and consistent about values rather than hypocritical. While the primary mission of a group may not relate to social change, leaders in a wide variety of contexts, such as business, sports, theater groups, or a group classroom assignment, can benefit from these approaches to working with others.

Regardless of whether social change is a major aspect of a group's mission, an approach to leadership that maintains a sense of responsibility for the welfare of others as the group goes about its business is called *socially responsible leadership*. Socially responsible leadership means operating with an awareness of the ways in which the group's decisions and actions affect others. Socially responsible leaders are concerned about the well-being of group members and about the impact of the group's decisions on the community. A socially responsible outdoor adventure club will always make sure it leaves campsites as clean as it found them. A sorority would make sure that its traditions and ways of socializing are welcoming to students from a diversity of social classes, ethnicities, and religious backgrounds. A socially responsible approach to leadership will influence the group's purposes, decision making, and how members work together.

There are many examples of socially responsible leadership in the corporate business field. While the primary goal of any business is to make a profit in order to continue to exist, many companies are able to do so while also adhering to other shared values. Companies such as Timberland and The Body Shop have published values statements that make clear their awareness of their impact on the community and their desire to have a positive influence through their ways of doing business. These companies and others like them have operating procedures as well as standards for their suppliers and business partners concerning values such as protecting the environment, defending against animal cruelty, and supporting suppliers from disadvantaged communities (www.timberland. com, www.thebodyshop.com). Organizations like these are not sacrificing profits in order to be "do-gooders." Rather, they are future oriented, recognizing their interdependence with their communities. "Organizations with a social imperative that links their survival to the well-being of society may be better positioned in the long run to maintain their human and economic viability" (Hickman, 1998, p. 561).

SOCIAL CHANGE AND LEADERSHIP

By their very definitions, working for social change and doing leadership both imply collaborative effort, or people working together toward shared goals. Leadership is clearly not an act done in isolation from others. Similarly, one person acting alone cannot solve problems that members of a society hold in common. Paul Loeb (1999) asserts, "Our most serious problems, both the public ones and those that seem most personal, are in the large part common problems, which can be solved only through common efforts"(p. 7). If both social change and leadership are group efforts, then being able to do them requires effective approaches to working in groups. The SCM addresses these approaches.

Julie Owen, Leadership Studies Professor at George Mason University, often asks an important question: "Do leaders create social movements or do the movements create leaders?" (personal communication, 2008). The Social Change Model of Leadership Development calls attention to the strong connection between getting involved in social change and learning to do leadership. The chapters that follow address the values that are explored and refined as a person gets involved with others to solve common problems.

Juana Bordas often describes the day she was sitting outside her residence hall in 1963 when she saw her political science professor and a long line of people walking toward the administration building. When she asked what was happening, she was invited to join them on a protest march to racially integrate the University of Florida. Juana says, "I stood up and said, 'Yes I'll go.' On that day, I became a leader" (personal communication, 2008). It is in this spirit that social change and leadership are connected here. It is through working with others for common benefit that people learn just how much they are capable of. "We regard a leader as one who is able to effect positive change for the betterment of others, the community, and society. All people, in other words, are potential leaders"(HERI, 1996, p. 16).

CONCLUSION

Working for social change means working to make a positive difference for the common good in ways that are collaborative and that address the root causes of problems. People are inspired to do social change for a variety of reasons and are able to get involved at the campus, community, national, and global levels.

DISCUSSION QUESTIONS

1. In what ways have you been involved in social change efforts? What social issues or what communities are you drawn to?

2. Can you think of an example of an organization (that you have been involved with or not) that did a particularly good job of collaborating with others and addressing the root causes of problems?

3. What is your motivation for being involved in social change efforts? What holds you back?

4. Describe someone you would consider a hero in terms of their commitment to making a positive difference for others. In what ways can you see yourself being like them? In what ways does their achievement intimidate you?

5. Unfortunately, many early volunteer experiences involve one of the potential pitfalls described in this chapter. Do

you have any personal experiences with one or more of the pitfalls that you are willing to share? What did you learn from that experience?

6. Think of a group you belong to that is not defined by its goal to do social change, such as a residence hall community, sports team, or academic club. How does that organization affect its members? How does it affect others in its community? How could that organization practice socially responsible leadership?

7. Do you think leaders create social movements or do social movements create leaders? How have your experiences with leadership shaped your motivation to work for the common good? How have your experiences trying to make a difference for the common good affected how you approach leadership?

JOURNAL PROBES

On Becoming

Preeminent psychologist Carl Rogers (1961) said that people are always in a process of *becoming*. The first two journal probes are intended to help you reflect on how you see yourself becoming a leader for social change.

1. In what ways can you see how you are becoming aware of your motivations to work for social change and how those experiences are shaping you as a leader?

2. Can you remember a time when you thought about social change differently than you do now? How is your current approach different from your approach then?

Learning Through Experience

The ensemble that created the Social Change Model believed the best way to learn to do leadership was through experience and reflection. This involves challenging yourself to have new experiences that test your ability and awareness **and** to spend time thinking about what you have learned from that experience. The remaining journal probes are designed to maximize learning through experience by guiding your reflective journal writing through Kolb's (1981) four processes of experiential learning.

1. **Concrete Experience.** Describe a specific situation when you had an experience that relates to social change as it has been described here. What was the social issue or community problem involved? What happened? What details stand out to you? Describe briefly the situation, what you did and how you felt. What was the outcome?

2. **Reflective Observation.** Why were you motivated to be involved with that experience? Did any of the potential pitfalls of social change emerge? What responses from yourself and others worked in this situation? Why was that effective? What did not work? Why?

3. **Abstract Conceptualization.** What lessons about working for social change can you draw from this specific experience

that could apply more generally? Given both your reflections and the information in this chapter, what would you do if a similar situation presented itself? What general guidelines would you create for handling future situations like this?

4. **Active Experimentation.** What opportunities might you seek out that would give you the chance to apply what you have learned here? How might you test the lessons or guidelines you created in #3 to see if they work?

References

Bellah, R. N, Madsen, R., Sullivan, W. M., Swidler, A., & Tipton, S. M. (1985). *Habits of the heart: Individualism and commitment in American life*. Berkeley: University of California Press.

Bordas, J. (2007). *Salsa, soul, and spirit: Leadership for a multicultural age*. San Francisco: Berrett-Koehler.

Coles, R. (1993). *The call of service: A witness to idealism*. Boston: Houghton Mifflin.

Edelman, M. W. (1999). *Lanterns: A memoir of mentors*. Boston: Beacon Press.

Fajnzylber, P., Lederman, D., & Loayza, N. (2000, Fall). Crime and victimization: An economic perspective. *Economia*, 219–302.

Gerber, R. (2002). *Leadership the Eleanor Roosevelt way: Timeless strategies from the first lady of courage*. New York: Penguin.

Haley, A., & Malcolm X. (1964). *The autobiography of Malcolm X*. New York: Ballantine.

Hernandez, A. (2007, September 12). Campus denounces hate. *The Diamondback*. Retrieved June 2, 2008, from http://media.www. diamondbackonline.com/media/storage/paper873/news/2007/09/12/ News/Campus.Denounces.Hate-2963158.shtml

Hickman, G. R. (1998). Leadership and the social imperative of organizations in the twenty-first century. In G. R. Hickman (Ed.), *Leading organizations: Perspectives for a new era* (pp. 559–571). Thousand Oaks, CA: Sage.

Higher Education Research Institute. [HERI] (1996). *A social change model of leadership development* (Version III). Los Angeles: University of California Los Angeles, Higher Education Research Institute.

Jacoby, B. (Ed.) (1996). *Service-learning in higher education: Concepts and practices*. San Francisco: Jossey-Bass.

Kiesa, A., Orlowski, A. P., Levine, P., Both, D., Kirby, E. H., Lopez, M. H., & Marcelo, K. B. (2007). *Millennials talk politics: A study of college student political engagement*. College Park, MD: Center for Information and Research on Civic Learning & Engagement.

Kolb, D. A. (1981). Learning styles and disciplinary differences. In A. W. Chickering & Associates (Eds.), *The modern American college: Responding to the new realities of diverse students and a changing society* (pp. 232–255). San Francisco: Jossey Bass.

Kretzmann, J. P., & McKnight, J. L. (1993). *Building communities from the inside out: A path toward finding and mobilizing a community's assets*. Chicago: ACTA Publications.

Loeb, P. R. (1999). *Soul of a citizen: Living with conviction in a cynical time*. New York: St. Martin's.

Morton, K. (1995, Fall). The irony of service: Charity, project and social change in service-learning. *Michigan Journal of Community Service-Learning*, 19–32.

Parks Daloz, L. A., Keen, C. H., Keen, J. P., & Daloz Parks, S. (1996). *Common fire: Leading lives of commitment in a complex world*. Boston: Beacon Press.

Rhoads, R. A. (1997). *Community service and higher learning: Explorations of the caring self*. Albany: State University of New York Press.

Rogers, C. R. (1961). *On becoming a person: A therapist's view of psychotherapy.* Boston: Houghton Mifflin.

Ross, F. (1989). *Conquering Goliath: César Chávez at the beginning.* Keene, CA: United Farm Workers.

Stanford University. (2005, April 3). Ocean ecosystems plagued by agricultural runoff. *Science Daily.* Retrieved June 18, 2008, from www.sciencedaily.com/releases/2005/03/050326010739.htm

Strain, C. R. (2006). Moving like a starfish: Beyond a unilinear model of student transformation in service learning classes. *Journal of College & Character, VIII,* 1–12. Retrieved September 5, 2008, from www.collegevalues.org/pdfs/moving.pdf

Takaki, R. (1993). *A different mirror: A history of multicultural America.* Boston: Little, Brown.

Tatum, B. D. (1997)."*Why are all the black kids sitting together in the cafeteria?" and other conversations about race.* New York: Basic Books.

Tutu, D. (2000). *No future without forgiveness.* New York: First Image Books.

AN OVERVIEW OF THE SOCIAL CHANGE MODEL OF LEADERSHIP DEVELOPMENT

Kristan Cilente

> *Once social change begins, it cannot be reversed. You cannot uneducate the person who has learned to read. You cannot humiliate the person who feels pride. You cannot oppress the people who are not afraid anymore. We have seen the future, and the future is ours.*
> CÉSAR CHÁVEZ

The Social Change Model of Leadership Development (SCM) was created specifically for students in college who want to learn to work effectively with others to create social change over their lifetimes (Higher Education Research Institute [HERI], 1996). Many diverse people are committed to social change goals. An underlying value and assumption of leadership for social change requires individuals to dig deeper and embrace the plethora of perspectives that exist in our changing world. Social change is happening everywhere and, as a result of the communication and technological revolution, everyone has the ability and responsibility to contribute to a better world (Allen, Bordas, Hickman, Matusak, Sorenson, & Whitmire, 1998; Allen & Cherry, 2000; Rost, 1991).

CHAPTER OVERVIEW

This chapter provides an introduction and overview of the Social Change Model and its seven core values. It also describes how the SCM was developed.

A NEW APPROACH TO LEADERSHIP

As a multi- and interdisciplinary subject, leadership has a plurality of definitions and approaches. The roots of leadership can be traced back to Egyptian times (Bass, 1990). For centuries in Western Europe, leadership was identified as the act of holding a position of power. The focus of leadership was how to acquire and maintain that position (Wren, 1995). It was assumed that only a select few people were born with the traits needed to be a leader, such as having higher intelligence. The measure of an effective leader was how long he or she stayed in power. This was the primary way in which leadership was viewed until the Industrial Revolution, when the study of leadership expanded beyond traits to more managerial approaches

The authors of the Social Change Model wrote:

A leader is not necessarily a person who holds some formal position of leadership or who is perceived as a leader by others. Rather, we regard a leader as one who is able to effect positive **change** for the betterment of others, the community, and society. All people, in other words, are potential leaders. Moreover, the **process** of leadership cannot be described simply in terms of the behavior of an individual; rather, leadership involves collaborative relationships that lead to collective action grounded in the shared values of people who work together to effect positive change.

The notions of leader as change agent and of leadership as collective action to effect social change suggest that a conscious focus on **value**s should be at the core of any leadership development effort. We believe that any new program in leadership development should focus not only on the value implications of any proposed social change, but also on the personal values of the leaders themselves. While some academic colleagues may be uncomfortable with our advocacy of a "values-based" approach, we feel strongly that any educational program is inevitably based on values, and that there is a need to embrace common human values such as self-knowledge, service, and collaboration to guide our common civic agendas. (HERI, 1996, p. 16) to leadership behavior and styles (Komives, Lucas, & McMahon, 2007; Northouse, 2007; Rost, 1991). During this time, notions about leadership largely focused on how the person in the leadership position got others to do what he or she wanted. Effective leadership was measured by determining which leader produced the most or the best products.

While aspects of these previous approaches to leadership continue in the early twenty-first century, there has been a significant shift in what leadership is understood to be. The shift began first with Robert Greenleaf's work on servant leadership (1977) and then in 1978, when historian James MacGregor Burns published the groundbreaking book *Leadership*, which has altered the way in which leadership is studied and taught in the United States. Burns's concept of transforming leadership espouses a relationship between leaders and followers in which each transforms the other. Leaders transform followers, helping them to become leaders themselves. Followers transform leaders by influencing them to pursue higher moral purposes. Burns made a significant statement with this theory by proposing that the aim of leadership is not just to reach a goal, but also to transform leaders and followers into better, more self-actualized people.

In 1991, leadership scholar Joseph Rost called attention to the shift that was happening in how leadership was defined. Rost described this as a paradigm shift from an industrial to postindustrial view. In the past, what Rost called the "industrial era," leadership was understood to be hierarchical, positional, directive, and one-way. Perspectives on leadership focused on the person who was the leader. The new way of understanding leadership approaches leadership as multidirectional, collaborative, networked, and process oriented. Rost emphasized that leadership came from anywhere in the group, was not only hierarchical, and happened among its members in a relational way that views leadership as a process among people.

In the late 1980s and early 1990s, there was a great amount of research on this collaborative, postindustrial approach to leadership (Allen & Cherry, 2000; Astin & Leland, 1991; Chrislip & Larson, 1994; Kouzes & Posner, 1995; Rost, 1991; Wheatley, 1999). Collaborative leadership is difficult to conceptualize; it deviates from the widely held norm of the positional leader and his or her followers. It calls for a new approach to leadership, in which leadership is the *process* that happens between people in groups, rather than just what the "leader" does. Within the group, there may be a hierarchical structure and a positional leader, but each member of the group has the ability (and even responsibility) to participate in the group's success. In collaborative leadership, every member acts to formulate and reach goals, to maintain authentic relationships, and to ensure that the group's process is ethical and inclusive of differing viewpoints. *This approach to leadership requires individuals and groups to let go of traditional notions of leaders as people who act upon followers and instead calls each person in the group to action* (Allen et al., 1998; Allen & Cherry, 2000; Astin, 1996; Astin & Astin, 2000; Astin & Leland, 1991; Bonous-Hammarth, 2001; Faris & Outcault, 2001; HERI, 1996; McMahon, 2001).

THE SOCIAL CHANGE MODEL OF LEADERSHIP DEVELOPMENT

Given the new definitions of leadership that developed during the 1990s, leadership educators recognized that students needed to learn different approaches to leadership. In 1993, the U.S. Department of Education funded grants for educational programs, institutions, and community organizations that would enhance youth and collegiate leadership. Upon receipt of one of these grants, Alexander and Helen Astin from the Higher Education Research Institute at the University of California, Los Angeles (UCLA) convened a group of national leadership educators to reconceptualize the way leadership was taught and understood by college students. Their goal was twofold: first, to enhance student learning and development of leadership competence; and, second, to facilitate positive social change. Team member Marguerite Bonous-Hammarth (2001) observed, "Our Ensemble discussed leadership as a process or way of channeling skills and energies to some ultimate purpose: that of contributing to the society and social outcomes" (pp. 35–36).

In 1996, the Social Change Model was widely distributed in the higher education community (Astin & Astin, 2000; Astin, 1996; Bonous-Hammarth, 2001; Faris & Outcault, 2001; HERI, 1996; McMahon, 2001; Outcault, Faris, & McMahon, 2001). Scholars have recently observed, "The social change model of leadership development . . . [has] played a prominent role in shaping the curricula and formats of undergraduate leadership education initiatives in colleges and universities throughout the country" (Kezar, Carducci, & Contreras-McGavin, 2006, p. 142).

It was important to these leadership scholars that their process of working together to create the model embodied a collaborative leadership approach. As they worked together, they identified an interesting tension between the needs of the individual and the needs of the collective group. They found that using music as a metaphor for their leadership experience was helpful for finding a balance to this dynamic tension. Almost any kind of music, from rock to jazz to country, is a mixture of melody (individual) and harmony (community), which requires both to produce the desired sound. Each instrument, even when playing the same note, contributes uniquely to the overall tune. The sum of a musical composition is somehow greater than the whole of its parts and, just as in the context of leading, demonstrates the importance of diversity, common purpose, self-knowledge, knowledge of others, feedback, listening, and the respect needed and necessary to practice collaborative leadership (HERI, 1996). Based on this metaphor, the group began referring to itself as an *ensemble*. They have been identified this way ever since. Throughout this book you will see quotes attributed to "the ensemble," referring to the original group of leadership educators who created the social change model.

The Social Change Model of Leadership Development is grounded in the work of the ensemble (Astin, 1996; Bonous-Hammarth, 2001; HERI, 1996) and in the work of Burns (1978) and Rost (1991). The model promotes the creation

The Social Change Model of Leadership Development approaches leadership as a purposeful, collaborative, values-based process that results in positive social change.

and development of social change agents. Research on collaborative leadership, particularly the work of ensemble members Helen Astin and Carole Leland (1991), who studied leadership in the women's movement and published *Women of Influence, Women of Vision*, greatly influenced the creation of the Social Change Model.

The Social Change Model of Leadership rests upon the following assumptions:

+ Leadership is socially responsible, it impacts change on behalf of others.
+ Leadership is collaborative.
+ Leadership is a process, not a position.
+ Leadership is inclusive and accessible to all people.
+ Leadership is values-based.
+ Community involvement/service is a powerful vehicle for leadership. (Astin 1996; Bonous-Hammarth, 2001; HERI, 1996)

A cornerstone of the model is the concept of a values-based process. The model is rooted in a commitment to core human values such as self-knowledge, service, and collaboration. Because the model assumes that leadership is not a position, the term *process* describes the way in which change (and ultimately leadership) occurs (HERI, 1996).

Leadership is not stagnant and does not happen through the efforts of a single individual alone; rather, it is dynamic and collaborative. It is an evolving process that takes place in connection to others. The foundation of this process is relationships. Connections to others through relationships are a core assumption of collaborative leadership and serve as a base for the leadership process. Finally, the intention of positive social change—the hope of helping to make a difference—is the goal of the leadership process. The intent of a leadership process must be for the benefit of others and should be focused on an improvement or alteration of the status quo.

The model provides a framework for individuals and groups to learn to engage in leadership for social change (see Exhibit 2.1). The model describes an interaction between seven key values that individuals, groups, and communities should strive for in order to create social change. Each value begins with a C, which is why the SCM model is sometimes referred to as the "Seven C's for Change." The seven values are grouped into three dimensions: community/society, group, and individual.

These values of the model do not represent a checklist or prescription of how to be a successful leader. One does not

EXHIBIT 2.1 The Social Change Model of Leadership Development

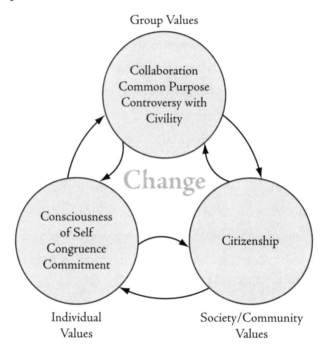

Source: Adapted from *A social change model of leadership development* (3rd ed., p. 20) by Higher Education Research Institute [HERI]. Copyright © 1996, National Clearinghouse for Leadership Programs. Reprinted with permission of the National Clearinghouse for Leadership Programs.

finish learning about one value and then start learning about the next. Rather, development in each value is ongoing. Applying the values in hands-on experiences of leadership results in understanding each value at a deeper level. The model works in this way because the values are interactive. Growth in one value increases the capacity for growth in the others. Although the Seven C's are presented here in a certain order, there are multiple entry points to the model. Depending upon a person's interest in learning about community issues, learning to work effectively in groups, or better understanding the self, he or she can start learning about and practicing the Seven C's at any of three dimensions: individual, the group, or the societal. Exhibit 2.2 describes each of these values in more detail.

Change (Chapter Four)
> *Believe and act as if it were not possible to fail.*
> CHARLES F. KETTERING

Social change is the ultimate goal of the Social Change Model (see Chapter Four). As shown in Exhibit 2.3, it is the hub around which the other elements interact. The model is grounded in the belief that everyone can contribute to making the world a better place for current and future generations. The *intention* of positive social change is at the heart of leadership, regardless of the outcome (HERI, 1996; Rost, 1991).

Change is not easy; it requires learning a new way of being and unlearning past habits, behaviors, and attitudes. It also requires some degree of risk, in order to challenge the status quo and go in a new, untested direction. The courage involved in social change is great, and the willingness to take a leap of faith toward a novel idea or a different tactic requires a comfort with ambiguity, transition, and even discomfort. While this is a difficult call to action, leadership requires that change (small or large scale) be attempted, and ideally, enacted. Change is explored in greater detail in Chapter Four.

EXHIBIT 2.2 Values of the Social Change Model of Leadership Development (The Seven C's of Change)

Value	Definition
Change	As the hub and ultimate goal of the Social Change Model, Change gives meaning and purpose to the other C's. Change means improving the status quo, creating a better world, and demonstrating a comfort with transition and ambiguity in the process of change.
Citizenship	Citizenship occurs when one becomes responsibly connected to the community/society in which one resides by actively working toward change to benefit others through care, service, social responsibility, and community involvement.
Common Purpose	Common purpose necessitates and contributes to a high level of group trust involving all participants in shared responsibility towards collective aims, values, and vision.
Collaboration	Collaboration multiplies a group's effort through collective contributions, capitalizing on the diversity and strengths of the relationships and interconnections of individuals involved in the change process. Collaboration assumes that a group is working towards a Common Purpose, with mutually beneficial goals, and serves to generate creative solutions as a result of group diversity, requiring participants to engage across difference and share authority, responsibility, and accountability for its success.
Controversy with Civility	Within a diverse group, it is inevitable that differing viewpoints will exist. In order for a group to work toward positive social change, open, critical, and civil discourse can lead to new, creative solutions and is an integral component of the leadership process. Multiple perspectives need to be understood, integrated, and bring value to a group.
Consciousness of Self	Consciousness of self requires an awareness of personal beliefs, values, attitudes, and emotions. Self-awareness, conscious mindfulness, introspection, and continual personal reflection are foundational elements of the leadership process.
Congruence	Congruence requires that one has identified personal values, beliefs, attitudes, and emotions and acts consistently with those values, beliefs, attitudes, and emotions. A congruent individual is genuine and honest and "walks the talk."
Commitment	Commitment requires an intrinsic passion, energy, and purposeful investment toward action. Follow-through and willing involvement through commitment lead to positive social change.

Source: Adapted from Astin (1996); HERI (1996); & Wagner (2007).

EXHIBIT 2.3 The Social Change Model and Change

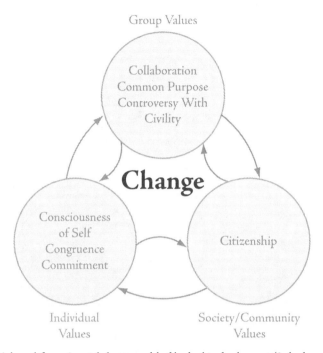

Source: Adapted from *A social change model of leadership development* (3rd ed., p. 20) by Higher Education Research Institute [HERI]. Copyright © 1996, National Clearinghouse for Leadership Programs. Reprinted with permission of the National Clearinghouse for Leadership Programs.

Society/Community Values

Even if I knew that tomorrow the world would go to pieces,
I would still plant my apple tree.
MARTIN LUTHER KING JR.

The Social Change Model calls for leadership directed toward a purpose greater than self for a societal end as illustrated in Exhibit 2.4. Social change occurs because diverse groups in a community work together to benefit the common good. This

EXHIBIT 2.4 The Social Change Model and Society/
Community Values

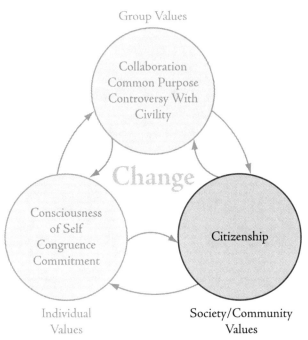

Source: Adapted from *A social change model of leadership development* (3rd ed., p. 20) by Higher Education Research Institute [HERI]. Copyright © 1996, National Clearinghouse for Leadership Programs. Reprinted with permission of the National Clearinghouse for Leadership Programs.

level of leadership encompasses all communities of which one is a member, whether that is the campus, the county, the state, the country, or the world; it is necessary that leadership be connected to a larger social purpose.

Citizenship (Chapter Five)

While it may seem overwhelming to work toward positive social change at the community/societal level, the C of

Citizenship calls all individuals to see themselves as part of a larger whole. Through this value, individuals and groups are able to see how their efforts for social change, large or small, play an important role when joined with the many others working toward the same goals in a global effort. Citizenship relies on caring and is characterized by active engagement in service to the community. *Community* can be defined broadly or specifically, such as a student organization, office, classroom, campus, neighborhood, town, nation, or the world. Service and community involvement are vehicles for implementing this value of the model (HERI, 1996).

Citizenship requires awareness of local and global issues, active engagement in one's community, and participation in interests beyond oneself. Building relationships with others in the community and working across difference are integral components of citizenship. There is great privilege in being part of a community, and as a result, a great responsibility to be an active participant in that community as part of the leadership process. Other dimensions of Citizenship are examined in Chapter Five.

Group Values

While communities vary in size, individuals often find themselves as members of multiple groups within a community. Leadership for social change occurs at the group level, whether with a student organization, a group of friends, a group project for a class, or a sports team. Three specific values, noted in Exhibit 2.5, interact to support the group being effective in

EXHIBIT 2.5 The Social Change Model and Group Values

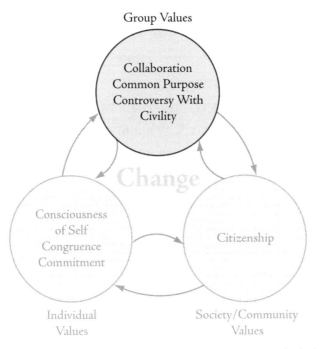

Source: Adapted *from A social change model of leadership development* (3rd ed., p. 20) by Higher Education Research Institute [HERI]. Copyright © 1996, National Clearinghouse for Leadership Programs. Reprinted with permission of the National Clearinghouse for Leadership Programs.

leadership ability: come to Common Purpose, engage in Collaboration with others, and embrace Controversy with Civility.

Collaboration (Chapter Six)

> Collaboration means working together toward common goals by sharing responsibility, authority, and accountability in achieving these goals. . . . It multiplies group effectiveness because it capitalizes on the

multiple talents and perspectives of each group member and the power of that diversity to generate creative solutions and actions. (HERI, 1996, p. 48)

Collaboration is a core value of the Social Change Model. Collaboration is also a necessity when working toward a Common Purpose, requiring individuals to work together. When groups value collaboration, individual members make a choice and a commitment to act in concert with others. Without collaboration, a group will not be effective at accomplishing its shared vision.

Additional benefits of collaboration include contributing to the diversity of a group and multiplying a group's effort through collective contributions. Collaboration necessitates mutually beneficial goals, engaged participants, shared responsibility, and self-aware individuals. The multiple perspectives that collaborative relationships and groups contribute to the change process are essential to leadership (HERI, 1996). Collaboration is explored in greater depth in Chapter Six.

Common Purpose (Chapter Seven)

Group leadership success rests upon a common purpose. All members or partners in a group need to participate in developing the shared vision of the group, even though each individual may work to accomplish that goal in a different way. Individuals must be engaged in the visioning process and agree upon a collective set of aims and group values. Common purpose is strongest when a group explicitly examines its implicit, or unspoken, values.

When looking at a student organization on campus, it is often easy to identify the common goal of that organization. For example, fraternities seek to build brotherhood among their members centered on a core set of values unique to each chapter. Or the public relations society is organized to promote opportunities for students to practice their PR skills outside of the classroom setting. This Common Purpose unites not only individuals within the campus student organization but brings together all organizations across the country. For more examples of Common Purpose as well as a more in-depth look at this value, see Chapter Seven.

Controversy with Civility (Chapter Eight)
Many different ideas and perspectives help group members make sound decisions. It is inevitable in any group that disagreements will arise. While individuals may have discomfort with conflict, it is necessary for all groups to experience the value of Controversy with Civility. Controversy with Civility allows for thoughtful and considered difference of opinion to be heard within a group (HERI, 1996). If a group does not welcome Controversy with Civility, there are many voices that may not be heard or perspectives that might be lost because individuals do not feel comfortable introducing ideas different from the norm of the group. Avoiding groupthink, the tendency to just go along with others even if one holds other views, and engaging in critical dialogue in a respectful manner is crucial for a group's development and ability to achieve Collaboration, work toward a Common Purpose, and achieve

positive social Change. Controversy with Civility rests upon the notion that civil discourse can lead to new, creative solutions and is an essential element of leadership.

Individual Values

No journey carries one far unless, as it extends into the world around us, it goes an equal distance into the world within.

LILLIAN SMITH

EXHIBIT 2.6 The Social Change Model and Individual Values

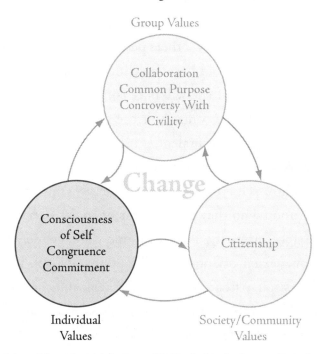

Group Values

Collaboration
Common Purpose
Controversy With
Civility

Change

Consciousness
of Self
Congruence
Commitment

Citizenship

Individual
Values

Society/Community
Values

Source: Adapted from *A social change model of leadership development* (3rd ed., p. 20) by Higher Education Research Institute [HERI]. Copyright © 1996, National Clearinghouse for Leadership Programs. Reprinted with permission of the National Clearinghouse for Leadership Programs.

In order for leadership to occur at the group and societal levels, one must do inner work and reflect on leadership at the individual level. The values of this level, shown in Exhibit 2.6, include developing Consciousness of Self, being Congruent with one's beliefs, and making Commitments that follow those beliefs.

Consciousness of Self (Chapter Nine)

Awareness of self and interactions with others are interrelated. The concept of the looking-glass self was introduced in the early twentieth century by sociologist Charles Horton Cooley (1902), who posited that how individuals perceive themselves influences how others perceive them. For example, if a person has been told her whole life that she is a talented pianist; it is likely that she will have confidence in her piano-playing ability. On the contrary, if the same person has been told she has little musical talent, it is likely that she will avoid opportunities to sing or perform musically. In addition to this concept of how self is defined, individuals also must take time to reflect upon who they are in terms of social identities (for example, race/ethnicity, socioeconomic class, gender/gender expression, sexual orientation, religion, or ability), personal identities (sister, parent, friend, or partner), and core values.

In addition to self-awareness, Consciousness of Self involves the ability to observe oneself in the moment. Sometimes referred to as *mindfulness*, it includes being aware of one's current emotional state and making considered responses rather than reacting without thinking. Each of these pieces of the self intersects to define an individual and may evolve or change over time, but self-reflection and mindfulness are critical to the development of leadership. Each individual needs to understand the values, beliefs, motivations, and perspectives that form how he or she approaches working with others (HERI, 1996; Jones & McEwen, 2000).

Consciousness of Self requires continual growth and reevaluation. Because the levels of the Social Change Model are interconnected, as an individual interacts with others and engages in the community his or her character will likely be influenced. This results in the need to reflect and make meaning of how the sense of self is impacted. This continual process is a lifelong endeavor and is essential for the leadership process. Further details and strategies for self-reflection are presented in Chapter Nine.

Congruence (Chapter Ten)

Acting consistently with espoused values, or *walking the talk,* demonstrates the genuineness or authenticity of a person. Everyone can think of a person who has not done what they said they would do or acted in ways inconsistent with what they claim to stand for: a friend who professes to be open-minded but then tells a racist joke is acting inconsistently with his or her espoused beliefs. Lee and King (2001) describe three ways one holds values: values that are held internally, values that one talks about or states, and values that are "reflected in . . . actions" (p. 62). One of the greatest challenges of leadership is acting consistently, even when no one is looking.

People whose actions are Congruent with their espoused values instill trust and trusting relationships support working collaboratively with others. Trustworthy people create safe spaces in groups to engage in Controversy with Civility. Congruence is not only integral to leadership, but it influences how an individual is perceived by others, thereby affecting the other C's of the model (HERI, 1996). Congruence is presented in greater detail in Chapter Ten.

Commitment (Chapter Eleven)
Commitment is also grounded in an individual's sense of self. One's passions fuel the desire to contribute to the group, community/society, and world. Commitment demonstrates each person's responsibility to service and leadership and contributes to the group's Common Purpose. The majors and future careers students choose may give insight into their passions.

Commitment is demonstrated by significant involvement, the investment of time, and emotional passion. It is crucial in advancing the collective effort. Commitment is the energy that drives action and is a necessary component of change (HERI, 1996). The value of Commitment and its importance to the Social Change Model is explored in further detail in Chapter Eleven.

INTERACTIONS IN THE SOCIAL CHANGE MODEL

For me, a landscape does not exist in its own right, since its appearance changes at every moment; but the surrounding

*atmosphere brings it to life—the light and the air which
vary continually. For me, it is only the surrounding atmosphere which gives subjects their true value.*
CLAUDE MONET

As Monet indicates, there is a connection between subjects
of a piece of art and the environment in which they exist. The
reverse is also true; the subjects influence the environment. In
the Social Change Model, each level interacts with and influences the other and each value is interconnected to the others.
While each C is a distinct component of the model, positive social change is not possible without the interaction and
connection of all of the values. As an individual gains better
Consciousness of Self, acts Congruently, and demonstrates
Commitment, the individual's ability to contribute to the
group's Common Purpose, work with others Collaboratively,
and engage in Controversy with Civility increases (as illustrated by arrow **a** in Exhibit 2.7). Similarly, learning to collaborate, work toward a common purpose, and civilly engage
with others will help the individual clarify his or her own values and commitments and learn to act in ways that are congruent with them (see arrow **b**). This reciprocity exists among
all of the values and dimensions of the model. For example,
awareness of and involvement in community issues challenges
groups (arrow **d**) and individuals (arrow **f**) to continue to clarify and collaboratively act upon their values and common purposes. Interaction and intersections at each dimension move
together to create and facilitate positive social change.

EXHIBIT 2.7 Interactions in the Social Change Model

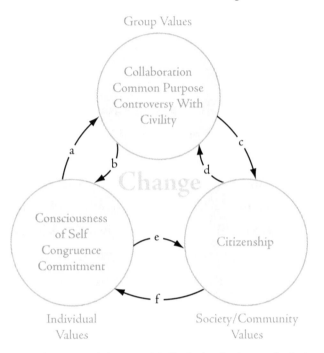

Source: Adapted from *A social change model of leadership development* (3rd ed., p. 20) by Higher Education Research Institute [HERI]. Copyright © 1996, National Clearinghouse for Leadership Programs. Reprinted with permission of the National Clearinghouse for Leadership Programs.

IMPLEMENTING THE SOCIAL CHANGE MODEL

The interactions within the model are only part of the leadership process. An interaction also exists among one's knowledge, attitudes, and skills around leadership and social change. In order to implement the Social Change Model, it is important that one acquires knowledge (knowing), integrates that knowledge into beliefs and attitudes (being), and applies knowledge and beliefs in daily life (doing). This knowing-being-doing framework works especially well for the Social Change Model; Exhibit 2.8 highlights key knowledge, attitudes, and skills rooted in social change and in each value of the model (National Association of Student Personnel Administrators and American College Personnel [NASPA & ACPA], 2004; Komives et al., 2007).

SOCIAL CHANGE ON CAMPUS

If you ever think you're too small to be effective, you've never been in bed with a mosquito!
AMERICAN PROVERB

As described in Chapter One, social change is often thought to be large in scope and scale. Popular examples of social change agents are of heroic people like Rosa Parks and Martin Luther King Jr. within the civil rights movement or Gandhi's peaceful liberation in India. Grand-scale change can be overwhelming to consider when one is starting as one person in college! While large-scale revolutions do happen, smaller acts can also make a difference and start a person on a path to deeper commitment to social change.

There are numerous examples of social change by college students, including working with university administrators to document the nutrition information for food served in the dining hall, Take-Back-the-Night rallies, or participating in a student protest of university investments.

EXHIBIT 2.8 Knowing, Being, Doing

Value	Knowing (Knowledge Acquisition)	Being (Attitudes; Knowledge Integration)	Doing (Skills; Knowledge Application)
	Understanding …	Having …	Demonstrating …
Change	That change is a process Resistance to change at the community/society, group, and individual levels Strategies for overcoming resistance Motivations for engaging in change	Positive perceptions of change Comfort with ambiguity and transition Self-confidence Patience Willingness to step outside of one's comfort zone	An ability to influence systems The creation of a sense of urgency An ability to articulate a change vision Willingness to take a risk to make a difference
Citizenship	Community building Collaboration Social responsibility and larger social issues Personal and community values Rights and responsibilities Social justice/equality	A belief in one's personal ability to make a difference A sense of belonging to one's communities Patience with self and others Optimism and pragmatism Appreciation for diversity Interdependent thinking An ethic of care Tolerance for ambiguity Respect for self and others	An ability to work with others across difference Reflective thought/meaning making Self-motivation/determination Diplomacy Empathy Creativity Critical thinking Interpersonal communication An ability to challenge assumptions Advocacy

Common Purpose	How change occurs The role of mission, vision, and core values How groups function Personal core values	A commitment (to the group, the vision, and social responsibility) A visionary approach Inclusive attitude	Ability to identify goals Decision-making skills Creative thinking Ability to work with others and collaborate
Collaboration	Intercultural awareness and competence Personal values and perspectives That multiple perspectives are both efficient and educational	Belief that working together can generate stronger, more creative win-win solutions Willingness to work toward group trust Willingness to put personal agendas aside to create shared visions	Strong listening, speaking, and reflective dialogue skills Trust and trusting relationships Shared ownership toward a Common Purpose
Controversy with Civility	Attitudes, biases, and values Various communication styles Difference in viewpoints is inevitable and contributes to the leadership process	Civility and commitment Inclusive attitude Patience Purpose	Active listening skills Communication skills Engagement in dialogue Ability to mediate and negotiate
Consciousness of Self	Values of self and others How change happens Personal strengths and weaknesses	Self-confidence Openness to feedback Readiness for change Commitment to positive social change	Ability to reflect Meaning-making skills Ability to give and receive feedback Active listening skills

(Continued)

EXHIBIT 2.8 Knowing, Being, Doing (Continued)

Value	Knowing (Knowledge Acquisition)	Being (Attitudes; Knowledge Integration)	Doing (Skills; Knowledge Application)
	Understanding . . .	Having . . .	Demonstrating . . .
Congruence	Personal values That values are relative to an individual	A commitment to self-evaluation Respect for values different from one's own	Action consistent with personal values An ability to work toward a shared purpose in a group
Commitment	One's personal values and passion The goals or target of a group That change is needed	Self-awareness of personal values Congruence with values and actions Passion Internal motivation Engaged attitude Discipline Energy to move motivation from "should" to "want"	Follow-through on commitments Engagement and involvement Devotion of time and energy Willful action

Source: Adapted from HERI (1996); NASPA & ACPA (2004); Komives, Lucas, & McMahon (2007).

More manageable examples include:

+ Reducing personal electricity use by turning off lights during the day

+ Programming concerts on campus to improve the sense of community or morale

+ Starting a recycling program in the residence halls or community

+ Producing or performing in a political play like the *Vagina Monologues* to raise money for a local women's organization

+ Making sure committees in student government represent diverse interests

+ Working with a professor to create undergraduate teaching assistant position in one's department

+ Participating in a community clean-up to rid a neighborhood of trash and protect the environment, or

+ Choosing a major that will prepare for a life of meaning: being a teacher to help children; being a lawyer to protect people's rights; being a journalist to reveal the truth; being a musician to lift the spirit; being a biologist to protect the environment; or being an agriculturist to feed the world

The world is changing, and with greater abilities to communicate across difference and distance in this networked era of connection and technology, there is a call to action. The Social Change Model provides a framework within which to mobilize oneself and others to address such needed changes.

CONCLUSION

The Social Change Model approaches leadership as a dynamic, collaborative, and values-based process grounded in relationships and intending positive social change. Designed with college students in mind, this model is relevant to student organizations, campus change, and personal development. The model is not a checklist or a prescription for successful leadership; it is a framework for continual exploration of personal values in working with others to attempt change. This approach to leadership requires continuous reflection, active learning, involvement, and action. The discussion questions at the end of each chapter in this book guide the reader to explore the values of Change, Citizenship, Collaboration, Common Purpose, Controversy with Civility, Consciousness of Self, Congruence, Commitment (HERI, 1996) and in becoming a change agent.

DISCUSSION QUESTIONS

1. How have you become aware of the various approaches to leadership that you encounter daily?

2. How do multiple perspectives and diversity fit into the Social Change Model?

3. What is the role of ethics in this approach to leadership?

4. How would this approach to leadership work in an organization with clearly defined hierarchical positions of

leadership? What benefits would it bring? What would be challenging to implement?

5. How did you come to leadership? Did you seek out opportunities to lead? Did your desire to make a difference on a particular issue bring you to leadership?

6. How do you want your life to matter? What passions can you identify that are driving any of your actions, such as the major or future career field you are choosing?

JOURNAL PROBES

On Becoming

Preeminent psychologist, Carl Rogers (1961) said that people are always in a process of *becoming*. The first two journal probes are intended to help you reflect on how you see yourself becoming a leader for social change.

1. How are you becoming more effective at doing collaborative leadership?

2. Can you remember a time when you defined leadership differently than you do now? How is your current approach different from your approach then?

Learning Through Experience

The ensemble that created the Social Change Model believed the best way to learn to do leadership was through experience

and reflection. This involves challenging yourself to have new experiences that test your ability and awareness **and** to spend time thinking about what you have learned from that experience. The remaining journal probes are designed to maximize learning through experience by guiding your reflective journal writing through Kolb's (1981) four processes of experiential learning.

1. **Concrete Experience.** Describe a specific situation when you had an experience that relates to leadership as it has been described here. What happened? What details stand out to you? Describe briefly the situation, what you did, and how you felt.

2. **Reflective Observation.** Why did this situation have the outcome it did? What caused the situation to occur in the first place? What responses from you and from others worked in this situation? Why was that effective? What did not work? Why?

3. **Abstract Conceptualization.** What lessons can you draw from this specific experience that could apply more generally? Given both your reflections and the information in this chapter, what would you do if a similar situation presented itself? What general guidelines would you create for handling future situations like this?

4. **Active Experimentation.** What opportunities might you seek out that would give you the chance to apply what you have learned here? How might you test the lessons or guidelines you created in #3 to see if they work?

References

Allen, K. E., Bordas, J., Hickman, G. R., Matusak, L. R., Sorenson, G. J., & Whitmire, K. J. (1998). Leadership in the twenty-first century. In G. R. Hickman (Ed.), *Leading organizations: Perspectives for a new era* (pp. 572–580). Thousand Oaks, CA: Sage.

Allen, K. E., & Cherry, C. (2000). *Systemic leadership: Enriching the meaning of our work.* Lanham, MD: University Press of America.

Astin, A., & Astin, H. (2000). *Leadership reconsidered: Engaging higher education in social change.* Battle Creek, MI: W.K. Kellogg Foundation.

Astin, H. S. (1996, July/August). Leadership for social change. *About Campus*, 4–10.

Astin, H. S., & Leland, C. (1991). *Women of influence, women of vision: A cross-generational study of leaders and social change.* San Francisco: Jossey-Bass.

Bass, B. M. (1990). *Bass & Stogdill's handbook of leadership: Theory, research, & management* applications (3rd ed.). New York: Free Press.

Bonous-Hammarth, M. (2001). Developing social change agents: Leadership development for the 1990s and beyond. In C. L. Outcault, S. K. Faris, & K. N. McMahon (Eds.), *Developing non-hierarchical leadership on campus: Case studies and best practices in higher education* (pp. 34–39). Westport, CT: Greenwood.

Burns, J. M. (1978). *Leadership.* New York: Harper & Row.

Chrislip, D. D., & Larson, C. E. (1994). *Collaborative leadership: How citizens and civic leaders can make a difference.* San Francisco: Jossey-Bass.

Cooley, C. H. (1902). *Human nature and social order.* New York: Scribner's.

Faris, S. K. & Outcault, C. L. (2001). The emergence of inclusive, process-oriented leadership. In C. L. Outcault, S. K. Faris, & K. N. McMahon (Eds.), *Developing non-hierarchical leadership on campus: Case studies and best practices in higher education* (pp. 9–18). Westport, CT: Greenwood.

Greenleaf, R. G. (1977). *Servant leadership: A journey in the nature of legitimate power and greatness.* New York: Paulist.

Higher Education Research Institute. [HERI] (1996). *A social change model of leadership development* (Version III). Los Angeles: University of California Los Angeles, Higher Education Research Institute.

Jones, S. R., & McEwen, M. K. (2000, July/August). A conceptual model of multiple dimensions of identity. *Journal of College Student Development, 41*(4), 405–414.

Kezar, A. J., Carducci, R., & Contreras-McGavin, M. (2006). *Rethnking the "L" word in higher education: The revolution in research on leadership.* ASHE Higher Education Report (Vol. 31, no. 6). San Francisco: Jossey-Bass.

Kolb, D. A. (1981). Learning styles and disciplinary differences. In A. W. Chickering & Associates (Eds.), *The modern American college: Responding to the new realities of diverse students and a changing society* (pp. 232–255). San Francisco: Jossey Bass.

Komives, S. R., Lucas, N., & McMahon, T. R. (2007). *Exploring leadership: For college students who want to make a difference* (2nd ed.). San Francisco: Jossey-Bass.

Kouzes, J. M., & Posner, B. Z. (1995). *The leadership challenge.* San Francisco: Jossey-Bass.

Lee, R., & King, S. (2001). *Ground your leadership vision in personal vision: Discovering the leader in you: A guidebook to realizing your personal leadership potential.* San Francisco: Jossey-Bass.

McMahon, K. N. (2001). An interview with Helen S. Astin. In C. L. Outcault, S. K. Faris, & K. N. McMahon (Eds.), *Developing non-hierarchical leadership on campus: Case studies and best practices in higher education* (pp. 3–8). Westport, CT: Greenwood.

National Association of Student Personnel Administrators and American College Personnel Association. (2004). *Learning reconsidered: A campus-wide focus on the student experience.* Washington, DC: Author.

Northouse, P. G. (2007). *Leadership: Theory and practice* (4th ed.). Thousand Oaks, CA: Sage.

Outcault, C. L., Faris, S. K., & McMahon, K. N. (Eds.). (2001). *Developing non-hierarchical leadership on campus: Case studies and best practices in higher education*. Westport, CT: Greenwood.

Rogers, C. R. (1961). *On becoming a person: A therapist's view of psychotherapy*. Boston: Houghton Mifflin.

Rost, J. C. (1991). *Leadership for the twenty-first century*. Westport, CT: Praeger.

Wagner, W. (2007). The Social Change Model of leadership: A brief overview. *Concepts & Connections, 15*(1), 8–10.

Wheatley, M. J. (1999). *Leadership and the new science: Discovering order in a chaotic world*. San Francisco: Berrett-Koehler.

Wren, J. T. (Ed.). (1995). *The leader's companion: Insights on leadership through the ages*. New York: Free Press.

APPLYING THE SOCIAL CHANGE MODEL

A Case Study Approach

José-Luis Riera

Leadership is a process that is learned. It is learned from reflections on experience, from observation, and from applying new concepts like those presented in the Social Change Model of Leadership Development (SCM). The case studies in this chapter are provided to illustrate the Social Change Model in action. Since leadership is expressed differently in different environments, these cases are set in the context college students are probably most familiar with: the college campus. As readers consider the Seven C's throughout the book, they are encouraged to look back at the case studies—both individually and with peers—and discuss them critically in light of the content of each chapter.

PUTTING THE MODEL TO WORK

The creators of the Social Change Model intended it to be applied by individuals or groups. As a collaborative model of leadership, SCM encourages students to get involved in group efforts regardless of whether the students hold formal positions of leadership or not. While initiating change is important, it is also necessary to sustain the group's efforts over time. This means leadership will often need to be passed on from those who initiate the change to those who plan on keeping that change alive. In the college or university context, this is best understood by thinking about how one's time on campus is finite. So, if an individual or group initiates change, eventually, he or she will leave and depend on future generations of students to sustain this change (Higher Education Research Institute [HERI], 1996). For example, think of the student organization with an ongoing tutoring program at a nearby elementary school and how they perpetuate a sustained relationship. We encourage you to think of approaches to these cases that produce self-sustaining systemic change.

PLANNING FOR CHANGE

The elements of planning can be very helpful when thinking through the case studies presented throughout this text. The elements can serve as a framework for analyzing and

 The ensemble highlights seven elements that are important to consider when planning any project whose aim it is to affect social change. In no particular order, they include:

+ Physical setting
+ Preliminary task definition
+ Involvement/recruitment of student participants
+ Task research/redefinition
+ Division of labor
+ Mode of group functioning and
+ Legitimizing the project. (HERI, 1996)

understanding the case studies. With each element, think through how a change project that you are attempting either to initiate or sustain can best thrive. A more detailed explanation of the elements of planning follows.

+ **Physical Setting.** Is the change effort at a college or university campus, the greater community, or a workplace? Within those areas, where exactly will the change be best initiated and/or sustained?

+ **Preliminary Task Definition.** What is the need or problem? How do you know this is a need or problem? What changes are needed? How can students best serve or solve the problem? What needs to get done?

+ Involvement and Recruitment of Student Participants. What personal and shared values can be identified? Are the students or participants involved in the change process those with diverse talents and background?

+ Task Research or Redefinition. What other information is needed about the problem or task, and how might this information reshape the task?

+ Division of Labor. How can tasks be divided most wisely among the talent that is held by the individuals in the group? What resources exist within the group of those initiating or sustaining the change?

+ Mode of Group Functioning. What is the role of each group member? How can the group best collaborate? How can the group foster an environment where openness and honesty is valued? What knowledge and skill development does the group need? How will the group assess its progress and improve its processes through feedback?

+ Legitimizing the Project. Is the community for which the social change is intended included in the change efforts? Who is the project intended to benefit? What are their perspectives on this issue? On the project? How can they be actively involved? Has the impact of this change been evaluated?

USING A CASE STUDY

Before beginning to explore each case study, it is useful to consider how to use a case study effectively. Case studies are not meant to lead to one correct answer, but to provide opportunities to apply new knowledge and practice analyzing the issues from different perspectives. This is why it is helpful to examine case studies both individually and with a group—the more diversity present in the group, the more perspectives that may be present in the analysis of the case study.

The following steps are useful when analyzing a case study:

1. Identify the characters in the case study. What is each of their roles?

2. Analyze the environment or context of the case study.

3. Apply the Seven C's to illuminate the case study.

4. Design a plan to intervene or understand what is happening in the case study.

5. Compare the experience of the characters to your own experience.

A first step is to identify the characters in the case study. Who are the players? What is each player's role? The second area of analysis is often the context or environment of the case study. Although the case studies presented here all take place on a college campus, there is a wide array of college and university environments, so it will be important to take note of the type of campus on which the particular case study is set. Then, consider how the Seven C's are represented in the case study. What issues affect the members' ability to work collaboratively toward a common goal? Fourth, design a plan to intervene and propose potential solutions. Last, compare the case study to one's own experience. How is it similar or different? How might the setting of the case study differ from the environment of one's own campus? Is it realistic to imagine what is happening in the case study?

It is helpful to consider the benefits of using case study analysis to understand how the Social Change Model might be implemented effectively. This type of analysis can help to provide challenges to conventional habits, promote the incorporation of multiple perspectives, understand the issue within a wide range of environments, consider the constraints that may be placed on the change makers by institutional or political forces (Stage & Dannells, 2000), and promote personal reflection.

The first set of general questions may be the most important. Their aim is to challenge one's instinctual reactions or thoughts about a solution for a given problem:

+ What is my first impulse on this issue?
+ What are the positive implications of that first impulse?
+ What are the negative implications of that first impulse?
+ How might the Social Change Model apply to this situation?
+ How might knowledge of the Social Change Model modify that first impulse? (Stage & Dannells, p. 9)

The next set of questions fosters the consideration of multiple perspectives. Each person involved in the case will be affected by the situation in different ways.

+ Who are the actors in the case?

+ What roles do these actors play?

+ What is the view of each actor on the issues?

+ Which of the actors are also decision makers?

+ What would be the scope of each of their decisions?

+ Would some "invisible" actors be affected by the decision?

+ What would be their perspectives?

Considering the environment where the case study takes place is also important. These questions will help shed light on how the unique environment of the case affects the issues being raised.

+ What is the history of the institution or place being considered in the case study?

+ What is the relationship between the characters of the case study?

+ What is the relationship of the characters with the environment around them?

+ How can you find good sources of information about the environment?

Finally, it is important to consider how the institution's governance puts constraints around potential solutions or provides supports for those solutions.

- What is the mission of the institution or place in question?
- Are there particular aspects of governance that need to be considered?
- What is the history of the institution with this issue?
- Do any political figures have any particular interest in this issue?

Particularly when one examines issues of social change, social justice, and inequality, it is important to analyze case studies with a critical eye. Analysis should include consideration of what is missing from the case as well as what is presented. For example, are there individuals affected by the issue who have not been represented in the case study? Why were they excluded? How do characters present themselves in the case study? Is this so because of who they are?

Working with case studies can be a very insightful way to help fully grasp concepts of the Social Change Model. Working within the parameters of a case study provides a safe place to try on different identities and consider alternatives in response to the presented issues as you learn how you would respond in a real-world scenario.

INTRODUCTION TO THE CASE STUDIES

Three case studies are presented in this book. The first study, entitled "An Inconvenient Truth," is presented in full in this chapter. A series of questions appear throughout this case study, as a model for how the other two case studies might be approached. The second and third case studies, entitled "Starving for Attention" and "Clear Haziness," are introduced here and evolve throughout each of the remaining chapters in the text. The "Zoom In" feature of each chapter serves as an opportunity to apply the topics covered in each chapter to the case study.

Case Study #1: An Inconvenient Truth

You attend State University, a mid-sized public university, and you have just wrapped up the summer after your first year as a student. After working for the summer, you are excited and looking forward to the beginning of classes for your sophomore year. You are especially excited about your sophomore seminar series class this semester. One of your favorite classes last year was your first-year seminar. As part of your general education requirements, State requires students to take interdisciplinary seminars each year on topics of their choice. You are thrilled because this year you will be in the seminar entitled "An Inconvenient Truth" and you have become passionate about environmental sustainability.

Based on Al Gore's popular documentary on climate crisis, your seminar will focus on issues of global warming and the impact it is having on our society as a nation and worldwide. Your professor, Dr. Yangklov, is a journalism professor who has been tracking the media's impact on the dissemination of information on global warming for many years. The first day of class you learn that you are required to perform three service hours every week in various community organizations whose mission in some way involves educating their communities about the impacts of global warming. You have been assigned to work with A Better Tomorrow, a grant-funded nonprofit agency in an urban setting whose mission is to reach out to members of lower socioeconomic backgrounds and help them understand issues around global warming and how they can contribute to the solution of the problem.

Your service will be performed in a group that was assigned by Dr. Yangklov. Your group consists of yourself; Tonya, an education and French double major; Greg, a government and politics major; Jensen, an environmental science major; and, Nina, an English major who is also pre-law.

Your first task is to go to the office of A Better Tomorrow and meet with your site supervisor, Lee. Lee will brief you on exactly what you will be doing for your time with the organization. You all meet as a group on campus and car pool together. Greg notices right away that the neighborhood where the agency is located is different than what he is used to. The homes are predominantly row-style housing and the

> Based on what you know about change, think about what change needs to happen here. Why is this change issue an important one? Notice the dynamics that might exist in this case study—a group of students is working together on a shared issue in the context of service. How might each student's opinion or approach to working on this project differ? How does this change related to the dangers presented in Chapter One?

businesses seem very small and not well maintained. There are many signs in different languages, some that look familiar, and others that no one in your group recognizes. You sense that a lot of people that you pass are staring at your car as you drive slowly down the road looking for your destination.

> How might the various majors of the students come into play? What is your major and how does that impact your approach to this project? How could diverse perspectives help this project's goal?

Lee is a really nice woman. She seems very intelligent, and you connect with her immediately. She is excited to have such a motivated group of college youth at her disposal in this way and poses a challenge to the group. She asks you each to introduce yourselves and tell her your majors and why you're interested in working on this project.

Lee wants your group to create a comprehensive way to address issues of global warming in this community. She stresses that "the sky is the limit" and that "we will give you as much support as we can to help you be successful in completing this project." She summarizes the charge for your project: "As you may have noticed this is a very diverse community.

> Look for how the concept of Citizenship might be represented throughout the case studies. Given that your institution is located in this city, do you consider yourself to be a member of this community? Do you identify with a sense of responsibility to promote positive change in a community such as this?

You name it, we got it here—friends from Africa, Asia, South America—all over the world. Our goal at A Better Tomorrow is to come alongside this community, and in particular this neighborhood, to educate around issues of global warming. You see, contrary to popular belief, it's not that these folks aren't smart or that they don't care, but unfortunately, they do not have the same resources that folks in the suburbs have. Reducing, reusing, and recycling are worthy goals, but there is no doubt that it takes resources to do this. So, these are the things we'd like your group to focus on: (1) Find out what types of things community members need, you know, what types of support they need, to be successful in living a more eco-friendly lifestyle; (2) Determine effective ways to educate the community about global warming and becoming environmentally friendly citizens; and (3) I would really like you to think about how to reach both young people and the elderly." Lee is exceptionally passionate about what she does and her enthusiasm is rubbing off on some of your group members.

Does this "charge" give your group Common Purpose? What questions might you ask Lee to fully understand your project? Do group members share a vision for what Lee's challenge involves?

Your group begins to work on developing a number of initiatives that might fit the goals that were laid out by Lee. Everyone is at a different place as you sit down to talk about the development of your service project. Greg understands why global warming might be important but does not see why working with lower socioeconomic communities is going to fix the problem. Tonya is excited about possibly using her French skills as she is informed that there is a Senegalese population in the neighborhood, though she is nervous about saying something wrong. Nina is wondering if an assignment in the inner city is the best place for her to be.

As the semester pushes forward, you start making observations about how your fellow group members are reacting to the project. Jensen is very excited about solving global warming. With his interest in environmental science, he is passionate about all the issues that this very project addresses. Though he took the class because of his passion for this subject area, he realizes that this project involves a lot more than this. He vocalizes this by stating, "I take so much for granted. I never have to worry about half of the things that these people have to worry about. Wow, we all have so much privilege to be able to be at a place like State."

Nina shares Jensen's passion for global warming. After watching Al Gore's documentary and seeing him speak live, Nina is concerned about how the United States in particular seems to be ignoring this issue. She struggles as to why the project has to be in this community. She counters some of Jensen's thoughts by saying, "Your parents worked for what they have. Why should they care about global warming when they should be trying to better themselves?"

One day after your service hours, the group decides to just hang out and go to a coffee shop. You are sincerely wondering how others are experiencing this project, so you ask, "What do you think about this project—do you like it?" Nina is the first to speak: "I'll be honest—I feel like I am the most out of place, but I'm also frustrated and mad—at my parents, my family, and my community. I almost feel cheated, like, why didn't anyone ever tell me more about people who live in this country but don't have access to the same types of things we do?"

Tonya is frustrated by how everyone acts. She says, "I don't want to offend anyone but I feel like we all act one way when we're on site for this project and another way on campus—not only you guys but the whole class. Like look at all the people in class who buy individual bottles of water or throw their soda cans in the trash. It's as if we don't take back what we're learning and let our lives be different at home—like that's not cool or something."

Commitment is an important concept in the Social Change Model. How does the passion evoked by a number of students in this case study contribute to Commitment? How does Commitment tie into being a change agent? How do you react to Nina's comment?

What are the issues of Congruence being expressed here? Do you see fellow students being incongruent in their espoused values versus their actions on your campus? How does this make you feel? How does one grow to have a Consciousness of Self and come to understand what one's values, beliefs, and attitudes are? Why is this important? How about the concept of Collaboration? Would you categorize how this group approaches this project as collaborative? Why or why not? How does collaboration strengthen the process of social change?

After careful thought, you realize you totally agree. In fact, you want them to really care about making a change and the people that you are all serving. You begin to introduce this idea to the group and you start to realize that some do not agree with you—you worry that if you "rock the boat" the group will not be able to finish the class project.

> How might you go about continuing this conversation in a way that promotes Controversy with Civility? Is it possible to continue engaging the group in this discussion without everyone becoming frustrated? How are the other C's related to Controversy with Civility—for example, how would having Common Purpose impact the ability to discuss something controversial *with* civility?

As the semester closes, you are thankful that you had such an experience. Your own reflections on the experience make you decide that you want to continue working with the community where you had your service hours and that you want to continue educating folks on campus and beyond about global warming.

> How are you affected on an individual level by this experience? How can one help his or her peers understand the need for change in a given social context?

Here are some general questions to consider as you evaluate the case study:

+ How might you continue to develop as a change agent for global warming beyond the scope of this class?

+ What other social issues can you identify as affecting the context of this project?

+ How might you learn more about communities you know very little about?

+ After looking at each C, how do you see it play out in the development of the group? How might you describe the main character's (your) process of leadership?

+ How about each group member's process of leadership?

+ Do you see the three dimensions (societal/community, group, and individual) of the SCM playing roles here? How did one influence the other and vice versa?

+ Global warming and working with urban populations might not be your "cause." If you were to substitute your own passions for seeking justice in the world, what might they be? Review the reasons why people develop their passions in Chapter One.

+ How might each student, from his or her unique academic vantage point, approach this service project?

+ Do you consider the members in this group to be leaders? Were they practicing leadership? If so, how? If not, why not?

+ What role did reflection play in helping each group member to grow?

You can imagine that there are countless ways to get at what's happening in a case study. In the context of learning more about leadership and the Social Change Model, we encourage you to reflect on the situations individually as well as to seek input from your peers on their thoughts of the case study. Relate the case study elements to the C's as often as you can, and when you think about how you see leadership represented in the case studies, do so based on the definition of leadership that is presented in Chapter Two.

Background of Case Study #2: Starving for Attention

Taylor, a sophomore at a private elite university, has just completed a Sociology of Poverty course as part of his core curriculum and is moved by a whole new world that is opened up to him through this class. Of the various facets of poverty that were discussed in class, Taylor begins to grapple with and understand the political and economic implications of wage distribution in U.S. society. Taylor is ready to do more and begins looking for opportunities to get involved. He approaches some upper-class students whom he has met through his classes and gathers some suggestions. The same day he encounters a rally for the Living Wage Campaign on the campus mall. He is somewhat familiar with the term *living wage*, but he stops by to learn more.

At the rally, Taylor learns more about the disparity between the legal minimum wage and the cost of living in this and many regions of the country. He learned about how housing, fuel, and food prices have escalated, but the minimum wage has not kept pace. One student mentioned that at the minimum wage, the campus's day care workers cannot afford to put their own children in day care. Noticing Taylor's interest, one of the rally coordinators invites him to attend the organization's next meeting.

After attending the organization's meeting, Taylor finds himself heavily involved in the Living Wage Campaign: he writes an article for the group's Web site, raises money for the next activity, and meets other members at 7 a.m. to put up flyers, and chalk the campus for the next rally. He identifies with this cause because he has learned so much about it and because, though he realizes the issue is large in scope, he begins to understand how change can begin on his own campus.

One of the issues discussed at the organization meeting is the undercompensation of the university's service staff. One of the organization officers brought information about the current staff wages, as well as average costs in the area for rent, gas, health care, insurance, and other household expenses. Taylor tried everything he could think of to get the numbers to add up, considering ways to live as inexpensively as possible. But even with two wage earners, and not accounting for day care, he cannot make the staff income meet the typical monthly expenses. Though he feels he learned a lot of the basics in his Sociology of Poverty class, this exercise really hits home as he realizes that this affects the housekeepers he knows who clean his residence hall.

Background of Case Study #3: Clear Haziness

This case study asks you to put yourself in the role of the main character. In each chapter of the book, you will be asked to make decisions about your response to the situation in the case study based on what you are learning in that particular chapter.

It is the end of summer and you are returning to college for your junior year. You are enjoying your experience at State University. As you begin to think about your year, you are most looking forward to your involvement on staff with the school newspaper, *The Weekly*. *The Weekly* is one of the strongest traditions at your college and is named after the college's founder, Lou Weekly. It is published once a week and is very popular among all constituents. Your college is located in a town that finds most of its identity in the college. Students, staff, faculty, and community members alike read the paper. *The Weekly* has won a number of awards throughout its eighty-five-year existence. It is no coincidence that your college has one of the strongest journalism programs in the country.

During your first year at *The Weekly*, you were involved with the paper in a noncommittal way. You freelanced for the paper as a photographer and op-ed writer. You spent very little time in *The Weekly's* offices and showed up to hand in your work if requested, though usually, you submitted everything electronically right from your computer. Sophomore year you became a lot more involved and as an official staff member spent a lot of time in *The Weekly's* office. As a junior you are returning to *The Weekly* as an editor. You were initially assigned to be the op-ed editor, but received a call from the executive editor a week before returning to school asking you to be the photography editor. This was very significant, as the photography in *The Weekly* has been the most consistent award-winning component of the paper.

Though your greatest strength is not in photography, you accept the position knowing it will be a tremendous opportunity and a step closer to becoming the executive editor your senior year. One of your greatest apprehensions is your relationship with the returning photographers. The executive editor tells you that you were chosen because the executive board believed that your leadership was such that it would keep the photographers "in line." Though the executive board knows that there are photographers more gifted than you, they did not feel that any of them could lead the department like you could.

As soon as you are back on campus you begin meeting with your staff, and in addition to compiling the first edition of the semester, you spend most of your time planning your biggest priority—recruitment of new staff photographers. You feel very positive about the coming year; after just three weeks of the fall semester you have a full staff of photographers who are willing and eager to be part of the paper's team. You pair up each new photographer with a returning photographer so that your new photographers will be trained and "learn the ropes."

After several weeks, you have a sense that things are going well. One night after the paper went to print for the week, you spend some time relaxing on Facebook. As you are viewing the profiles of some of your junior photographers, you notice that there are a number of inappropriate pictures posted in their albums. This disturbs you and you begin to wonder why this is so consistent across the profiles of all junior photographers. Coincidentally, you receive an instant message from Wendy, one of your junior photographers, requesting to meet with you. You agree and let her know that you are available immediately.

After meeting with Wendy, you are truly dismayed. Wendy describes to you that she has a series of inappropriate pictures that she has taken and is supposed to post them to her Facebook account, though she is very apprehensive to do so. She explains that the senior photographers gathered all the incoming photographers and gave them a number of assignments to photograph inappropriate things. The senior photographers made it clear that in order for them to have the privilege of being part of *The Weekly*'s photography staff they would need to complete this assignment throughout the semester. Some of the photos involved trespassing in offices on campus and taking pictures on site and others involved taking pictures of random students without their knowledge in situations that violated their privacy. Additionally, each junior photographer was given a list of five students on campus; they were instructed to photograph them as much as possible. All five of these students Wendy mentions are students who are not part of the mainstream culture on campus.

Very upset with the actions of your senior photographers, you call a meeting and confront them without disclosing Wendy's name. They explain to you, "This has been happening for years." One of the more respected senior photographers says, "For years this same or similar type of assignment has been given out to junior photographers as a way to prove ourselves. If you rose through the ranks, you would know about all this—it's nothing that they should complain about, it's just the way it is." You question them as to whether they think it is appropriate and they accuse you of overreacting and not understanding the culture of the photography staff.

ZOOM IN

At the end of each chapter there is a "Zoom In" section for each case study that gives you details as the study pertains to what you are learning in that chapter. Apply the SCM to these case studies by diagnosing the cases based on key elements of the model as well by the actions of the characters (and consider what you would do) in those same circumstances.

References

Higher Education Research Institute [HERI]. (1996). *A social change model of leadership development* (Version III). Los Angeles: University of California Los Angeles, Higher Education Research Institute.

Stage, F. K., & Dannells, M. (Eds.). (2000). *Linking theory to practice: Case studies for working with college students* (2nd ed.). Philadelphia: Accelerated Development.

CHANGE

Nurredina Workman

If you want to truly understand something, try to change it.
KURT LEWIN

As described in Chapter Two, the goal of the Social Change Model (SCM) is fostering positive social change (Higher Education Research Institute [HERI], 1996).

At the simplest level, change is a shift or move to something different. This can occur suddenly or over a long period of time and can occur both intentionally and unintentionally. Hultman (1998) noted, "By itself, change is inherently neither good nor bad" and at the same time, "Change is not

 *Change* is the "hub" of the Social Change Model and focuses on making "a better world and a better society for self and others." (HERI, 1996, p. 21)

neutral, people will be better or worse off because of it" (p. 98). Whether a change is good or bad often depends on one's perspective. For example, think about the changing membership of student organizations each year. While this change is neither bad nor good, different members and officers change the organization, resulting in the need for team building, values clarification, training, goal setting, and more. Remodeling on campus is another example of change that is not neutral, as it can both improve campus ecology and cause a lot of issues for campus members, such as noisy classroom environments, loss of space, or having to find a new entrance during construction. The advent of air conditioners certainly improved comfort in the hot summer months, but it also took people off their front porches where they readily greeted and talked with neighbors.

CHAPTER OVERVIEW

This chapter highlights key concepts that will help to answer the question, "What is change?" by exploring (1) transformative change, (2) several models that describe change on the individual, group, and the community/society levels, (3) new approaches to change, and (4) resistance to change. When reading this chapter, write down new things you are learning about change that will help you in your efforts to have a positive impact in your community.

TRANSFORMATIVE CHANGE

Boyce (2003) argued that there are two types of change: single-order change and second-order change. *Single-order change* involves structural or procedural changes that can be made within the organization's current framework of rules, procedures, and leadership roles. Sometimes however, the current rules, procedures, or approaches to leadership are creating the problem. These situations call for *second-order change*, or changing the organization's fundamental values and assumptions (Boyce). Second-order change has also been referred to as *transformative change* (Eckel, Hill, & Green, 1998). Transformative change "(1) alters the culture of the institution by changing select underlying assumptions and institutional behaviors, processes, and products; (2) is deep and pervasive, affecting the whole institution, (3) is intentional; and (4) occurs over time" (p. 3).

A common challenge for student organizations is managing a smooth leadership transition as new executive officers are elected and outgoing officers graduate. It is not rare to find the incoming student officers at a loss about what worked and did not work for the officers the previous year. A single-order change might be to create a resource binder for each of the officer positions that could be added to each year to create a record of information and rational for decisions that were made over time. A second-order or transformative change might involve a gradual shift in how the organization thinks about leadership. Rather than holding closed-door executive meetings, the officers would work to create an environment where ideas and contributions come from any member. Rather than focusing on the powers and responsibilities of the elected few, they would consider leadership to be an act of mentoring and empowering the general membership to contribute to the organization. An organization with a more transparent approach to what the officers do and more collaborative values, newly elected officers would be quite familiar with the direction of the organization and with the responsibilities of their new role, with or without an updated binder.

O'Toole (1996) asserts that the ineffectiveness of leaders in making change rarely occurs because they utilized flawed procedures or did not follow the "recipes for success" provided by experts. In the previous example, the resource binder system could be implemented flawlessly, but it still might not result in smooth officer transitions. As long as executive board decision making and actions are kept hidden from the general membership, new officers will always be unclear about their responsibilities. O'Toole argues that "when change fails to occur as planned, the cause is almost always to be found at a deeper level, rooted in the inappropriate behavior, attitudes, and assumptions of would-be leaders" (p. x).

Fullan (2001) emphasizes the need for a change of culture or "reculturing" that "activates and deepens moral purpose through collaborative work cultures that respect differences and constantly build and test knowledge against measurable results—a culture within which one realizes that sometimes being off balance is a learning moment" (p. 44). Strategies may help to define what is or is not working in efforts toward transformative change but alone do not provide an accurate picture of the process. That is why O'Toole (1996) argues for transformative values-based leadership, stating:

> Learning to lead is thus not simply a matter of style, or how-to, of following some recipe, or even of mastering "the vision thing." Instead, leadership is about ideas and values. It is about understanding the differing and conflicting needs of followers. And it is about energizing followers to pursue a better end state (goal) than they had thought possible. It is about creating a values-based umbrella large enough to accommodate the various interests of followers, but focused enough to direct all their energies in pursuit of a common good. (p. xi)

Individual Change

Since the 1980s, change has emerged as one of the primary tasks of leaders (O'Toole, 1996) and a shared responsibility of group members. Becoming a transformative change agent at the group and societal levels requires some level of self-transformation (Goleman, Boyatzis, & McKee, 2002). Without consciousness of self (discussed in Chapter Nine) and self-transformation, a leader is likely to continue using the same knowledge, skills, and lack of awareness that may have been part of the problem to begin with.

Each person's self-transformation is an important aspect of groups and communities seeking to make change. Pulsifer (2008) shares the story of a wise monk who said:

When I was a young man, I wanted to change the
world. I found it was difficult to change the world, so
I tried to change my nation. When I found I couldn't
change the nation, I began to focus on my town. I
couldn't change the town and as an older man, I tried
to change my family. Now, as an old man, I realize
the only thing I can change is myself, and suddenly I
realize that if long ago I had changed myself, I could
have made an impact on my family. My family and I
could have made an impact on our town. Their impact
could have changed the nation and I could have indeed
changed the world. (p. 1)

Senge, Scharmer, Jaworski, and Flowers (2005) believe
that "when people who are actually creating a system start to
see themselves as the source of their problems, they invariably
discover a new capacity to create results they truly desire" (p.
45). Consider the earlier example of executive officers changing the way they viewed leadership. In order for a transformative change to occur, the individuals in the organization
need to change their own fundamental assumptions about
what leaders do. When leadership is not done in secret and
imposed upon followers but is a collaborative and empowering process between leaders and followers, the organization
can accomplish more than ever thought possible.

Developing insight into personal change processes is
empowering because once people know who they are in relation to change, they will have a greater ability to make changes

within themselves. Quinn (1996) noted that while there is a general consensus that deep change must be made by organizations to remain competitive, it is rarely mentioned that individuals must also change. Sometimes, Quinn shared, "We need to alter our fundamental assumptions, rules, or paradigms and develop new theories about ourselves and our surrounding environment" (p. 7). Much like finding and polishing a diamond in the rough, *deep change is about unearthing the hidden assumptions that one has about oneself, others, organizations, and society.*

Transformative change is much easier said than done. Changing a behavior, attitude, or belief is challenging, ongoing work. For example, creating a new anti-hazing policy and calling it done may not lead to less hazing. Instead it might lead to more secrecy. To make a deep change, organizations would have to address the values of the individuals who hold pro-hazing beliefs, such as believing the best way to build strong organization is "break them down so that you can build them up." Merely creating policies will not address these deeply held beliefs; changing those beliefs is a more complicated process.

Prochaska and DiClemente (1982) developed a model describing the process of change for smokers who were attempting to quit. While the model was designed specifically for changing health-related habits, it provides insight for those who are curious about making any behavioral change. An example of a student leader, Sayid, who wants to stop procrastinating, will be used to illustrate each stage in the model.

Stage Model of Personal Change

Thinking about a habit we would like to change is a great way to analyze who we are and how open we are to self-transformation. Attempting to change the habit can provide great insight into our internal responses to change. Reflecting on the personal process of changing a behavior is particularly important to those who are interested in becoming more effective leaders. Are there things that you have been trying to change but have yet to figure out? My friend Sayid (pseudonym) wanted to stop procrastinating so that he could improve the quality of his life as well as role-model effective leadership for the newer members of his organization. He had noticed that his organization was not doing as well as it had before and that they were losing members. His example is used to illustrate Prochaska and DiClemente's (1982) model.

Although this model describes the change process for health-related habits, its concepts have relevance and applicability to other change processes.

STAGES OF PERSONAL CHANGE

1. Precontemplation
2. Contemplation
3. Preparation
4. Action and,
5. Maintenance (Prochaska & DiClemente, 1982)

In *precontemplation*, no change is planned in the near future, as there is little or no awareness about the need for change. People in the precontemplation stage are thought to be in denial because they do not recognize a need for change. They may also feel stuck in the behavior or believe that change is beyond their control. Sayid shared that during the precontemplation phase, his motto was "Ignore the problem." While there were several events that may have encouraged him to change, he felt that there were so many things going on his life that it was hard to get everything done; it was out of his control. Eventually, Sayid lost an opportunity to be promoted at work as result of his decision to call in sick so that he could free up some time to get a class assignment done. Additionally, an event that his organization put on was poorly attended because members procrastinated on advertising. After the initial disappointment, he started to realize that he would have to change if he wanted to hold others accountable as an officer in the organization and be someone that others could rely on.

In the *contemplation* stage, people are aware that a change needs to happen and are thinking about what they could do to make that change, but they have yet to commit to taking action. People in this stage struggle with the amount of time and energy that it would take to change and tend to favor current behaviors over developing new ones. Sometimes they do not know what to do to make the change. In Sayid's case, he started to notice how often he said yes to projects in the organizations he was involved in on top of his coursework and job on campus. In addition to all of these responsibilities, he also noticed that every time his friends invited him to play Ping-Pong, he said yes. Sayid noticed that part of the reason he always said yes was that he enjoyed feeling popular with his friends. After weighing the pros and cons of his current behavior, he decided that he needed to make a change if he ever wanted to be promoted at work and take the organization to the next level. This was in part a lesson on Commitment, which is discussed further in Chapter Eleven.

While not fully committed to taking action, *preparation* involves making small changes in preparation for the big change. In an effort to better understand how he spent his time, Sayid took a break from Ping-Pong one night so that he could make a weekly schedule. As a visual learner, Sayid knew that it would be helpful to draw a picture of his procrastination cycle so that he could identify where he was getting stuck. In an effort to make his desired change more clear, Sayid wrote down his goals for the rest of the semester so that he had an idea of where he wanted to spend his time. Sayid went to bed ready to make a change. He deepened his Consciousness of Self, as described more fully in Chapter Ten.

Action, the next stage of the model, involves actively changing a behavior. Here, people alter their experiences, environments, or behavior in an effort to stay actively committed to change. Since Sayid had already written out his procrastination cycle, he had an idea of where he would get stuck. Sayid learned new strategies for getting his work done before playing Ping-Pong. In between classes, Sayid partnered with other members of the organization on projects to ensure that they got done in time. Then he went to the library and did homework until 8 p.m. As a reward for all this good work, he played Ping-Pong with his friends when he got home. Sayid knew that he had made positive change when he noticed how his life had improved for the better. He was much happier, doing better academically, got promoted at work, and his student organization was growing exponentially. In fact, a new leader in the organization commented that he was inspired to be a part of the team because of the way they collaborated on projects (something that increased with Sayid's individual change and leadership within the group).

In the last stage, *maintenance,* individuals actively work to maintain the change that they have made and avoid slipping back into old habits. As undesired behavioral patterns are replaced with desired behavioral patterns, individuals become more likely to stabilize the change. Sayid knew that it would be tempting to fall back into his old habits so he identified ways that he could maintain his new behaviors. Since he knew that he loved spending time with his friends, he started inviting them to come with him to the library. He also formed study groups with people in class and learned to finish projects before he started new ones. He was working effectively to be congruent with his values and new goals (see Chapter Ten).

Exhibit 4.1 illustrates how a person might identify with each stage and make progress through the model to accomplish personal change.

EXHIBIT 4.1 Action Steps for the Stage Model of Change

Stage of Change	Identifying Statements	Action Steps for Change
Precontemplation	I don't need to change anything.	Notice what you are unwilling to change in your life. Make a list of the messages you tell yourself about making a change.
Contemplation	I'm not sure that I want to make a change.	Weigh the pros and cons of making a change. Envision what your life would be like if you did make the change.
Preparation	I'm going to make a change.	Map the cycle of your behavior that you would like to change. Make a goal to change. Identify your sticking points. Think of small steps that you can take toward your goal. Share your goal to change with others.
Action	I am actively changing.	Develop a rewards system for the change you are making. Visualize how you will respond to your sticking points and avoid situations where you know you will get stuck.

Source: Adapted from Prochaska and DiClemente (1982).

 Consider for a moment a change you most desire to see within yourself. How do you know what to change? What do you notice yourself saying about this need for change? What are the positive and negative messages you send yourself about your ability to change? How do you act in the critical moments involving change? How do you reward and punish yourself for making or not making change?

Group Change

While a belief that individuals have the power to influence social change is important, it is equally important to recognize the strength in working in conjunction with groups and communities who also want to affect change. Reflecting on the civil rights movement, then-Senator Barack Obama (2008) noted:

> What Dr. King understood is that if just one person chose to walk instead of ride the bus, those walls of oppression would not be moved. But maybe if a few more walked, the foundation might start to shake. If a few more women were willing to do what Rosa Parks had done, maybe the cracks would start to show. If teenagers took freedom rides from North to South, maybe a few bricks would come loose. Maybe if white folks marched because they had come to understand that

their freedom too was at stake in the impending battle, the wall would begin to sway. And if enough Americans were awakened to the injustice; if they joined together, North and South, rich and poor, Christian and Jew, then perhaps that wall would come tumbling down, and justice would flow like water, and righteousness like a mighty stream. (Obama, 2008, ¶ 6)

For example, not long ago, the Board of Trustees at Mills College in Oakland, California, determined that the only way to make this women's college financially viable was to admit men and become coeducational. The students, alumni, faculty, and community members who had experienced firsthand the power of an all-women's college experience worked together to raise funds, recruit more students, and demonstrate to the board that Mills could remain all women. It took all of those groups working together to accomplish this shared purpose (Rhoads, 1998).

Working together can be a powerful way to move toward more inclusive communities founded on equality and justice. Some of the benefits of working effectively in a group or with several groups include the joy of collaborating with people who feel similarly, sharing the demands of the work load, coming up with new ideas, and creating a critical mass of concerned individuals for a significant cause. Some of the challenges are learning to share resources, agreeing on a common goal and a path to reach that goal, holding one and each other accountable, and creating a space for different viewpoints without

The Magnolia Project at the University of California, Berkeley began as a result of an alternative break relief trip to New Orleans following Hurricanes Katrina and Rita. What began as a spring break trip has expanded to a 15-year commitment of year-long service opportunities in New Orleans as well as an internship exchange program to assist in making change in a city still devastated by the broken levees of 2005.

alienating. Scholars have studied change processes extensively. The rest of this chapter concerning change at the group level explores a few concepts that may aid in effectively working in groups.

Kotter's Process of Creating Major Change

Although Fullan (2001) argued that recipes for change do not necessarily lead to change, it is still helpful to look at models that make it easier to understand what is working and not working in approaches to change. John P. Kotter (1996), a professor and a scholar in the Harvard Business School, based his eight-stage model on many years of research and insight from organizations that have been successful in making change. While several stages of the model may occur at the same time, each stage of the model builds on the previous stage, and a skipped step may result in an undesired outcome.

Although this appears to be a "top-down" approach to change and assumes that those who are attempting to make change have the necessary authority to do so, it can also be useful to members of a group who are trying to organize a change initiative. Refer back to the case study, "Starving for Attention," introduced in Chapter Three, and how the students in the Living Wage Campaign group could work toward meaningful change toward a living campus wage. This case is briefly illustrated using the Kotter model.

Following are the eights steps in Kotter's (1996, p. 21) process of creating major change:

1. **Establish a Sense of Urgency.** Without urgency there is complacency. Creating urgency can sometimes be risky because there is a subtle implication that the status quo is no longer effective. *The Living Wage Campaign group might compile comparison data of wages paid on and off campus for similar jobs and bring such actions as evictions and foreclosures from lower-paid campus staff to the attention of senior administrators.*

2. **Create the Guiding Coalition.** Without coalitions, there is a lack of importance. Kotter observed that no single individual is able to orchestrate every stage of the model alone; thus a group with enough power to facilitate the change must be organized. Further, the group must work like a team in order to be considered a working coalition. *The campaign might form a coalition with Amnesty International, the student government campus life committee, and the employee union.*

3. Develop a Vision and Strategy. Without a vision, there is confusion, false starts, and misalignment. Good visions function in three important ways: they (1) clarify the general direction for change, (2) motivate people to take action in the right direction, and (3) help coordinate the actions of different people (pp. 68–69). *The coalition would spend ample time at early meetings to identify realistic outcomes they can all agree are important to address.*

4. Communicate the Change Vision. Without communication, there is inaction and resistance. Once a vision has been created, it should be communicated continually in as many ways as possible. Metaphors, analogies, and examples are all helpful ways to communicate complicated ideas and accompanying strategies quickly and effectively. Nothing sends a better message than leading by example; leaders should be sure to model the way. *The coalition might identify a media plan for how to get the word out about the urgency for the campus to act and the purposes and plans of the project.*

5. Empower Broad-Based Action. Without empowerment, there is frustration. Structures and obstacles that get in the way of making the desired change a reality should be removed. Training should be provided when needed to help members see how the change will benefit them and to "encourage risk taking with nontraditional ideas, activities, and actions" (Kotter, 1996, p. 21). *The coalition needs to keep members trained but also needs to link with official offices that would also like to improve the wage environment for staff.*

6. Generating Short-Term Wins. Without short-term wins, there is cynicism and a loss of momentum. Major change does not occur overnight; short-term wins keep people motivated to continue the change effort over long periods of time. A good short-term win is "(1) visible; large numbers of people can see for themselves whether the result is real or just hype; (2) it's unambiguous; there can be little argument over the call; and (3) it's clearly related to the change effort" (Kotter, 1996, pp. 121–122). Recognizing and rewarding the people who make the change possible will also help build morale and motivation. *Celebrate when the human resource office agrees to a campuswide study of wages. When the vice president for business affairs office agrees to bring this issue forward in the new strategic planning process, celebrate. When ten new members join the campaign, celebrate. Recognize the individual efforts of Campaign members.*

7. Consolidating Gains and Producing More Change. Without reinforcement, there is wasted effort. Resistance to change is never fully eradicated. Kotter (1996) offers one cardinal rule: "Whenever you let up before the job is done, critical momentum can be lost and regression may follow" (p. 133). Thus, members of the guiding coalition should use increased credibility to change all systems, structures, and policies that are counter to the vision. Further, more people should be brought into the change process. *The coalition has prepared a report on all the individual changes and presents a revised agenda for next steps in the campaign. They seek an audience with the director of physical plant to update him or her and reinforce the importance of the campaign.*

8. Anchor New Approaches in the Culture. Without anchoring, there is dissipation. Kotter observed, "Alterations in norms and values come at the end of the transformation process" (1996, p. 157). To facilitate a change in culture, leaders should discuss the benefits of changes and relate these changes to the success of the organization. They should also be sure to create promotional strategies that solidify the right leadership to keep the change going. *The coalition creates many ways to sustain attention to how the campus treats the staff. It creates a business affairs liaison role in the coalition to provide a steady flow of information to the campus business affairs office. They work with the human resources office to create a campuswide award for exceptional staff-centered good practices to praise those offices known to be responsive to their employees. They approach the student newspaper to do a series of articles on these issues.*

Throughout the steps in Kotter's (1996) model, those involved need to assess progress and scan the environment for evidence of its impact. This constant assessment shapes more effective practices at each succeeding stage.

 Students at a large urban university successfully convinced the University Senate to initiate and uphold a ban of Coca-Cola products in response to a 2004 incident in Columbia where workers at a bottling plant were killed after trying to unionize.

Community/Society Change

Large social systems are comprised of interconnected organizations and individuals. It is not uncommon for student leaders selected for a senior class council or a senior honor society to look around the room at their first meeting and realize the phenomenal influence they can have; they represent student government, athletics, fraternities and sororities, political organizations, cultural organizations, and more. Mobilizing the resources of this newly networked system can bring a lot of influence on any desired change.

> Students at Illinois Wesleyan University (IWU) worked closely with the dining services management team to encourage the use of locally grown foods on campus. Now, IWU is the largest consumer of organics in their region.

According to Lukensmeyer and Stone (2006), there are five characteristics of large social systems that differ from those of the typical organization:

1. **Boundaries are more permeable.** Much of what occurs in society happens in the space between individuals and groups. Individuals are members of multiple organizations that may hold different perspectives on shared issues. This can make it both difficult to define the problem and

to identify key stakeholders who should be involved in the change process. Stakeholders can be people who are affected by the issue, have an interest in or have expressed an opinion about the issue, are in a position to exert positive or negative influence, or ought to care about the issue (Luke, 1998).

2. Ensuring participation can be more difficult. Authorities can require participation in the change process within organizations. Outside of organizations, a direct penalty does not exist for a lack of participation. Thus, motivating individuals and groups to commit voluntarily to making change at the societal level is very difficult.

3. Decision makers are in fact accountable. Since members of a democracy believe that elected officials should be held accountable, it is easier to persuade political figures to become involved in the process.

4. The process is inherently political. Within formal organizations, management generally has control over what is communicated. Within society and within higher educational institutions, those who are in power do not directly control communication. Processes for change must withstand scrutiny in order to be legitimized.

5. The issues are complex. Members of society have the full range of life experiences that represent the human condition, whereas organizations have a more limited perspective. Further, stakeholders in society are typically more diverse than stakeholders within an organization, which may include differences in language, ability, race, gender, class, religion, and sexual orientation. Careful consideration must be made to ensure that all community members are included.

These characteristics of large social systems highlight potential roadblocks to affecting positive change at the societal level. Complex social issues such as those concerning class, ethnicity, gender, religion, sexual orientation, size, and age are all interconnected like a giant mass of tangled yarn. As a result, it is difficult to pinpoint what societal changes will have unintended consequences, both positive and negative, on other social issues. For example, according to Rothstein (2004), school reform alone cannot solve the achievement gaps in the K–12 system. Instead, Rothstein argued that social class differences also impact the academic performance of children, and to affect real change, school reform must occur alongside closing the gaps in income, health, and housing. As Allen and Cherrey (2000) argued, "Change occurs through a coordinated nudging and waiting by many people intentionally influencing toward a shared goal" (p. 47). It is difficult to pinpoint both the causes and solutions to the social issues that affect our society, but one can increase his or her understanding of the different approaches toward change so that one can let go of rigid strategies and begin to influence change where one is able.

NEW APPROACHES TO CHANGE: UNDERSTANDING NETWORKED SYSTEMS

In recent decades, many people in the Western world have come to understand organizations and change differently than before (Allen & Cherrey, 2000; Senge, 1990; Wheatley,

1999). In order to understand new approaches to change, it is first necessary to understand organizations in a new way. Allen and Cherrey describe one aspect of this understanding as a shift from viewing the world as fragmented to seeing it as networked and connected.

A Fragmented View of Organizations

Allen and Cherrey (2000) explain that a fragmented approach to understanding organizations has several key characteristics.

1. It emphasizes separation and boundaries. People and responsibilities are kept separated into parts (such as divisions, committees); sales is independent of manufacturing or student affairs is separate from academic affairs. Further, the organization itself is understood as a distinct unit independent from the outside community. A fragmented view understands an organization by breaking it down into its parts and examining them each separately. Much like a mechanic looks at a car, determining which part is defective, replacing it, and reassembling the parts into a car again identifies the problem.

2. It assumes linear causality. Cause and effect is assumed to happen in a straight line: A caused B, and then B caused C. It assumes that one can easily determine what went wrong and fix it.

3. It assumes that control happens from a certain point in the system. Cars have one driver, and organizations have one leader. The organization leader is believed to have control over what happens to and in the organization.

4. It assumes that change happens incrementally in small even steps. Each year, new car designs represent a few new variations on the last year's model. Over the years, this adds up to bigger changes, such that a car from 1980 is quite different from a 2010 car. In organizations too, change is often introduced gradually, even when leaders know where they want to be many years down the road.

A Networked or Systems View of Organizations

While a car was a useful example of a fragmented view, the Internet is a good example of the systems view. A *system view* is the view of the bigger picture of an organization, including how all of its parts connect and how it connects to the outer world beyond the organization. Students of mathematics will recognize a matrix structure, where changes in any element of the matrix affect all the other elements.

Networks can only be understood from the perspective of the whole system. There are so many interconnections that it is meaningless to isolate one part in order to understand the whole. How each part connects is critical. Organizations can be understood in similar ways. It is not the talent of individual players that makes a team great, but each player connecting with the others. Each person's performance is improved by their connections with the others, which increases their ability to improve others in return.

Networks are nonlinear. Networks are more like a three-dimension spider web than a straight line. A tug on a string in one area has an impact all over the web. Cause and effect are less simple. A has an impact on Z, B has an impact on Z, C has an impact on Z. In fact, A can have an impact on C that makes C's impact on Z a little different than it would have been without A. In other words, networks are complex, and it isn't possible to predict specific outcomes. When a change is initiated, a string on the spider web is pulled. It is not possible to predict the unintended effects on other areas of the web. Networked systems require a "learn as you go" mentality. One should get used to not knowing everything there is to know before making a decision. Groups must ask, "What other areas of our organization may have an interest in the decision we are about to make; how do we get their input since this will affect them?"

Networks can be influenced, but not controlled. Unlike cars, the Internet has no driver. Change can come from anywhere. Anyone can set up a new Web site, add to a wiki, and connect it to others; anyone can publish their ideas for millions to see. A networked view of organizations also recognizes that any active member can make a difference in how the organization operates, with or without having been elected to an office. Networked systems do not respond to force. In fact, force can create more resistance. Consider how placing an idea out there and waiting, rather than forcing it on others without their input, can make change in an organization.

Networks are always in "dynamic flux" (Allen & Cherrey, 2000). With influence coming from so many places on the spider web, and initiative coming from any participant rather than a single driver, networks continually change, and that change can sometimes be large. The Internet does not increase in small steps each year like the design of a car. A Web site with new content can go from ten hits to half-a-million hits in a single day; a YouTube video can be posted and be on the nightly news the same day. An organization whose members are well connected to each other and to their community can make huge changes in a small amount of time.

Viewing individuals, groups, and organizations as networked in larger systems provides a more useful and resourceful approach to change. Systems views help identify those shareholders and stakeholders who should be involved and who can come together in coalitions to work toward common purposes. This view empowers the individual or the small group to see how others may share their goals and build coalitions for change.

THREE APPROACHES TO CHANGE

Change is around everyone all the time. People seem to take one of three different approaches to change—(1) making change, (2) surviving change, (3) and organic change—each of which has different focuses, values, and meaning (Allen & Cherrey, 2000).

Making change involves pushing and controlling the change process with force or positional power. The focus in this approach to change involves staying in control by fixing broken parts and setting long-term goals and objectives.

It assumes the chair of the organization can know all the information and control all the people and events involved to produce the desired outcome. Change is initiated from the top, in a strategic plan that describes each incremental step that, through the predictability of linear cause and effect, will achieve the leader's goal. This approach may be needed in a crisis and, if the authority uses the power of their position for good, can accomplish worthwhile outcomes. Allen and Cherrey (2000) noted that the problems with this approach are (1) it takes time to think through and plan this type of change, which slows one's ability to respond quickly when the unexpected arises; (2) there is an invalid assumption that organizations can control their environments; and (3) the head of the organization has to be able to predict the outcomes of the changes, which is impossible to do in a complex networked world where problems have multiple causes.

Surviving change involves surviving and adapting to change as an uncontrollable force, much like responding to unexpected weather. Members of the organization who are able to adapt to change are valued more than the members who are unable or unwilling to face the next challenge. Meaning is found in searching patterns for emergent threats and opportunities and being prepared for them before they happen. The strengths of this approach are to maintain stability in the face of many changes; not everything can be addressed at once and the individual and the organization have to select which changes to address and survive the others. Allen and Cherrey (2000) noted that the problems with this approach are (1) something is lost when organizations respond to outside pressure without striving to play an active role in influencing society as a whole, (2) there is too much emphasis on responding to daily crisis, and (3) this mode breeds frustration and stress, which can lead to burnout.

Organic change involves recognizing that individuals and organizations are a part of an interconnected system. Although systems cannot be controlled, they can be influenced. Organizations that utilize this type of change envision "relationships with the external environment as opportunities for mutual shaping" (Allen & Cherrey, 2000, p. 54). Leaders take time to develop strategic partnerships, consider new ways to influence change and value ongoing learning. Meaning is found in the use of collective wisdom in which the dynamic connections and relationships between many variables are discovered and explored. Allen and Cherrey argued that this approach works because it encourages the idea that one person cannot do it alone and allows organizations to develop structures that "increase the flexibility and find new ways of maintaining cohesion without traditional forms of control" (p. 56). This approach relies on trusting relationships across a system and takes energy to maintain; people come and go in that system.

Allen and Cherrey (2000) advised, "Becoming effective at organic change requires an appreciation of how a networked system works, a realization of what is controllable and what is not, and an ability to work in partnership with the dynamics of the system to facilitate change" (p. 60). They suggested that one could envision the nature of networked systems by imagining what the Internet might look like if one were to draw it. Systems have many active players, cannot be controlled by any one person, and are in continuous flux; consequently, "a network cannot be forced to follow a specific set course because the interconnections allow for many different ways to get from one place to another"(p. 45). To assist in this process, several metaphors are provided to help us understand the organic change concept. The four metaphors Allen and Cherrey used to elucidate the dynamics of networked systems are (1) wet sand, (2) birds on a wire, (3) yeast, and (4) beneficial virus.

1. *Wet sand* illustrates the concept the "relationship between force and resistance" (p. 56). When individuals and organizations use force, much like attempting to slam one's foot into wet sand, they may be met with hard resistance. Allen and Cherrey noted that organizations resist when "positional power forces a direction on us without adequate time to understand or be involved in the change process" (p. 57). However, if change is slowly introduced to the system, it is likely to be embraced, much like one's foot when resting and gently sinking into the sand.

2. The concept *birds on a wire* demonstrates the power of individuals and organizations that decide to do things differently. To better understand this concept, imagine a flock of birds sitting on a telephone wire. A few will take off and circle back. The birds that stay on the wire may ruffle their feathers and inch closer to one another. Then a few more will

take off, and return. Eventually, however, the remaining the birds all take off together. Much like these birds on a wire, in creating change, a few individuals experiment with new ways of doing things and may even return to the original way when they do not receive support from their colleagues. Each time they experiment, however, several others will join them until the whole organization is ready to make large-scale change. The image of a bird on a wire is a reminder that although change can be slow and often takes time, with patience and persistence the system can be influenced.

3. Allen and Cherrey use the metaphor of *yeast* to highlight the role of "individuals in organizations who could be active agents and in combination with other people and under the right conditions, provide the leaven for change" (p. 58). Rather than focusing on positional leadership, organizations should spend time seeking out individuals who could provide a variety of qualities that would help shift the system and create the right conditions for them to maximize their contributions to the organization.

4. Last, the *beneficial virus* concept by Allen and Cherrey is used to illustrate that "any influencing process (or resistance) in a networked system can spread quickly throughout the system depending on the quality of the network" (p. 59). Where the first three metaphors were used to illustrate how change can be triggered, this concept is meant to highlight how change can be accelerated or resisted. A cold or a virus represents the negative messages that are spread rapidly through an organization, whereas positive messages represent

Can you think of a time when you accomplished something you wanted by the gentle approach of *wet sand* (maybe like getting the car keys from your mom)? Can you think of a time when change came slowly like *birds on the wire*? What early efforts toward change finally resulted in the change happening? Who do you know that epitomizes *yeast*; their ideas and positive energy spark others to action? What *virus* have you seen spread and get adopted widely on campus, perhaps a commitment to service or campus recycling?

the beneficial virus that could be spread. To do this, one needs to learn how "to see the social, technical, and organizational connections of systems, and work with them to spread beneficial viruses" (p. 59).

RESISTANCE TO CHANGE

Understanding reasons for resisting change is critical to effective leadership at the individual, group, and community levels. People, organizations, and society resist change for many reasons. Developing an appreciation of resistance is critical to making change. The deeper the understanding of resistance and where it is coming from, the more likely it is that energy behind the resistance can be shifted into a productive force in the change process. When encountering resistance, one of the first steps to take is to find out as much as possible about what the resistance is about and where it stems from. As noted by Fullan (2001), "We are likely to learn something from people who disagree with us more than we are from people who agree" (p. 41). When individuals ignore, avoid, or minimize resistance messages that they are receiving from within or from others, they miss an opportunity to learn.

According to Hultman (1998), symptoms of resistance can be found in active and passive behaviors (see Exhibit 4.2). These behaviors are indications that there is resistance, but they do not tell us why.

It is important to note that resistance itself is not necessarily positive or negative; it is how it is *interpreted* that makes it so.

EXHIBIT 4.2 Examples of Active and Passive Resistance

Active Resistance	Passive Resistance
Being critical Blaming/accusing Blocking Finding fault Sabotaging Undermining Ridiculing Intimidating/threatening Starting rumors Appealing to fear Manipulating Arguing Using facts selectively Distorting facts	Agreeing verbally but not following through Failing to implement change Procrastination/dragging feet Feigning ignorance Withholding information, suggestions, help, or support Standing by and allowing the change to fail

Source: Original Copyright © Davies-Black Publishing, 1998. Copyright © 2005, Kenneth E. Hultman. Reprinted with permission of the author.

 Where in your life have you used these types of resistance for both positive and negative reasons? Are you more likely to use some methods in certain situations? Where have you noticed others using these types of resistance? What have you learned about change thus far that may help in working through resistance at the individual, group, and societal levels?

The underlying motives for resistance are complex. Hultman (1998) identifies a number of key causes of resistance.

When they encounter resistance, leaders should spend some time reflecting on the images of organic change and use the chart in Exhibit 4.3 to formulate a strategy. Fullan (2001) argued that when leading in a culture of change, "the goal is to develop a greater feel for leading complex change, to develop a mind-set and action set that are constantly cultivated and refined" (p. 34). These principles of change provide a framework to plan a successful change and identify problems you may encounter if you do not embrace the principle.

CONNECTION TO THE OTHER C'S

The Social Change Model "seeks to develop a **conscious** and **congruent** person who can **collaborate** with others, who can become a **committed** participant in the shaping of the group's

COMMON CAUSES OF RESISTANCE

1. People believe their needs are being met already.
2. People believe the change will make it harder for them to meet their needs.
3. People believe the risks outweigh the benefits.
4. People believe change is unnecessary to avoid or escape a harmful situation.
5. People believe the change process was handled improperly.
6. People believe the change will fail.
7. People believe change is inconsistent with their values.
8. People believe those responsible for the change can't be trusted. (Hultman, 1998, p. 142)

In 2008, the World Economic Forum partnered with YouTube to provide an opportunity for people to answer the Davos Question: "What one thing do you think that countries, companies, or individuals must do to make the world a better place?" What is your answer to this question?

EXHIBIT 4.3 Principles and Strategies for Change

Principles of Change	When you are …	Try …
Just because you have a good idea does not mean that anyone is going to listen.	Overly attached to your own "good ideas"	Focusing on garnering an internal commitment from others through collaboration
Appreciate the implementation dip. Change is a process, not an event.	Frustrated by resistance	Increasing empathy by asking questions and listening
Redefine resistance. Good ideas come from resistors as they have ideas that planners have missed. Resistors are critical to the politics of implementation.	Only listening to those who agree with you	Seeking out those who would disagree with you, they might have ideas that you missed. Involving them on the front end of shaping a change works best.
Re-culturing is the name of the game. Changing the way things are done around here is the main point.	Adopting innovations one after one	Developing the capacity to seek, critically assess, and selectively incorporate new ideas. Recognize the norms of how the group is functioning are changing.
Never a checklist, always complexity. While recipes for change are helpful in stirring one's thinking, they should not be the sole basis for transformative change.	Constricting around a set agenda for change	Brainstorming and forecasting other possibilities

Source: Adapted from Fullan (2001), 34–46.

common purpose, who can help to resolve **controversy with civility** and be a responsible **citizen**" (Bonous-Hammarth, 1996, p. 4). The goal in this chapter was to provide a basic understanding of what change is at the individual, group, and community/societal levels. As each of the C's is explored in Chapters Five through Twelve, reflect back on the "hub" of the Social Change Model—change—and think about what the process of change might look like if that C was missing.

CONCLUSION

Becoming a change agent involves understanding that change is a process that typically involves active or passive resistance that can be transformed through the Seven C's. Individuals and groups must also develop positive perceptions of change, comfort with ambiguity, confidence that change can happen, and a willingness to step out of one's comfort zone. Last, change requires increasing one's skills in influencing systems and larger communities, creating a sense of urgency, an ability to articulate a shared vision for the future, and the willingness to take a risk and make a difference.

DISCUSSION QUESTIONS

1. What is a change you would like to promote in an organization or community you are a part of? Is it a single- or second-order change?

2. What is something you could change about yourself that would make you more effective at leadership in groups? What would the "stages of personal change" look like to make that change?

3. What organic change metaphors do you find yourself drawn to? Can you think of an example from your experience working in groups that was like that metaphor?

4. What role has resistance played in the advancement/or stagnation of a change effort in an organization with which you are involved?

JOURNAL PROBES

On Becoming

Preeminent psychologist, Carl Rogers (1961) said that people are always in a process of *becoming*. The first two journal probes are intended to help you reflect on how you see yourself becoming a leader for social change.

1. How are you becoming more effective at both responding to change and promoting change?

2. Can you remember a time when you approached change differently than you do now? How is your current approach different from your approach then?

Learning Through Experience

The ensemble that created the Social Change Model believed the best way to learn to do leadership was through experience

and reflection. This involves challenging yourself to have new experiences that test your ability and awareness **and** to spend time thinking about what you have learned from that experience. The remaining journal probes are designed to maximize learning through experience by guiding your reflective journal writing through Kolb's (1981) four processes of experiential learning.

1. Concrete Experience. Describe a specific situation when you had an experience that relates to change as it has been described here. What happened? What details stand out to you? Describe briefly the situation, what you did and how you felt.

2. Reflective Observation. Why did this situation have the outcome it did? What caused the situation to happen in the first place? What responses from yourself and others worked in this situation? Why was that effective? What did not work? Why?

3. Abstract Conceptualization. What lessons can you draw from this specific experience that could apply more generally? Given both your reflections and the information in this chapter, what would you do if a similar situation presented itself? What general guidelines would you create for handling future situations like this?

4. Active Experimentation. What opportunities might you seek out that would give you the chance to apply what you have learned here? How might you test the lessons or guidelines you created in #3 to see if they work?

APPLYING THE CASE STUDIES

Go back to Chapter Three for more context on each of these case studies. Apply the material on change from Chapter Four to these cases.

Zoom In: Starving for Attention

In this case, Taylor has become involved in an organization that is challenging the university to pay its service workers a wage that better reflects the cost of living in the area. Taylor learned so much through his Sociology of Poverty class. He realized that in many ways the United States has an unspoken social class system that affords the wealthy great privilege. He learned to recognize instances when the wealthy control policy that affects low-wage earners.

As Taylor begins to read some of the information he received at the Living Wage Campaign organization meeting, he feels guilty because he realizes he had never stopped to think about many of the financial issues that the work force at his university have. He began to engage his roommates and classmates about these issues. He heard many differing opinions. Many of the students he talked to say that the primarily Latina/o workforce should learn English first and then demand higher wages. Others wonder why they were here and why they are taking jobs from American workers. When he goes home that weekend, he attempts to start a conversation at dinner with his family and is frustrated by the lack of response that his family has to his concern over this issue.

Taylor begins to truly understand the concept of injustice for the first time in his life. He realizes that though there are many privileged students on his campus, many of them do not realize the very conditions the university is condoning and how the university treats its workers. He begins to make a commitment to befriend the housekeepers in his residence hall. He introduces himself and tries to get to know them. He also starts urging the students on his floor to keep the bathrooms and lounges clean and to respect the housekeepers that have to clean the facilities.

Think About It

- What is the issue of social change being considered in this situation?

- What personal changes has Taylor attempted given what he has learned about working conditions at his university? What group changes is he promoting? What other personal or group changes could he promote? How might he go about promoting change at the campus level?

- Apply Kotter's (1996) model to the change Taylor would like to make. What would each of the eight stages entail?

- How might a systemic perspective on change apply to this case? What would it look like to foster an organic change in this situation?

- What kinds of resistance did Taylor experience to the social change he is interested in?

Zoom In: Clear Haziness

In this case, you are the photography editor of the campus paper, *The Weekly*, where a tradition of hazing new members of the photography staff has been uncovered. You are now facing a very important decision: to identify a need for change or to justify the actions of your senior photographers based on their feedback and response to you. Think through and plot both responses—engaging a change process or ignoring it. What are the implications of both decisions? Thinking through what you learned in this chapter, what would a single-order change look like? In what ways would a single-order change be effective or ineffective? What are potential areas for transformational change? If organizational change begins with changing the individual, what does that mean for the group?

Examine the scenario from a systems perspective. What are the multiple factors influencing the situation—what nudges could happen? Who, if anyone, is victimized and/or marginalized in this situation? Should you choose to change the organization, what types of resistance might occur and why? How is your definition of leadership or leader challenged by this situation? Are you a leader because you hold a position as photography editor? What would qualify as leadership based on the definition presented in Chapter Two?

References

Allen, K. E., & Cherrey, C. (2000). *Systemic leadership: Enriching the meaning of our work.* Washington, DC: University Press of America.

Bonous-Hammarth, M. (1996). Developing social change agents: Leadership development for the '90s and beyond. *Concepts and Connections,* 4(2), 1, 3–4.

Boyce, M. (2003). Organizational learning is essential to achieving and sustaining change in higher education. *Innovative Higher Education,* 28(2), 119–136.

Eckel, P., Hill, B., & Green, M. (1998). *On change: En route to transformation.* Washington, DC: American Council on Education.

Fullan, M. (2001). *Leading in a culture of change: Being effective in complex times.* San Francisco: Jossey-Bass.

Goleman, D., Boyatzis, R., & McKee, A. (2002). *Primal leadership: Learning to lead with emotional intelligence.* Boston: Harvard Business School Press.

Higher Education Research Institute. [HERI] (1996). *A social change model of leadership development* (Version III). Los Angeles: University of California Los Angeles, Higher Education Research Institute.

Hultman, K. (1998). *Making change irresistible: Overcoming resistance to change in your organization.* Palo Alto, CA: Davies-Black.

Kolb, D. A. (1981). Learning styles and disciplinary differences. In A. W. Chickering & Associates (Eds.), *The modern American college: Responding to the new realities of diverse students and a changing society* (pp. 232–255). San Francisco: Jossey Bass.

Kotter, J. P. (1996). *Leading change.* Boston: Harvard Business School Press.

Luke, J. S. (1998). *Catalytic leadership: Strategies for an interconnected world.* San Francisco: Jossey-Bass.

Lukensmeyer, C. J., & Stone, D. (2006). Working in very large social systems: The twenty-first century town meeting. In B. B. Jones & M. Brazzel (Eds.), *The NTL handbook of organization development and change:*

Principles, practices, and perspectives (pp. 302–316). San Francisco: Jossey-Bass.

Obama, B. (2008). Retrieved February 1, 2008 from http://www.barack-obama.com/2008/01/20/remarks_of_senator_barack_obam_40.php

O'Toole, J. (1996). *Leading change: The argument for values-based leadership.* New York: Ballantine Books.

Prochaska, J. O., & DiClemente, C. C. (1982). Transtheoretical therapy: Toward a more integrative model of change. *Psychotherapy: Theory, Research and Practice, 20,* 161–173.

Pulsifer, C. (2008). *I wanted to change the world.* Retrieved February 1, 2008, from http://www.wow4u.com/change-world/index.html

Quinn, R. E. (1996). *Deep change: Discovering the leader within.* San Francisco: Jossey-Bass.

Rhoads, R. A. (1998). *Freedom's web: Student activism in an age of cultural diversity.* Baltimore: Johns Hopkins University Press.

Rogers, C. R. (1961). *On becoming a person: A therapist's view of psychotherapy.* Boston: Houghton Mifflin.

Rothstein, R. (2004). *Class and schools: Using social economic and educational reform to close the Black-White achievement gap.* Washington, DC: Economic Policy Institute.

Senge, P. (1990). *The fifth discipline: The art and practice of the learning organization.* New York: Doubleday.

Senge, P., Scharmer, C. O., Jaworski, J., & Flowers, B. S. (2005). *Presence: An exploration of profound change in people, organizations, and society.* New York: Currency.

Wheatley, M. J. (1999). *Leadership and the new science: Learning about organization from an orderly universe* (2nd ed.). San Francisco: Berrett-Koehler.

PART 2

Societal/
Community
Values

Community is the binding together of diverse individuals
committed to a just, common good through shared experi-
ences in a spirit of caring and social responsibility.
NATIONAL LEADERSHIP SYMPOSIUM

All that is necessary for the triumph of evil is that good
[people] do nothing.
EDMUND BURKE

Membership in any group brings with it the rights of membership and the responsibilities to serve the good of the group. These groups are the communities each individual engages with in daily life—from the smallest unit, such as the community of one's family, residence hall suite, seminar class, work staff, campus, religious institution, local neighborhood, professional colleagues, to the nation and world.

Feeling responsible to those communities and moving those communities positively to address change in the arenas they influence is a responsibility of membership. This indeed is the inherent nature of being a citizen of those communities. Communities must "continually participate in conversations about the questions 'Who are we' and 'What matters?'" (Wheatley & Kellner-Rogers, 1998, p. 17). The process of that engagement is Citizenship.

Former Secretary of Health, Education, and Welfare and President of Common Cause, John Gardner (1997) viewed communities as networks of responsibility:

All citizens should have the opportunity to be active, but all will not respond. Those who do respond carry the burden of our free society. I call them the Responsibles. They exist in every segment of the community— ethnic groups, labor unions, neighborhood associations, businesses—but they rarely form an effective network of responsibility because they don't know one another across segments. They must find each other, learn to communicate, and find common ground. Then they can function as the keepers of the long-term agenda. (p. 5)

In Part Five, the Social Change Model examines leadership development from the societal or community perspective. This section examines the importance of people coming together in community to address their shared needs and address shared problems. The ensemble asked, "Toward what social ends is the leadership development activity directed? What kinds of service activities are most effective in energizing the group and in developing desired personal qualities in the individual?" (Higher Education Research Institute, 1996, p. 19). The value explored in the societal or community perspective is Citizenship.

References

Gardner, J. (1997). You are the responsibles. *Civic partners.* Charlottesville, VA: Pew Partnership for Civic Change.

Higher Education Research Institute [HERI]. (1996). *A social change model of leadership development* (Version III). Los Angeles: University of California Los Angeles, Higher Education Research Institute.

National Leadership Symposium. (1991). *Summer Leadership Symposium Invitational June 12–14(1991). Symposium Proceedings.* College Park, MD: National Clearinghouse for Leadership Programs.

Wheatley, M. J., & Kellner-Rogers, M. (1996). *A simpler way.* San Francisco: Berrett-Koehler.

CITIZENSHIP

Jennifer Bonnet

Humankind has not woven the web of life. We are but one thread within it. Whatever we do to the web, we do to ourselves. All things are bound together. All things connect.
CHIEF SEATTLE

The term *citizenship* is often perceived as a nebulous notion, centering solely on voting, government, and political parties. College students often comment on the challenges of incorporating this grand idea of "citizenship" into their lives at school, at home, and among friends. For many students, citizenship seems to be much more than casting a ballot during an election year, but what it is beyond that is not always clear. This chapter addresses the "much more" of civic life for college students.

CHAPTER OVERVIEW

This chapter presents an overview of citizenship through the lens of the Social Change Model (SCM). Several facets of citizenship are explored, including the definition and historical roots of citizenship, the processes of civic engagement, and the new look of citizenship in today's world.

DEFINITION OF CITIZENSHIP

Within the Social Change Model, *Citizenship* centers on active community participation as a result of a sense of responsibility to the communities in which people live.

The concept of civic responsibility is pivotal to this description of Citizenship and further defines the attributes of being a citizen through accepting the responsibility of active engagement in one's community. This connection is also exemplified in former Indiana University President Tom Ehrlich's (2000) statement that "civic engagement means working to make a difference in the civic life of our communities and developing the combination of knowledge, skills, values and motivation to make that difference. It means promoting the quality of life in a community" (p. vi).

CIVIC ROOTS IN THE UNITED STATES

The United States has a long history of people working together as citizens to address their common needs. In the 1830s, French historian Alexis de Tocqueville traveled throughout the United States and wrote about his surprise at

Since "citizenship" can have several different meanings, it is important to understand the special sense in which it is being used as a component of the Social Change Model of Leadership Development. To speak of an individual as a "citizen" requires us to think in terms of multiple communities, large and small, to which the individual belongs. But "citizenship," in the context of the model, means much more than mere membership; rather, it implies active engagement of the individual (and the leadership group) in an effort to serve that community, as well as a "citizen's mind"—a set of values and beliefs that connects an individual in a responsible manner to others. Citizenship, in other words, implies social or civic responsibility. It is the value that responsibly connects the individual and the leadership group to the larger community and society. At a more basic human level, citizenship is about another "C," the value of caring about others. (Higher Education Research Institute [HERI], 1996, p. 65)

the extent to which Americans worked together to solve their common problems. "Americans of all ages, all conditions, and all dispositions constantly form associations. . . . Wherever at the head of some new undertaking you see the government in France, or a man of rank in England, in the United States you will be sure to find an association" (Tocqueville, 1835/1956,

p. 198). Tocqueville observed communities forming associations to create hospitals, schools, places of worship, and to provide entertainment like musical groups and community theaters. He believed that community building was one of the keys to making a democratic society work.

In 1915, John Dewey defined what it meant to live in a democracy: "A democracy is more than a form of government; it is primarily a mode of associated living. . . .Each has to refer his own action to that of others, and to consider the action of others to give point and directions to his own. . ." (p. 87). At a fundamental level, Dewey's concept of democracy refers to people working together so that communities can function. Such essential functions include volunteer fire departments, community youth programs, the Chamber of Commerce, and the Parent-Teacher Association.

African American, Asian American, American Indian, and Latina/o American communities have a long history of working together to build strong communities (Takaki, 1993). Active citizenship in these cultures grew in part from a cultural expectation that one should support fellow community members the way one would support a family member. Juana Bordas (2007) described this as the *all my relatives* principle, referring to a Cherokee tradition of acknowledging others as "all my relatives" and the Lakota greeting "*Mitakuye oyasin*," which means "We are all related" (p. 145). Similarly, Bordas described the concept of *la familia* in Latina/o culture as an elastic one, that stretches to include many honorary aunts and uncles, all of whom can expect to both give and receive support from "la familia."

Bordas also describes the African American value of strong community connections, such that a person's identity is not fully understood in isolation from those with whom they share their lives. Throughout U.S. history, African Americans have faced personal, social, and political challenges by "sticking together" (Bordas, 2007, p. 53). Asian American culture also tends to value collaborative leadership efforts and attending to group needs over individual desires (Liang, Lee, & Ting, 2002). In all of these cultures, there is high value placed on community members helping one another, being responsible for the welfare of others, and standing stronger by standing together (Takaki, 1993).

WHAT CITIZENSHIP LOOKS LIKE

Even when defined as working with others to make a positive difference in one's communities, what that work looks like might be different from person to person. For some, this means voting and holding elected officials accountable to what the people want (through political engagement such as circulating petitions and attending protest marches). For others, it means being an active member of community organizations, creating new initiatives to make a positive difference for everyone. For still others, the term "good citizen" harkens back to the days of elementary school, where the "Good Citizen Award" went to the student who helped a classmate in need, remembered to recycle the milk cartons, or obeyed the rules. As adults, we now connect these approaches to citizenship with our awareness of our impact on larger communities, for example, by participating on one's residence hall floor, volunteering with Habitat for Humanity, or boycotting clothing made in sweatshops.

COMMUNITY DEFINED

If citizenship is approached as working with others in one's community to make a difference for the common good, then it is important to explore what is implied by the word *community*. Various dimensions of community comprise the locality where a group of people live; society at large; shared identity with others; and "sharing, participation, and fellowship" ("Community," 2007). Exemplifying this definition, a student in an American Indian leadership course at the University of Maryland wrote:

> A community is a group of people tied together through some defining link such as ethnicity or geographical region. I belong to the University of Maryland community, the College Park community, the upperclassman community, the Prince George's County community, the activist community, and the American Indian student community.

Another student in that course noted:

Citizenship is reflected through my participation in student groups on campus, through my voting in elections, when students become actively involved in the classroom by participating in class, building relationships with professors, and working with classmates in or out of class. This happens any time I take part in an academic or extracurricular activity.

Following a series of thefts and assaults in off-campus apartment properties, students at Arizona State University responded by working with university staff and city police to create the "Be a Good Neighbor Program." The program included generating and distributing public relations announcements and publications to better educate and inform students and community members of safety and security issues. In addition, a series of town hall meetings was held. To this day, there is a bi-annual safety campaign that highlights community safety tips, as a result of engaged students, community members, university and city police, and university staff.

Political scientist Melissa Williams (2005) supported the concept of "citizenship as membership in a community of shared fate" (p. 209). When describing communities, Williams asserted that there is not simply one place where one is "supposed" to engage in citizenship; that it can be practiced anywhere. She further maintained that multiple experiences and worldviews comprise the concept of citizenship.

For example, a student may belong to Circle K International (2006), a service-based student organization whose mission is to foster "responsible citizens and leaders with a lifelong commitment to community service worldwide" (www.circlek.org/circlek/). This student may participate in community service on a regular basis as a member of this organization; however, this type of action is not the only defining feature of civic engagement, nor is this the sole organization through which a student can participate in civic activities. As members of the Black Student Union, several students may promote a campus movie series about the history of civil rights and segregation at their land grant institution, thus serving their campus community through educational programming. In the current dialogues concerning global warming trends, many students are engaged in awareness campaigns for environmental stewardship and sustainable practices. Such students may coordinate an e-mail campaign to apprise campus constituents of their carbon footprint (www.carbonfootprint.com), to encourage students, their roommates, family, and friends to get an estimate of their greenhouse gas emissions, how-to action plans for reducing emissions, and a subsequent cost-benefit analysis. Within Williams's definition of citizenship, everyone has the capacity to be engaged in their communities and practice citizenship in myriad ways and manifestations.

I always thought a good citizen voted for the president. Through my introductory leadership class, I realize that I'm also a good citizen when I help my roommate with her math homework or when I volunteer for freshmen orientation.

—A junior criminology major

Furthermore, Williams (2005) suggested that an understanding of one's place within a community varies and that the same perspective does not have to be adopted by all members within a community. What is instrumental to this concept is that there may be various interpretations within a community regarding its shared fate, and that members must identify in *some* way with the community, but not necessarily in the *same* way (Williams).

On a college campus, the prevalent notion, or "shared fate," of preparing students for leadership and active citizenship in

In response to proposed budget cuts to the California State University (CSU) system, CSU Channel Islands students and staff collaborated to form a statewide organization called "Access Denied?" which organized a rally on the capital, resulting in an increase of funds into the CSU system.

society may mean that the academic curricula support students' knowledge and skill building. It may also mean that student groups like the Latina/o student union, Omicron Delta Kappa honor society, or the student programming board foster leadership development, and that employment and internship opportunities provide experiential learning environments that develop transferable skills to postgraduation endeavors.

 Consider the communities to which you belong. How do you actively involve yourself in these communities? What values and beliefs connect you to others within these communities? What about these communities is important to you? How do you feel responsible to these communities? Think about communities in which you are a member without even being conscious of that membership. To what extent do your friend groups, families, teams, classes, religions, and/or cultures influence how you engage in Citizenship?

THE PROCESSES OF COMMUNITY ENGAGEMENT

People have the opportunity to engage in their communities in many different ways. Exhibit 5.1 presents a range of forms of engagement that support communities and their needs.

EXHIBIT 5.1 Forms of Individual Civic Engagement

Direct Service	Giving personal time and energy to address immediate community needs. Examples include tutoring, serving food at a shelter, building or repairing homes, and neighborhood or park clean-ups.
Community Research	Exploring a community to learn about its assets and how it is being affected by current social problems. This form of civic engagement provides knowledge that other efforts can build upon.
Advocacy and Education	Using various modes of persuasion (e.g., petitions, marches, letter writing) to convince government or corporate decision makers to make choices that will benefit the community. Raising public awareness of social issues by giving speeches to community groups, distributing written materials to the general public, or providing educational activities in schools.
Capacity Building	Working with the diverse constituencies of a community, building on existing assets, to solve problems and make it a better place. Creating a space for everyone in the community to have a say in what the community should be like and how to get there.
Political Involvement	Participating in processes of government, such as campaigning and voting. This includes keeping informed about issues in the local, national, and global communities in order to vote responsibly and engaging in discourse and debate about current social issues.
Socially Responsible Personal and Professional Behavior	Maintaining a sense of responsibility to the welfare of others when making personal or professional decisions. Using one's career or professional training to benefit the community. This category describes personal lifestyle choices that reflect commitment to one's values: recycling, driving a hybrid car, or bicycling to work; buying or not buying certain products because of unjust corporate policies or choosing to work for companies with socially just priorities.
Philanthropic Giving	Donating funding or needed items, organizing or participating in fundraising events.
Participation in Associations	Participating in community organizations that develop the social networks that provide a foundation for community-building efforts, including civic associations, sports leagues, church choirs, and school boards.

Source: Used with permission. © Julie E. Owen and Wendy Wagner, 2007.

ENGAGING IN CITIZENSHIP

Citizenship is not often an activity undertaken on one's own. The fact that citizenship involves working with others is what links citizenship and leadership so closely. While anyone can be involved in her or his community for the common good, there are skills and knowledge that can make that involvement more effective. Some of these include understanding social capital, awareness of the issues and community's history, empowerment, empathy, multicultural citizenship, an understanding of community development, and the ability to build coalitions.

Social Capital

Alexis de Tocqueville believed the strength of democratic communities in the United States was due to the large numbers of citizens working together in community associations (Tocqueville, 1835/1956). Indeed, the principles of democracy rely on the social contract of shared responsibility. More than 150 years later, social scientists can confirm this belief with empirical research. Whether aims are better schools, a safer college campus, effective government or economic development, a community's chances at success are more likely if the citizens are actively engaged with each other (Putnam, 2000). Harvard professor Robert Putnam (1999) defined this engagement, or *social capital*, as "networks, norms, and social trust that facilitate coordination and cooperation for mutual benefit" (p. 573). In other words, communities with social capital have citizens who have worked together, socialized together, and who *know* and *trust* each other. Citizens who build social capital attend public meetings, political speeches or rallies, serve on committees, belong to local organizations, participate in community sports groups, choirs, book clubs, professional societies, fraternal groups, faith-based groups, and service clubs. Even spending a social evening with a neighbor strengthens social capital.

Putnam (2000) described two dimensions of social capital: bonding and bridging. *Bonding* refers to social networks that are limited to people who are similar, like an all women's book club, or a student organization for business majors. Exclusive social networks like these have many benefits for those who are in them and can be a particularly meaningful source of support and strength for members. However, they can also be limiting. These types of groups can put an emphasis on "us" and "them" that limits opportunities to expand social networks and draw strength and knowledge from external groups. *Bridging* refers to social networks among more diverse people. The student government association that brings together students of all majors and backgrounds to address common concerns for the campus is an example. Bridging social capital tends to have many benefits for both the individuals and the community. In fact, bonding has been described as useful for getting by, but bridging is what is needed to get ahead (Putnam).

Examples of social capital exist in all communities and can easily be found on the college campus. Compare a residence hall floor where neighbors do not interact to one that has a vibrant social events committee, a floor-sponsored intra-mural sports team, active participation in floor meetings, and neighbors who often eat together. Residents of the latter floor are more likely to trust each other, help each other, and more easily resolve their common problems. Putnam (1999) said that for many reasons, "life is easier" (p. 573) for those who are living in communities that have worked to foster social capital.

 What groups do you belong to that build social capital through bonding? Which build it through bridging?

Awareness of the Issues and Community History

Staying informed about the community and its issues is some-times called *passive activism* (Lopez, Levine, Both, Kiesa, Kirby, & Marcelo, 2006). It includes making conscious decisions to engage in activities such as reading the paper or participating in online chat groups about important issues. It is also useful to initiate conversations with others in the community about opportunities to work together to develop new initiatives and make the community stronger.

An important aspect of keeping informed is to inform oneself about a community's history as well as its current sta-tus. It is incredibly useful to know how things have come to be how they are and what approaches have been tried in the past. When a fraternity struggles with decisions about some of its current programs, it is useful for the group to remember why they were created and what their mission and vision are. Understanding the nature of the ongoing relationships between individuals in the community is also useful. Who has been involved in conflicts with each other in the past? Who has had positive, successful working relationships?

Samuel Ryan, a sophomore at DePaul University, is a youth organizer committed to improving the quality of education in Illinois. He worked with others to coordinate forums for political candidates throughout the state, focusing on education as a means to engage high school students in the civic process.

Empowerment

When working with others to shape community, it is important to keep in mind that some members of a community may feel empowered, and others disenfranchised. This can have real consequences when envisioning the possibilities and limitations to development. For example, the undergraduate student group, Students as Parents, may collaborate with Graduate Student Life to draft a well-intentioned and thoughtful plan to start a campus day care center for students who are parents. Potential obstacles to achieving this goal may be financial resources, staffing, space, and liability issues. Student parents who have not felt that their interests were valued in the past may feel that establishing campus day care is an impossible and unrealistic goal. In this situation, active listening, collaboration, and empathy may help members of Students as Parents navigate this situation. When examining their reactions to the change process, members of Students as Parents may realize that they hold some constraining beliefs that inhibit their progress and also have empowering beliefs that move them forward.

In collaboration with other local universities, Rachel Osuna, a student at the University of San Diego, organized a regional conference called C.A.S.E.: *Collaborative for Action, Service and Engagement.* Each year for three years the group picked a topic and created a community project to raise awareness of its significance. In her senior year, that issue was educational inequity. As community volunteers, they saw the gap that existed between low- and high-income public schools and sought to empower students and parents to speak up for change. Rachel shared, "Often when discussing issues of educational reform, parents, school officials and politicians talk about what should be done to 'fix' the problem, but they rarely ask the children what they would change. That night, the voices of the children were heard."

Exhibit 5.2 illustrates some of the constraining as well as the empowering beliefs that many students embody. Being aware of these viewpoints will be important as students work through differences and attend to power structures in order to be thoughtful, inclusive, understanding, and collaborative in building campus communities.

Empathy

Williams (2005) completed her definition of citizenship with Yale political science professor Seyla Benhabib's assertion that "an enlarged mentality" (p. 237) is necessary to understanding one's place in a larger community, and that this translates into community members' honing their ability to empathize with others. Irvin Yalom (2002), a professor of psychiatry at Stanford University, referred to empathy as looking through someone else's window in order to try and see the world from a different and distinct vantage point. In this sense, truly listening to others and understanding perspectives other than one's own are critical components to participating in a community. Williams contended that this enlarged thinking can be broken down to (1) a capacity developed through its exercise, which (2) depends on experiences with diverse practices and beliefs, and (3) is cultivated through "discursive exchange between different perspectives, that is, through dialogue with different others" (p. 237). It is often through the free discourse of ideas, including those that conflict, that communities seek shared solutions (see Chapter Eight on Controversy with Civility).

EXHIBIT 5.2 Constraining and Empowering Beliefs in Campus Community Building

Constraining Beliefs

Individual Internal Beliefs	Individual External Actions	Implications for Individual Development
I don't have time to get involved. Faculty don't value my contributions. I don't have anything to offer student organizations. Other students don't support my interests.	Individual students are not engaged in campus life. Individual students are passive learners. Individual students self-select out of student organizations.	Individual students are not viewed as major stakeholders or change agents and are therefore overlooked for opportunities to develop community. Individual students are less self-aware of their talents and opportunities to be part of campus life.

Group Internal Beliefs	Group External Actions	Implications for Group Development
This campus doesn't care about students. Students do not have enough experience to engage in major campus community-building efforts.	Students and student groups are not involved in shared responsibilities for effecting growth. Fragmentation exists among student groups.	Students do not learn collaborative models of community building which embrace: 1. Shared purpose 2. Inclusion 3. Commitment 4. Group learning 5. Coalition building 6. Working with diverse populations

Empowering Beliefs

Individual Internal Beliefs	Individual External Actions	Implications for Individual Development
I can manage multiple roles and tasks so that I can make a difference on campus. As a campus citizen, I have a responsibility to help shape matters that affect me and my peers. Individual students have the ability to shape their futures. Each student has the capacity to engage in community building.	Individual students are engaged in a wide array of activities inside and outside the classroom. Individual students take the initiative to become involved in the life of the campus.	Individual students have opportunities for community development through formal and informal programs and experiences.

Group Internal Beliefs	Group External Actions	Implications for Group Development
Students are viewed as major stakeholders. Students are viewed as change agents. Student community building can make a difference on campus.	Students build coalitions with other campus groups to advance a shared vision and purpose. Students actively participate in shared campus governance. Students involve and prepare other students for community responsibilities.	Students and student groups model collaborative leadership. Students learn how to work interdependently to effect change. Students learn how to influence and shape the future of their campuses.

Source: Adapted from Astin and Astin (2000), pp. 24–25.

In 2006–2007 the "common reading" at the University of Texas at Arlington was *The Kite Runner*, which promoted campuswide discussion of the situation in war-ravaged Afghanistan. Freshmen Leaders On Campus (FLOC), a student organization that promotes leadership and involvement in the campus and local community, participated in the *Seeds for Afghanistan* project. More than 500 packages of seeds were collected and sent to the Afghani people so that they could raise products for market sales and for their personal survival.

In fact, the Multi-Institutional Study of Leadership (Dugan & Komives, 2007)—a fifty-two-campus research study of more than 50,000 undergraduate students—found that "engaging in discussions about socio-cultural issues was the single strongest environmental predictor of growth across the Social Change Model values as well as self-efficacy for leadership" (p. 15). Conversations centered on sociocultural issues refer to "the frequency with which students talked about different lifestyles, multiculturalism and diversity, major social issues such as peace, human rights, and justice and had discussions with students whose political opinions or personal values were very different from their own" (pp. 14–15).

How often do you have conversations with others who think, look, and live differently than you? Do you talk about these differences? Why, or why not? What do these conversations mean for your understanding of others and the world around you? Do you agree with Williams that empathy is integral to a sense of belonging within a community? What connections do you find between Williams's definition of Citizenship and communities in which you are a member?

Multicultural Citizenship

As communities develop, associations form, and communities work toward their shared fate, an important dimension of citizenship is the integration of diversity and a commitment to multicultural citizenship. Director of the Center for Multicultural Education at the University of Washington, James A. Banks (2001) stated that "multicultural citizens take actions within their communities and nations to make the world more humane" (p. 6). He emphasized several essential questions in developing oneself as a member of a democratic society. These have been adapted here to reflect the development of oneself as an engaged, conscientious member of a community. Questions to consider as an active member of a community include

(1) Who gets to participate

(2) To whom the community belongs

(3) Whom the community benefits

(4) Who defines the boundaries of the community

(5) Who makes the decisions in how the community develops, and redevelops, itself, and

(6) How the community redevelops when some within the community feel alienated or marginalized

These are critical questions for leaders to contemplate when examining the communities in which they participate, the diversity and inclusiveness of their communities, and the members who feel empowered, and who feel powerless, in those communities.

Use Banks's (2001) questions as guidelines for observing existing student groups in which you participate. Think about the classes, clubs, student organizations, athletic teams, committees, or work groups in which you have participated. How did each of these questions influence the communities in which you were involved? How did the culture of your group and/or the culture of your campus support or stifle your organization's development? How did students respect different leadership and communication styles? Did your student group commit time to discuss discrimination and/or oppression?

An Understanding of Community Development

Involvement in one's communities can be more effective when one has an understanding of the typical development of community groups. Peck (1987) presented a fourfold process for community development categorized by stages. The stages comprise pseudocommunity, chaos, organization or emptiness, and community. As you read through the stages, think of ways your communities share some of their characteristics and ways that your communities may differ in their development.

The first stage, *pseudocommunity*, is characterized by a false sense of getting along, such that harmony is sought at all costs, often at the expense of true relationship building. "The basic pretense of pseudocommunity is the denial of individual differences" (Peck, 1987, p. 89). This may be evidenced in a residence hall floor meeting near the beginning of the semester, at which time floormates instantly agree on proposed ground rules, such as study times, late night noise regulations, and overnight guest policies. Peck cautions against instant community without deliberation, suggesting that community building takes time and patience. In the example given, what might be some consequences of floormates making quick decisions about rules and regulations for each other?

The second stage is *chaos*; it involves unconstructive struggle. This tension lies in opposition to struggle that is engaged by fully developed communities once they have learned how to effectively communicate through conflict (see Chapter Eight on Controversy with Civility for more on this concept). Individual differences are prevalent in this stage as are efforts to normalize them; thus, there is vying for what is considered "normal" and who defines "normal" for the group.

Additionally, individual agendas are advocated. This may manifest when taskforces within a work team argue about which unit deserves more funding or staff, or when the student class councils argue over which group should get the more visible tables at the student involvement fair.

The third stage in community development, *organization* or *emptiness*, is the most critical, in Peck's (1987) estimation. Organizing out of a problem is symptomatic and occurs when groups bandage an issue rather than aim for preventive care. For example, consider that the Asian American Student Union and the Indian Students Association do not agree on a venue and theme for the Asian American History Month event they are coordinating. In haste, the president of one of the organizations decides that the groups will do separate events to move ahead with their plans. This immediate "solution," rather than a resolution of underlying issues, may allow the tension to continue to build between the two groups. Emptiness centers on community members' shedding or emptying themselves of potential obstacles to effective communication and working through constructive conflict (see Chapter Seven on Collaboration). These obstacles include assumptions, biases, stereotypes, and personal motivations that block listening and understanding among the members of a community. If the College Democrats talk about the College Republicans as insensitive and money grubbing, and the College Republicans speak of the College Democrats as hypocritical and money squandering, their preconceived notions and stereotyping may mask their common interests, purpose, and shared enthusiasm for societal change and political discourse.

The fourth and final stage of community development is, appropriately, *community*. Within this stage, members continue to have conflict and disagreements, and sometimes to fall back into previous stages of development, but they have strategies for allowing various voices to be heard and ideas to be considered. Members have learned how to collaborate and work *with* differences of opinions and ideas, rather than to avoid or quash them. Not all groups reach the community stage, and many in fact remain in pseudocommunity, where cooperation rather than collaboration maintains functioning; however, Peck's (1987) stages of community development highlight the great potential for genuine community building. Thus, Peck described these stages as flexible, meaning that different groups of people may move through the process in different ways and not in a linear fashion.

Coalitions

When several distinct organizations decide to formally join together around a common goal, a *coalition* is born. A coalition

 To what extent has one of your communities developed similarly to this process? How has it differed? How might this model be useful to you? To what extent is a sense of responsibility valuable in this model?

allows groups to join resources and expertise in order to solve problems they share in common, while letting each organization retain its autonomy. Organizations in coalitions each preserve their unique missions, identity, and values. In fact, sometimes organizations within a coalition may disagree on many issues, but they do not let those disagreements deter them from uniting on the issues they do have agreement on (Mizrahi & Rosenthal, 1993).

Coalition building is an important aspect of citizenship because most community problems are too complex to be solved by one approach or one group acting alone. Successful groups and organizations rely on collaboration with other groups as an essential skill for progress in developing community (Peck, 1987). Coalition building has become an oft-used collaborative tool for communities to reach out to community members from diverse backgrounds.

A student intern from Illinois Wesleyan University worked with a neighborhood in Bloomington, Illinois, to create a community garden. In order to succeed, the student partnered with neighbors, the Boys & Girls Club, a local corporation, and the community's historical society. The resulting garden added beauty to the area and also served as an educational tool for local children.

Community development specialist Thomas Wolff (2001) outlined several salient characteristics of an effective coalition:

> It is composed of community members. . . . It addresses community needs, building on community assets; it helps resolve community problems through collaboration; it is community-wide and has representatives from multiple sectors; it works on multiple issues; it is citizen influenced if not necessarily citizen driven; and it is a long term, not ad hoc, coalition. (p. 166)

This assertion strengthens Peck's statement that community building is time intensive and collaborative in nature. Furthermore, this statement reflects the growing trend for communities to build on members' strengths to develop well-functioning communities (Morse, 2004).

THE NEW LOOK OF CITIZENSHIP

Global Citizenship

References to how the world is growing smaller and interdependent are based on such things as a global economy, a global

 Consider the communities to which you belong—how are coalitions formed and for what reasons? How might you see coalition building as a useful skill to develop?

human rights agenda, and the impact of pollution on global warming. A burgeoning topic in discussions of citizenship is the significance of global citizenship. Japanese educator and Buddhist Tsunesaburo Makiguchi (as cited in Ikeda, 2005) "considered the identity of a global citizen on the three levels of local, national, and global community. . . . As the individual grows, the sphere of what that individual experiences as her or his local community expands to a national and then global scale" (p. x).

It is important to consider how this might look on a specific campus as an institution of higher learning, and how institutional citizenship might parallel global citizenship. Perhaps a student who welcomes his new roommate to the residence hall and takes care to make sure he is comfortable in his new home also recognizes the sense of belonging and well-being his new roommate develops as a result of the student's outreach. The roommate's satisfaction may lead him to become a resident assistant in his residence hall, in order to extend a hand to other students new to campus who are building communities to call home. Continuing in this vein, this student may choose to volunteer with the orientation staff on campus in order to expand his scope of outreach to nontraditional students residing off campus, realizing that he has the power to positively affect the people in his larger campus community. In this sense, the growth of one's identity within Makiguchi's concepts of local, national, and global communities becomes the extension of one's outreach through growing campus networks and communities.

Atem Deng and Abraham Awolich, two University of Vermont students who are emigres and "Lost Boys" from Sudan, cofounded the nongovernmental organization NESEI (the New Sudan Education Initiative [nesei.org]), an international organization dedicated to building twenty schools for secondary education by 2015 as southern Sudan reemerges following the comprehensive peace agreement of 2005. Their first school, the New Sudan School of Health Sciences in Lainya County, near Yei, South Sudan, opened in May 2008. (www.uvm.edu/theview/article.php?id=2277)

Consumer Activism

A recent study on generational differences in civic engagement found that the current generation of college students is more actively engaged than were earlier generations in consumer activism (Lopez et al.). The researchers of this study referred to two such activities as "boycotting" and "buycotting" products and services. *Boycotting* involves opting out of certain purchases or services due to the conditions in which they were made or provided. For example, a student may choose to not purchase products from a campus bookstore or apparel outlet that uses sweatshop labor, and he or she may petition such companies to improve their workplace practices. *Buycotting* refers to intentionally purchasing products or services that are distributed by companies who share the consumer's social and political values. This may mean purchasing coffee from a vendor who sells free trade coffee, or supporting microlending firms that provide loans to entrepreneurs in developing countries, or purchasing gasoline from companies that are working toward reducing carbon emissions and developing green technologies. Both boycotting and buycotting support the idea that the everyday decisions people make have an impact on others, at home and abroad.

Use of Technology

College students shift their citizenship focus from local to global and can be informed from global to local, on a regular basis using information technology provided on the Internet. After the 2004 tsunami struck Southeast Asia, and within hours of media attention to this natural disaster, students worldwide had launched online aid groups to provide financial and emotional support to the many survivors throughout Asia and beyond.

Students use technology to have a voice in matters that affect themselves as well as others. When Facebook added a News Feed feature in 2006 that tracked in great detail user activity for anyone in a person's friend network, students took action. Within days of an anti–News Feed campaign, hundreds of thousands of students had consolidated their online efforts to effect change in the new policy they viewed as a breach of students' privacy rights (Bachioni, 2006). Starting what are termed "global groups," students were able to access anyone on the Facebook network. As a result of their online protests, the owners of Facebook issued an apology and introduced new methods for ensuring user privacy. Such action was witnessed worldwide because these protests took place in an online forum.

During the 2006 Gallaudet student protests of the president-elect Jane K. Fernandes, students opposed her appointment using pagers, text messaging, instant messaging, and blogs to reach both on- and off-campus constituents. This technology also assisted students in staying connected to the media and in rousing other students and staff to support their efforts. According to the president of the National Association of the Deaf, Bobbie Beth Scoggins, "Sidekicks and pagers did more than help students publicize their grievances. They also helped activists and protesters stay organized during a quickly evolving situation" (Farrell, 2006). During these protests, students consolidated their efforts to effect change in a broader, more "global" sense by reaching a greater audience as a result of their technological savvy.

CONNECTION TO THE OTHER C'S

Citizenship as the societal component of the Social Change Model of Leadership Development draws on the interconnectedness of the individual, group, and societal C's. The ensemble (HERI, 1996) stated that "Citizenship thus acknowledges the interdependence of all who are involved in or affected by these efforts" (p. 23), that is, individual, group, and societal attempts to effect change.

Attention to the Citizenship C builds capacity in the other C's as well. Experiences with citizenship often challenge people to make choices that require them to clarify their Commitments, clarify their values through Consciousness of Self, and examine whether their choices are Congruent with their beliefs. In addition to the individual-level C's, the group-level C's also are positively affected by citizenship. When actively participating in community endeavors, people have opportunities to practice Collaborating with others, reaching a Common Purpose, and learning to work through Controversy with Civility.

Just as experiences with Citizenship build capacity to engage in the other C's, experiences with the other C's improve one's ability to engage in citizenship. These experiences are discussed further in subsequent chapters.

CONCLUSION

According to an East African proverb, "The person who has not traveled widely thinks his or her mother is the only cook [the best cook]." The grand outcome of the social change model is Change, and involves stepping out of one's comfort zone and asking critical questions of oneself and others. The metaphor of traveling widely echoes this sentiment and directs the change agent to seek to understand self and others, challenge one's own worldview, engage in conversations across difference, and take risks that involve trying new things and meeting new people.

> Throughout this chapter, the Citizenship value of the Social Change Model has been discussed in its various dimensions. These facets of Citizenship have ranged from community building, to working toward a shared fate, to embracing multiculturalism, to supporting global interconnectedness. As the ensemble (HERI, 1996) recommends, one way to visualize these different "levels" of citizenship is to imagine a set of concentric circles with the smallest (most interior) circle representing the individual, the next large one representing the group, the next larger the institution, and so on, with the largest (most exterior) circle representing the society at large. (p. 68)

In this context, long-term, effective Citizenship will ideally intersect all circles in the set. Similar to the individual, group, and societal levels described earlier, Komives (1994) encouraged her readers to continually ask themselves three questions: "How am I like no one else here? How am I like some others here? And how am I like everyone here?" (p. 219). As you continue to learn and apply the Seven C's of Change, you are encouraged to personally reflect on where you and your communities enter the value of Citizenship, to think critically about how you and groups with which you are affiliated see yourselves using the model in your communities, and to ask questions along the way.

DISCUSSION QUESTIONS

1. What communities can you consider yourself a part of? What does citizenship in those communities mean to you?

2. What forms of citizenship and active community involvement appeal to you most? Are there any forms described here that you have never done?

3. Within the communities named in #1, how might you go about developing social capital and increasing your awareness of the issues in those communities?

JOURNAL PROBES

On Becoming
Preeminent psychologist, Carl Rogers (1961) said that people are always in a process of *becoming*. The first two journal probes are intended to help you reflect on how you see yourself becoming a leader for social change.

1. How are you becoming a more effective citizen in the groups you are a part of?

2. Can you remember a time when you thought about Citizenship differently than you do now? How is your current approach different from your approach then?

Learning Through Experience

The ensemble that created the Social Change Model believed the best way to learn to do leadership was through experience and reflection. This involves challenging yourself to have new experiences that test your ability and awareness **and** to spend time thinking about what you have learned from that experience. The remaining journal probes are designed to maximize learning through experience by guiding your reflective journal writing through Kolb's (1981) four processes of experiential learning.

1. **Concrete Experience.** Describe a specific situation when you had an experience that relates to Citizenship as it has been described here. What happened? What details stand out to you? Describe briefly the situation, what you did and how you felt.

2. **Reflective Observation.** Why did this situation have the outcome it did? What caused the situation to happen in the first place? What responses from yourself and others worked in this situation? Why was that effective? What did not work? Why?

3. **Abstract Conceptualization.** What lessons can you draw from this specific experience that could apply more

generally? Given both your reflections and the information in this chapter, what would you do if a similar situation presented itself? What general guidelines would you create for handling future situations like this?

4. **Active Experimentation.** What opportunities might you seek that would give you the chance to apply what you have learned here? How might you test the lessons or guidelines you created in #3 to see if they work?

APPLYING THE CASE STUDIES

Go back to Chapter Three for more context on each of these case studies. Apply the material covered in Chapter Five to these cases.

Zoom In: Starving for Attention

In this case, Taylor is a student who has become involved in an organization that is challenging the university to pay its service workers a wage that better reflects the cost of living in the area. Taylor is captivated by the idea of helping the Latina/o workforce at his university gain a living wage. As he begins to put together the information he has learned in class and the information he is now learning as part of the Living Wage Campaign, Taylor realizes that the organization must rise up to address this issue with university administration. He raises his hand during one of their meetings and tells the members that "we have an obligation to act and fight on behalf of these staff members." He tells group members that they must use their individual responsibility to advocate for the individual housekeepers of the service staff at the university.

Other students in the group agree and respond by letting all members know that "we can all work together to change this." Another student points out that "we must involve the service staff in this movement and not simply do it on our own." Taylor is feeling very encouraged by the response at the meeting and how all are beginning to understand their obligation to help their community.

Think About It

+ What processes of community engagement might be used to achieve the change this group is promoting?

+ How can this group increase its social capital on the campus?

+ What other groups might be approached in order to do coalition building?

Zoom In: Clear Haziness

In this case, you are the photography editor of the campus paper, *The Weekly*, where a tradition of hazing new members of the photography staff has been uncovered. How can you, through your role as photography editor, encourage active citizenship in others? What role might you play in building social capital on campus? Considering the important role that experienced staff photographers can play in campus community building, they are a valuable asset to the community. However, at the group level, the senior photographers are playing a less than positive role. How are the needs of the group balanced with the wider needs of the community in this situation?

References

Astin, A., & Astin, H. (2000). *Leadership reconsidered: Engaging higher education in social change.* Battle Creek, MI: W. K. Kellogg Foundation.

Bachioni, J. (2006, October 16). The new facebook story. *iMPrint Magazine.* Retrieved April 15, 2007, from http://www.imprintmagazine.org/2006/10/16/the-new-facebook-story/

Banks, J. A. (2001). Citizenship education and diversity: Implications for teacher education. *Journal of Teacher Education, 52,* 1–13. Retrieved from http://jte.sagepub.com/cgi/reprint/52/1/5.pdf

Bordas, J. (2007). *Salsa, soul, and spirit: Leadership for a multicultural age.* San Francisco: Berrett-Koehler.

Community. (2007). *The American heritage dictionary of the English language* (4th ed.). Retrieved April 15, 2007, from http://dictionary.reference.com/browse/community

Dewey, J. (1916). *Democracy and education: An introduction to the philosophy of education.* New York: Free Press.

Dugan, J. P., & Komives, S. R. (2007). *Developing leadership capacity in college students: Findings from a national study.* College Park, MD: National Clearinghouse for Leadership Programs.

Ehrlich, T. (2000). Preface. In T. Ehrlich (Ed.), *Civic responsibility and higher education* (pp. vi–x). Washington, DC: Oryx.

Farrell, E. F. (2006, November 1). At Gallaudet U., technology and influential blogs helped galvanize protests. *The Chronicle of Higher Education*. Retrieved May 14, 2007, from http://chronicle.com/daily/2006/11/2006110102n.htm

Higher Education Research Institute. [HERI] (1996). *A social change model of leadership development* (Version III). Los Angeles: University of California Los Angeles, Higher Education Research Institute.

Ikeda, D. (2005). Foreword. In N. Noddings (Ed.), *Educating citizens for global awareness* (pp. ix–xi). New York: Teachers College Press.

Kolb, D. A. (1981). Learning styles and disciplinary differences. In A. W. Chickering & Associates (Eds.), *The modern American college: Responding to the new realities of diverse students and a changing society* (pp. 232–255). San Francisco: Jossey Bass.

Komives, S. R. (1994). Increasing student involvement through civic leadership education. In C. C. Schroeder, P. Mable, & Associates (Eds.), *Realizing the educational potential of college residence halls* (pp. 218–240). San Francisco: Jossey-Bass.

Liang, C.T.H., Lee, S., & Ting, M. P. (2002). Developing Asian American leaders. In M. K. McEwen, C. M. Kodama, A. N. Alvarez, S. Lee, & C.T.H. Liang, (Eds.), *Working with Asian American college students* (New Directions for Student Services, no. 97). San Francisco, Jossey-Bass.

Lopez, M. H., Levine, P., Both, D., Kiesa, A., Kirby, E., & Marcelo, K. (2006). *The 2006 civic and political health of the nation: A detailed look at how youth participate in politics and communities*. College Park, MD: Center for Information and Research on Civic Learning and Engagement.

Mizrahi, T., & Rosenthal, B. S. (1993). Managing dynamic tensions in social change coalitions. In T. Mizrahi & J. Morrison (Eds.), *Community organization and social administration: Advances, trends and emerging principles* (pp. 11–40). New York: Haworth.

Morse, S. M. (2004). *Smart communities: How citizens and local leaders can use strategic thinking to build a brighter future.* San Francisco: Jossey-Bass.

Owen, J. E., & Wagner, W. (in press). Situating service-learning in the contexts of civic engagement and the engaged campus. In B. Jacoby (Ed.), *Establishing and sustaining the community service-learning professional: A guide for self-directed learning.* Providence, RI.: Campus Compact.

Peck, M. S. (1987). *The different drum: Community-making and peace.* New York: Simon & Schuster.

Putnam, R. D. (1999). *Bowling alone: America's declining social capital.* In B. Barber & R. M. Battistoni (Eds.), *Education for democracy* (pp. 553–557). Dubuque, IA: Kendall/Hunt.

Putnam, R. D. (2000). *Bowling alone: The collapse and revival of American community.* New York: Simon & Schuster.

Rogers, C. R. (1961). *On becoming a person: A therapist's view of psychotherapy.* Boston: Houghton Mifflin.

Takaki, R. (1993). *In a different mirror: A history of multicultural America.* Boston: Little, Brown.

Tocqueville, A. d. (1956). *Democracy in America.* (Heffner R. D., Trans.). New York: Penguin Books. (Original work published 1835.)

Williams, S. (2005). Citizenship as identity, citizenship as shared fate, and the functions of multicultural education. In K. McDonough & W. Feinburg (Eds.), *Citizenship and education in liberal-democratic societies* (pp. 208–248). New York: Oxford University Press.

Wolff, T. (2001). Community coalition building—contemporary practice and research: An introduction. *American Journal of Community Psychology, 29,* 165–172.

Yalom, I. D. (2002). *The gift of therapy: An open letter to a new generation of therapists and their patients.* New York: HarperCollins.

PART 3

Group
Values

Relationships are the connective tissue of organizations. . . .
Over time . . . relationships built on integrity are the glue
that holds organizations together.
KATHY ALLEN AND CYNTHIA CHERREY

The Social Change Model (SCM) recognizes that leadership is inherently a relational process. "Leadership involves collaborative relationships that lead to collective action grounded in the shared values of people who work together to effect positive change" (Higher Education Research Institute [HERI], 1996, p. 16). "[This] requires that individuals learn how to develop relationships among themselves that allow for collaborative action on issues in common" (Morse, 1994, p. 48). Indeed, leadership is all about relationships.

People come together in groups to accomplish shared purposes. Whether a study group, an academic class, a staff at work, or a student organization, groups are dynamic and evolve as the members within them develop a breadth and depth working together.

Part Three explores how leadership happens among individuals in groups as they seek to work toward change. Understanding groups is key to accomplish shared purposes.

Just as individuals grow and change, so do groups and organizations. Tuckman (1965; Tuckman & Jenson, 1977) studied the evolving nature of groups and observed that they go through predictable stages of

+ **Forming.** In the early process of individuals coming together around their shared purposes, individuals focus
  on determining how the group can address their interests
  and needs. Individuals figure out what their roles will be in
  the group and how engaged they will be in the life of the
  group.

+ **Storming.** As the group evolves, members identify differences of opinion about what process they will use, what
  their real purposes are; their individual expectations may
  conflict. Members may challenge each other and pull away
  from each other, the process, or the purpose.

+ **Norming.** Members may also recognize storming is a stage
  in the group's process and encourage everyone to return to
  the group's purposes and find ways to work through their
  controversies. At this stage the group established what
  they will expect of each other, how they will work together,
  and establish the culture of the group so all members know
  what to expect and how they can contribute.

+ **Performing.** The group settles into working together to
  accomplish their purposes. It maintains group processes.
  The group recognizes the need to bring in new members
  and incorporate them into the ongoing purposes of the
  group.

+ **Adjourning.** At some point many groups end and dis-
  band—a class is over or a service project ends. Often the
  structure of the group may continue (for example, a staff

or student organization has a large turnover) but the group has to start over in this cycle and form again.

In Part Three, the SCM examines leadership development from the group dimension. The ensemble asked, "How can the collaborative leadership development process be designed not only to facilitate the development of the desired individual qualities [that follow in the next section] but also to effect positive change?" (HERI, 1996, p. 19). The three values explored in this dimension are Collaboration, Common Purpose, and Controversy with Civility.

References

Higher Education Research Institute [HERI]. (1996). *A social change model of leadership development* (Version III). Los Angeles: University of California Los Angeles, Higher Education Research Institute.

Morse, S. W. (1994). Educating leaders for the responsibilities of a civil society. *Journal of Leadership Studies, 1*(3), 37–49.

Tuckman, B. W. (1965). Developmental sequence in small groups. *Psychological Bulletin, 63,* 384–399.

Tuckman, B. W., & Jensen, M. C. (1977). Stages of small group development revisited. *Group and Organizational Studies, 2,* 419–427.

COLLABORATION

Jordan England

> *When we perceive differences in personality and abilities as gifts and pieces of a magnificent puzzle, we put them together to form a masterpiece of power and creation truly larger than anyone's single vision.*
> THOMAS CRUM

Collaboration is a core value in the Social Change Model of Leadership Development (SCM)—in fact, it is part of the definition. Leadership is grounded in relationships between people; in these relationships one develops the ability to work collaboratively with others that is essential to the leadership process. The ensemble's definition of *collaboration* underscores the importance of relationships, the need for shared responsibility, authority, and accountability, and the benefit of having multiple perspectives and talents in a group process.

The ensemble defined collaboration as:

Working together toward common goals by sharing responsibility, authority, and accountability in achieving these goals. . . . It multiplies group effectiveness because it capitalizes on the multiple talents and perspectives of each group member and the power of that diversity to generate creative solutions and actions. Collaboration underscores the relational aspect in the model. It is about human relationships, how people work together, and how they value and relate to each other. Collaboration mobilizes and enhances the power of the group through the members' commitment to the common purpose. (Higher Education Research Institute [HERI], 1996, p. 48)

Our approach to leadership development views collaboration as more than merely coming together around a predetermined vision or approach. Rather, we see collaboration as being most centrally about how people value and relate to each other across differences in values, ideas, affiliations, visions, and identities (for example, race, gender, culture, religion, sexual orientation, class, and so on). Collaboration is not only an efficient and effective way to get the "task" accomplished, but it also a powerful way to learn about ourselves and others in the process. (p. 49)

CHAPTER OVERVIEW

This chapter explores the concept of Collaboration as it relates to the leadership process. First, the chapter looks at what collaboration is, and what it is not. Second, it will look at the role and impact of diversity in the collaborative process. Third, the chapter explores processes and competencies that are necessary for successful collaborations. Finally, it will look to how collaboration relates to the other C's in the Social Change Model of Leadership.

EXPLORING COLLABORATION

Crum (1987) studied the role of followers and group members in accomplishing group goals. Believing in empowered group members, he used the term *cocreation* instead of collaboration to describe the relationship among group members working toward shared goals. His definition is quite similar to the ensembles, but it draws attention to the importance of sharing in the creation of visions, goals, and solutions in a collaborative process. Crum asserted:

> Power arises when both parties participate in the cocreation process because they both begin to share (or be committed to) the common vision. Knowing that they have the same goal in mind, they are able to proceed

together to cocreate solutions . . . and when both sides participate in cocreating solutions, they both become responsible for carrying out those solutions. (p. 186)

Based on these definitions, collaboration involves:

+ Human relationships and how people relate to each other
+ A process of developing common visions, goals, and purpose
+ Shared responsibility, authority, and accountability in developing solutions and accomplishing goals
+ Creating synergy by capitalizing on the multiple perspectives and talents of group members

Collaboration, Competition, Cooperation, and Compromise

Fully understanding what collaboration is and is not requires an exploration of the relationships among collaboration, competition, cooperation, and compromise. The following is a discussion of each of these concepts and the relationships between them.

Competition seems embedded in many of our American structures. The adversarial legal system, sports teams, the game of bridge, and the competitive free market economy all illustrate the way competition permeates our shared lives (Komives, Lucas, & McMahon, 1998, p. 95). Many people believe that competition is the most effective way of working toward goals and motivating individuals to achieve their greatest potential;

however, the research on achievement has repeatedly refuted the myth that competition leads to greater productivity than cooperation (Kohn, 1986). Johnson, Maruyama, Johnson, Nelson, and Skon (1981) conducted a meta-analysis of more than 100 different studies measuring performance data in competitive, cooperative, or individualistic structures. In the analysis, 65 of the studies showed that cooperation resulted in greater achievement than competition, 36 studies found no statistically significant difference between achievement in cooperative and competitive environments, and 8 studies found that achievement was higher in competitive environments (Johnson et al.). Kohn notes that teachers often believe that competition is effective in educational environments because it sparks students' interest and holds their attention and in some contexts it may teach students to stand up for themselves. However, students' interest is often focused on the competitive game rather than the material itself, and students actually *learn* more when they cooperate rather than compete (Kohn). Some group competitions such as intramural sports can promote a bigger common goal of supporting healthy behaviors and productive leisure activities. For the purpose of this approach to leadership, the Social Change Model promotes the value that individuals working together in the same group toward a shared goal would accomplish more if they collaborate with each other instead of compete with one another for recognition, rewards, or for other motives.

The essence of the concept of competition is what Kohn (1986) calls "mutually exclusive goal attainment," meaning "one person succeeds only if another does not" (p. 9). Competition usually does not motivate people to do the best that they can; it only motivates them to do better than the others. It actually limits how high one's goals are set. It encourages a focus on beating others, rather than focusing on doing well. Winning is extrinsically motivated, and though it may produce short-term gain, a continued focus on beating others tends to erode one's intrinsic or internal motivation to strive toward excellence on a task (Kohn). Collaboration allows people to imagine a different paradigm, one in which great things can be accomplished in win-win situations. The much used phrase "Two heads are better than one" is a simple illustration of the fact that more can be accomplished when everyone's talents, skills, and efforts are brought together in working toward a shared goal.

In *The 7 Habits of Highly Effective People*, Covey (2004) refers to win/lose thinking (another term for a belief in mutually exclusive goal attainment) as inherently flawed. Covey recommends looking for and working toward synergistic, win-win solutions. He defines *win-win* as "a belief in the Third Alternative. It's not your way or my way; it's a *better* way, a higher way" (p. 207). The way to find Covey's "Third Alternative" is to learn to approach differences of opinion in a completely different way. Traditionally, each individual states their position and defends its merits. One person wants to go out for coffee at Starbucks, the other wants to go to College Perk, a locally owned coffeehouse. The two argue about why each is better, trying to convince the other they are right. With a

 Students With a Vision (SWAV) started at St. John Fisher College when Jackie Morrison and John Snyder met in their first year during the first week of class. They were both interested in running for class office, and their individual platforms consisted of engaging the freshman class in urban service work. The more they investigated the position, however, the more they realized that the best way to achieve their goals would be to start their own organization. They began to talk with the Office of Campus Life about creating a new service organization and concurrently were enrolled in a "Leadership Through Self-Development" course and were continually inspired by how motivated people united in a common goal can create widespread change. Discussions about transformational leadership and historical examples of social change made them realize their potential to do the same. They assembled other like-minded students and shared their ideas about how they could impact the community. Jackie and John realized, "Ultimately, we were empowering our peers by providing a space where they could work toward making their Visions reality."

win-win approach, each person would try to understand the criteria behind the other's choice. One person prefers to support locally owned businesses; the other wants to be able to sit outdoors on a patio. Once the criteria are established, it is not about opposing sides anymore. There is no longer a winner and a loser. Instead there are two people on the same side, solving the puzzle together: find a locally owned coffee shop, with outdoor seating.

Win-win requires each party to determine the criteria that would constitute a win for them, then to set aside "my way" and "your way" of doing things and try to create a whole new option that meets the "win" criteria of both parties. In the process of forming win-win agreements, Covey (2004) suggests keeping the option of "no deal" on the table. That is, if both parties are not able to come to an agreement that is mutually beneficial, then they agree to walk away peacefully rather than agreeing on a solution that favors the interests of one party over the other. Knowing that neither person will commit to interest in a "win" if it means a "loss" for the other person develops trust in working relationships. Win-win solutions are satisfying and beneficial to all parties involved and generate higher levels of commitment from group members.

Synergy is a term used to describe the point when the whole has become greater than the sum of its parts (Covey, 2004). For organizations, this means the unified efforts of the group working together achieves more than the combined result of same individuals working independently. *Reaching the point of synergy is the goal of a collaborative process.*

 Whom have you worked with who was skilled at finding win-win solutions? Have you been in a situation that resulted in a win/lose outcome? How could that situation have been reframed to engage in a win-win option?

Organizations that have synergy have a high degree of trust and truly value the differences in other people. When members see things differently, they think, "Good! Talking through different perspectives will help us make sure we've really thought this issue through." Members do not need to feel "right" or that they have "won" an argument, they just need to feel their perspective was understood and was taken into consideration in the search for the Third Alternative (Covey, 2004).

Cooperation is different from collaboration in a small but important way. The ensemble asserted that "collaboration differs from cooperation in the sense that collaboration is based on a relationship that tries to achieve mutual goals, while cooperation is based on a relationship that helps each party to achieve its own individual goals" (HERI, 1996, p. 48). Similarly, Chrislip and Larson (1994) asserted that the "purpose of collaboration is to create a shared vision and joint strategies to address concerns that go beyond the purview of any particular party" (p. 5). As such, win-win solutions can be a part of either cooperative or collaborative processes.

Consider an example of two different community service-based student organizations that are both trying to increase undergraduate participation in their respective community service projects. The two groups may decide to *cooperate* to help each group achieve their goals by doing a joint mailing to new students about their respective organizations. A *collaboration* between the two groups would require them to take a step back from their individual goals of increasing participation in their specific projects, to develop a common goal: increasing undergraduate participation in community service. Once that purpose has been decided upon, the organizations can join together to develop new strategies and interventions focused on the common goal.

Even while considering the possibility of win-win situations, people often believe that working together requires some level of *compromise* from each party. Crum (1987) says, "Often in life we are so intent on doing the 'fair' thing that we never look at what we are really going for. We never see the possibility that there is enough for each to have everything that he or she needs" (p. 177). Thus, groups often seek solutions that require each person to compromise a little rather than believing and striving for the possibility of a truly win-win solution. The ensemble asserts that

> collaboration is not about "compromise" in the traditional sense of the word. Compromise has traditionally meant that you have to "give something up" for the greater good. We prefer to see true collaboration as requiring each participant to hear and consider the ideas, values, and perspectives of others with the

ultimate aim of expanding or redefining individual
beliefs and viewpoints. (HERI, 1996, p. 49)

How Does Collaboration Work?

With a better understanding of what collaboration is, the
specific elements that lead to successful collaborations can
be explored. Chrislip and Larson (1994) identified five keys
to successful collaborations that the ensemble felt were
closely aligned with the Social Change Model of Leadership (HERI, 1996). First, group members have collectively
identified a clear need that they will address as a group. Second, there is broad-based involvement from members of the
group, and if appropriate, relevant stakeholders outside of
the group. Third, members of the group must believe that
the process is both credible and open, and believe that they
have a meaningful voice and role. Fourth, group members
put in the time and effort to overcome mistrust and skepti-
cism. Finally, the group has agreed upon group norms and
ground rules.

Straus's (2002) five principles of collaborative problem
solving also provide useful insight into means of developing
successful collaborations. Strauss suggests that:

1. Collaborations should be **inclusive** and involve all of the
   relevant stakeholders.

2. Decisions should be made by **consensus**—and consensus must be continually reached throughout the process.
   Additionally, a fallback means of decision making should

be decided upon in advance in the case that consensus cannot be reached in a certain phase of the process.

3. Groups should **design a process map** or flowchart—a visual representation of the collaboration process—early in the process to help group members understand where the group is headed.

4. Groups should **designate a facilitator** who will lead the process. This person helps facilitate the process and should not have positional power over the group.

5. Finally, groups should **create a visual record** of what happens at meetings using flip charts and markers to help members of the group keep up with all of the information. See an example in the "Zoom In" feature on the Starving for Attention case study at the end of the chapter.

Through a review of literature related to successful collaborations, the ensemble also identified a number of activities that enhance collaboration:

- Members of the group jointly explore their values, the reasons for their interest in the project at hand, and any problems they may foresee in implementing the project.
- The group agrees to make time for informal and celebratory occasions to strengthen their common bonds.
- Group members actively seek to identify mechanisms to maintain open communication and to share information.

+ The group agrees to establish and maintain trust (the essential ingredient in collaboration), not by avoiding controversy or conflict, but instead by dealing with it openly and with civility.
+ Trust is established in part by jointly engaging in conversation about what it means to have trust and by discussing what specific behaviors illustrate it.
+ Procedures are established to make sure that everyone in the group is being heard.
+ Group members learn to give feedback that describes rather than evaluates. (HERI, 1996, p. 52)

Meaningful conversation is clearly a central step in designing group norms that will support collaborative practices. The group also has to move beyond talk and into action. As the steps of an activity unfold, checking in on the process ensures that collaborative practices are reinforced and encouraged.

Diversity in the Collaborative Process

Diversity is an essential part of the collaborative process. The ensemble said that collaboration "multiplies group effectiveness because it capitalizes on the multiple talents and perspectives of each group member and the power of that diversity to generate creative solutions" (HERI, 1996, p. 48). Thus, diversity is an integral part of the collaborative process. Diverse groups can be more productive, make higher quality and more creative decisions, are better at adapting to changing conditions, and are less prone to groupthink than are groups with homogenous membership (Johnson & Johnson, 1994).

Understanding the role of diversity in the collaborative process requires some exploration of what diversity is. Smith and associates (1997) offer a useful definition of diversity as it relates to campus communities:

> Diversity on campus encompasses complex differences within the campus community and also in the individuals who compose that community. It includes such important and intersecting dimensions of human identity as race, ethnicity, national origin, religion, gender, sexual orientation, class, age, and ability. These dimensions do not determine or predict any one person's values, orientation, choices, or responses. But they are by definition closely related to patterns of societal experiences, socialization, and affiliation. They influence ways of understanding and interpreting the world. (p. 7)

It is important to keep in mind that each individual has multiple dimensions of identity (for example, race, ethnicity, national origin, sexual orientation, class, age, ability, and religion) that intersect with one another and must be understood in relation to one another and to the environment of the individual (Jones & McEwen, 2000). In addition to one's identities, each individual also brings values, personalities, opinions, attitudes, communication styles, working and learning styles, and strengths and weaknesses (Johnson & Johnson, 1994) often learned through the development of various identities. Diversity is both the strength and the challenge of collaboration. Try to imagine working in a homogeneous group where everyone has similar backgrounds, perspectives, strengths, and talents. It may be difficult to imagine such a group— and while such a group may get along well, it seems unlikely that it would be particularly creative or effective. Working in heterogeneous groups allows us to capitalize on the multiple perspectives and strengths of the various group members, enabling us to tackle problems with creativity and innovation (Johnson & Johnson).

While differences within groups are necessary and lead to stronger outcomes, they can also provide challenges in a group process. Individuals with different values, perspectives, and working and learning styles may come to a group with different ideas of what is important, different notions of how groups should function, and value different styles of communication. These factors can lead to increased conflict and misunderstandings among group members and can create barriers to group effectiveness. To make the most of the diversity in a group, it is important to create an organizational culture that openly communicates about the differences. If certain individuals feel their perspective has been ignored or their values slighted, they need to feel they can say so, and that others in the group will truly listen and empathize with their feelings. These can sometimes be uncomfortable conversations, the kind many people prefer to avoid. Some try to ignore these tensions hoping they will go away on their own. Others listen, but become defensive of their own behaviors, minimizing the feelings of others: "It isn't that big of a deal." To make the most of a diverse organization, it is

 Johnson and Johnson (2006) provide a useful set of guidelines for maximizing the positive outcomes of diversity in the collaborative process:

1. Recognize that diversity among group members is ever present and unavoidable.

2. Recognize that the more interdependent the world becomes, the more important it is to be able to work effectively with diverse groupmates.

3. Maximize heterogeneity among group members in both personal characteristics and abilities in order to maximize the group's productivity and success.

4. With heterogeneous membership comes increased conflict. Structure constructive procedures for managing conflicts among group members.

5. Identify and eliminate barriers to the utilization of diversity (stereotyping, prejudice, blaming the victim, cultural clashes).

6. Ensure that diversity is utilized as a resource by strengthening the positive interdependence within the group in order to create the context in which diversity is a resource, not a hindrance.

7. Ensure that diversity is utilized as a strength by uniting the personal identities of members of diverse groups. Create a superordinate identity based on a

pluralistic set of values. Encourage individuals to develop:

a. An appreciation for their gender, religious, ethnic, and cultural backgrounds

b. An appreciation for the gender, religious, ethnic, and cultural backgrounds of other group members

c. A strong superordinate identity of "group member" that transcends the differences among members

d. A pluralistic set of values concerning equality, freedom, the rights of individual members, and the responsibilities of group membership

8. Ensure that diversity is utilized as a strength by fostering personal relationships among members that allow for candid discussions that increase members' sophistication about their differences.

9. Ensure that diversity is utilized as a strength by clarifying miscommunication among diverse group members. (p. 448)

important that every member's point of view is treated as a valid perspective.

Diversity within a group does not guarantee a group process that is truly inclusive of diverse ideas and perspectives. Differences in communication styles may lead members of the group to share their perspectives in various ways. Some individuals communicate directly and assertively, while others may use body language to convey messages. Some people will use facts to convey a point, while others may use symbolism and metaphor. Additionally, some people may convey messages with passion and emotion, while others may be more reserved (Komives, Lucas, & McMahon, 2007). Additionally, because of our country's history and social structures, people with certain identities have become accustomed to being more dominant than others. Likewise, those with other identities have been historically excluded or marginalized and still seek to be understood in a group. It is ongoing work within a group to create a group culture in which everyone knows their ideas and contributions are equally valued. Just as an individual's background, perspectives, socialization, and assumptions influence the way they communicate their messages, these factors will also influence one's ability to hear and understand the messages that others convey, and may result in some voices

Try to think of an instance when a different perspective helped shed light on a challenging situation. What were the conditions that made that contribution possible? What was the environment like? How did the individuals involved create a comfortable space for people who "think differently"? What are some things that you can personally do in a group setting that would enable each group member to bring their full self (talents, perspectives, and identities) to the conversation?

and perspectives having more influence in the process than others. Inclusion of diverse voices is only effective if every voice has influence over the process.

Collaboration within diverse groups requires each of us to enhance our ability to work effectively with, listen to, and develop trust with people who are different from us. We can enhance our ability to work in diverse groups by developing intrapersonal and interpersonal competencies.

MAKING IT WORK

> Choosing cocreation is an obvious step to take in resolving conflicts. . . . So why do we often forget it when conflicts arise in our life? There is one simple reason. It takes time, energy, and work to cocreate when there are major differences in a relationship. Cocreation takes listening and understanding and a commitment to discovering a solution together. It means not having it be just your way, but rolling up your sleeves to create new possibilities. (Crum, 1987, p. 174)

The ensemble identified a number of processes and personal competencies that are necessary for effective collaboration, including doing personal work, building trust, and communicating clearly. The following is a discussion of each of these competencies and processes as they relate to a collaborative leadership process.

Personal Work

The ensemble defined *personal work* as involving "examining and clarifying one's values and perspectives; being willing to redistribute power and at the same time take responsibility for and ownership of the group process and its outcomes; being authentic and congruent; and being willing to take risks" (HERI, 1996, p. 50). Personal work is about developing Consciousness of Self and takes place largely at the individual level. However, self-awareness about one's personal beliefs, values, attitudes, and emotions are absolutely necessary in order to effectively engage in a collaborative process. In order to understand other perspectives and build trust with diverse groups of people, an awareness of one's own perspectives and beliefs is needed first. (For a greater discussion about the process of developing Consciousness of Self, see Chapter Nine.)

Building Trust

The ensemble identified trust as the essential ingredient for building and sustaining a collaborative effort (HERI, 1996). When groups come together for the first time, people often bring their own agendas. Differences in those agendas often lead to confrontation and mistrust. Chrislip and Larson (1994) remind us that trust and openness are essential for collaboration and that "trust takes time to develop, especially among diverse people who are not used to working together" (p. 91). Chrislip and Larson offer four suggestions for building and sustaining trust: informal exploring, sharing ownership, celebrating success, and creating powerful, compelling experiences.

Informal exploring asks members of the group to put aside preset agendas at the beginning of a group process in order to engage in a process of exploration. This exploration involves getting to know each other's backgrounds, interests, priorities, and perspectives on problems and issues. Chrislip and Larson (1994) identify informal exploring as an important and necessary step in the collaboration process as it allows the "opportunity to discover common interests, similar ways of defining the problem, and shared aspirations for solutions, as well as the opportunity to get to know individuals as people, is important enough that it must be deliberately built into the process for working together" (p. 92).

Sharing ownership involves each member of the group taking ownership for the leadership process. Struggles over control and ownership frequently undermine the trust of a group early in the collaboration process. Whether there is a preset positional leader or not, sharing ownership asks individual group members to take ownership of the process. This requires individuals who hold formal leadership positions and those who tend to take on leadership in leaderless groups to use their power and influence with the group to empower the participants to direct the process. Chrislip and Larson (1994) assert that "the more participants take ownership of the process, the more sustainable the collaborative effort will be" (p. 93).

Celebrating success is a means of group renewal. Leadership is ultimately about change, which can often be a slow and tedious process. Celebrating small success along the way is necessary to sustain the group's energy in the collaboration effort.

Creating powerful, compelling experiences can be a useful way to quickly build trust and establish respect among group members at the beginning of a group process. Examples of powerful, impelling experiences include (but are certainly not limited to) challenge courses like ropes courses and outdoor challenge trips. Chrislip and Larson (1994) assert that "a shared experience of this kind can transform a collection of individuals into a group and unify them around a set of values and a common purpose" (p. 96).

 Think of a group that you are a member of. What can you personally do to encourage each member to feel engaged in the group and share ownership of the group process?

Communicating

It would be very difficult to engage in a successful and sustainable collaborative process without open communication among group members. Earlier diversity was identified as both the strength and challenge of collaboration. Effective communication within a diverse group can make the difference between a frustrating, stagnating process, and a synergistic, dynamic process. There is a strong relationship between communication and Controversy with Civility—strong communication channels are often required for understanding and moving through controversy. When differences arise that seem to block the flow of ideas, effective communication can help us move through those differences in such a way that builds and maintains trust and takes us toward the creation of a shared vision and purpose, and synergistic solutions. While this chapter does not specifically address the role of controversy in the communication process, it will explore ways that one can improve upon both personal communication and group communication skills. (For a greater discussion of the role of communication as it relates to Controversy with Civility, see Chapter Eight.)

Often we do not attempt to develop and communicate in a common language. Even within our own families, we rarely have the same internal representation of various words. To one person the word *run* means health, jog, fun. To another the word conjures up images of shin-splints, boredom, and agony. Someone else sees elections, politicians, and handshakes—or another stocking ruined. (Crum, 1987, p. 38)

In a diverse group, differences of opinion, vision, and even meanings of words will inevitably arise. The Prayer of St. Francis encourages us that when differences arise, it is best first to understand, then to be understood. A good place to start in developing one's personal communication skills is listening. Lucas (2004) asserts that there is a difference between hearing and listening. Hearing is the "physiological process, involving the vibration of sound waves on our eardrums and the firing of electrochemical impulses from the inner ear to the central auditory system of the brain" (p. 56), while listening is our attempt to pay close attention to and really understand and make sense of what we hear. Most people only grasp about 50 percent of what they hear, even when they believe they are listening attentively (Lucas).

Lucas (2004) cites a number of things that contribute to poor listening. First, many people do not fully concentrate on the person that is speaking and their message, allowing their thoughts to wander instead of remaining focused on the conversation at hand. Other people listen too hard, trying to remember every word that is being said and, in the process, lose track of the main message that the other person is trying to communicate. Other times, people jump to conclusions, thinking that they know what people are about to say and either finish their sentence for them or tune out their actual message. In either case, a preconceived notion of what people are about to say prohibits people from being able to truly understand what they are trying to communicate. Finally, it is easy to become distracted by the delivery of the message or the person delivering it, and in the process tune out the actual message (Lucas).

Much of the listening done in life is passive listening—that is, half-listening to someone while being engaged in other activity: listening to a CD while doing homework, or listening to a professor while doing Sudoku or checking e-mail on a laptop, or having a conversation with a friend while cooking dinner or reading the newspaper. In each of these instances, only part of the individual's attention is focused on listening. Because listening is essential to understanding, which is in turn essential to the process of building trust, it is useful to spend some time thinking about how to improve one's listening skills.

Lucas (2004) asserts that people can become better listeners by improving skills in active listening. *Active listening* involves focusing one's undivided attention on the person speaking and a genuine effort to understand both the content and the feelings that he or she is trying to communicate. There are several keys to effective active listening:

+ Listen for both the content and the emotion of the message.
+ Occasionally paraphrase the speaker's message and feelings back to them, indicating a desire to be sure the message is being accurately understood.
+ Listen without interrupting or assuming you know what the person is about to say.
+ Probe for further information; ask questions to make sure you understand.
+ Do not simultaneously try to form your response while the other person is still speaking.

Active listening is especially important in diverse groups as it can help us to better understand individuals with communication styles different from our own (2004).

BE WILLING TO UNDERSTAND

Understanding

+ is the gift that comes from listening;
+ is asking questions rather than having the answer;
+ allows differences to fade and similarities to come forth;
+ naturally acknowledges and appreciates the other person;
+ moves us from issue to vision;
+ creates movement from stalemate to resolution. (Crum, 1987, p. 151)

In addition to developing skills in active listening, it is also important to learn how to clearly convey a message in a way that the listener can hear it. The language and tone that one uses to communicate a message will have a large impact on the listener's ability to hear the message. Rosenberg (1999) identified communication traits that can block the listener's ability or willingness to hear the message. These include making statements containing moralistic judgments about people or ideas such as "He's lazy" or "That's a stupid idea," which imply wrongness or rightness, or making statements that deny personal responsibility, such as "I'm only here because my friend made me come."

Rosenberg (1999) also offers a number of suggestions for clearly communicating a message in a way that others will be able to hear it. First, it is helpful to communicate using observations rather than evaluations. An example of an observation would be, "David has missed the last three meetings," where the evaluation might be, "David never comes to meetings," or "David isn't committed to this group." If you are David, which message would be easier to hear and respond to? Second, it is important to learn how to name and express our feelings. When we allow ourselves to be vulnerable to each other by expressing our out feelings, we can connect more easily with one another. Finally, people must learn how to make clear and specific requests about what they need from one another. It is important to distinguish a request from a demand. "Requests are perceived as demands when others believe they will be blamed or punished if they do not comply" (Rosenberg, p. 83). Demands make people feel as though they are backed into a corner with the options of submission or rebellion. In order for individuals to feel that they have ownership and shared power in a group, it is important for them to be able to enter into or decline a request freely. For example, a *demand* for David's attendance at an upcoming meeting might sound like, "David, we need your help with the part of the project we're tackling this week. We've set up a special meeting on Thursday and we need you to be there." A member of a group could *request* David's presence at the upcoming meeting by saying, "David, we really need your help with the part of the project we'll be tackling this week. We've set up a special meeting on Thursday; will you be able to be there?" This second example still clearly conveys the desire of the speaker, but allows David to say no if he cannot attend the meeting.

Both listening and clearly conveying a message are extremely important elements of successful communication. However, successfully collaborating in diverse groups requires a step further. In addition to talking and listening, group members need to develop their abilities to engage in reflective and meaningful dialogues to bring out deeper meanings and create shared understandings within groups. Juanita Brown, David Isaacs, and the World Café Community (2005) have developed a process of *reflective communication* aimed at achieving a deeper and more accurate understanding among group members. They offer suggestions for engaging in authentic conversations that help develop trust and harness the power of the group's collective intelligence. These suggestions include creating a *climate of discovery* where new ideas are encouraged and explored; being careful to listen fully and *suspend premature judgment*; taking the time to *explore underlying beliefs and assumptions* held by individual members and the group as a whole; encouraging and creating space for *a wide range of perspectives*; and taking the time to reflect on and *articulate shared understandings* that the group comes to throughout the conversation process.

Imagine Mike, Jason, and Will working on a time-consuming class project. After Will misses two project meetings, Mike and Jason begin to sense that he does not care as much about the project as they do, and they fear he will not do his share of the work. Now Will is saying he cannot go to city hall and pick up documents the team needs. Mike and Jason decide to talk to Will about his role in the project. They learn that Will is carrying seventeen credit hours and working two jobs to be able to remain in school and provide additional income to his mother. As much as he wants to do well in school and on this project, he cannot afford to lose his job, so missing work is not an option. Once Mike and Jason understand Will's situation, the three of them discuss what kind of tasks Will can do for the team. Will is appreciative and readily takes on doing the Web searches for information and designing the

Think of a time when you felt that someone listened and truly understood what you were saying. What was that experience like for you? What specifically contributed to your feeling of being heard? Think of a group that you are currently a part of. How much time does that group dedicate to reflective conversations? Think of a time that you engaged in a productive dialogue around a difficult issue. What contributed to the conversation being productive?

PowerPoint presentation. The team also decides to have virtual meetings and come early to class for in-person meetings. Will had to trust enough to share his personal circumstances, and through this authentic conversation Mike and Jason learned to rethink their assumptions about Will and expand their notions of how a project can be accomplished.

CONNECTION TO THE OTHER C'S

Collaboration is a core value in the Social Change Model of Leadership and positively influences people's capacity to do the other C's. It is intricately tied to the other two group values, Common Purpose and Controversy with Civility. It is through learning to do collaboration that purposes that are truly shared in common can be reached. It is the Commitment to having a collaborative process that gives groups the resolve to embrace Controversy with Civility.

The ensemble pointed out that "when individuals work together to build collaborative relationships, everyone involved is affected or changed by the process" (HERI, 1996, p. 49). Thus, throughout the collaborative process, individuals' Consciousness of Self, Commitment, and Congruence are likely to deepen and develop. Finally, the ability to work collaboratively within the diverse communities one is a member of positively influences a person's ability to do Citizenship.

Just as experiences with Collaboration build capacity to do the other C's, experiences with the other C's positively affect a person's ability to do Collaboration. This is described in more detail in other chapters.

CONCLUSION

The Social Change Model of Leadership Development is a model of collaborative leadership. Individuals must develop their individual capacities of working authentically and effectively with others toward shared purposes. After experiencing a SCM course including a project engaging in the local community, one San Diego State University student observed, "I've learned that leadership is really more about 'us' than it is about 'me,'" illustrating that students understand that leadership is more about a dynamic interpersonal relationship than it is about a position or the individual" (Robertson & Lubic, 2001, p. 98). Approaching others in a group to seek true understanding of their perspectives, and reciprocally, expecting that they will seek to understand one's own perspectives is key to working collaboratively.

DISCUSSION QUESTIONS

1. Why is collaboration so important to the leadership process?

2. What are your personal feelings and opinions about competition, cooperation, and compromise? Were the ideas

presented in this chapter in line with your opinions, or did they differ somewhat?

3. Think of a group that you are a part of. What are some things that you can personally do to help establish and maintain trust within the group?

4. Take a moment to reflect on your communication skills. What strengths and areas for growth can you identify?

5. How can you tell if a group is functioning *collaboratively* versus *cooperatively*? What are the distinguishing factors between the two? Is it possible to move a group from a cooperative effort to a collaborative effort? What would that process look like?

JOURNAL PROBES

On Becoming

Preeminent psychologist, Carl Rogers (1961) said that people are always in a process of *becoming*. The first two journal probes are intended to help you reflect on how you see yourself becoming a leader for social change.

1. How aware are you of the process of becoming more effective at being collaborative with others?

2. Can you remember a time when you worked differently in groups than you do now? Are you more or less collaborative

now? How would you describe the differences between your former and current approach?

Learning Through Experience

The ensemble that created the Social Change Model believed the best way to learn to do leadership was through experience and reflection. This involves challenging yourself to have new experiences that test your ability and awareness **and** to spend time thinking about what you have learned from that experience. The remaining journal probes are designed to maximize learning through experience by guiding your reflective journal writing through Kolb's (1981) four processes of experiential learning.

1. **Concrete Experience.** Describe a specific situation when you had an experience that relates to collaboration as it has been described here. What happened? What details stand out to you? Describe briefly the situation, what you did and how you felt.

2. **Reflective Observation.** Why did this situation have the outcome it did? What caused the situation to happen in the first place? What responses from yourself and others worked in this situation? Why was that effective? What did not work? Why?

3. **Abstract Conceptualization.** What lessons can you draw from this specific experience that could apply more generally? Given both your reflections and the information in

this chapter, what would you do if a similar situation presented itself? What general guidelines would you create for handling future situations like this?

4. **Active Experimentation.** What opportunities might you seek out that would give you the chance to apply what you have learned here? How might you test the lessons or guidelines you created in #3 to see if they work?

APPLYING THE CASE STUDIES

Go back to Chapter Three for more context on each of these case studies. Apply the material covered in Chapter Six to these cases.

Zoom In: Starving for Attention

In this case, Taylor has become involved in an organization that is challenging the university to pay its service workers a wage that better reflects the cost of living in the area. As his group continues to plan this upcoming event, Taylor realizes that the administration at this meeting will not respond to unintelligent and overly abrasive presentations; he wants the group to be able to communicate their points with passion, authenticity, and astuteness. He feels as if he is learning more about what he values and this is motivating him to invest more deeply in this cause, yet he cannot help but feel that as he becomes more invested, it affects what he values.

As the group collaborates to prepare together, a few members begin discussing a backup plan if the administration does not take the group seriously. Taylor begins thinking of ways to bring wider campus attention to the issue in order to educate others about it. Soon, he approaches the larger Living Wage Campaign organization with a suggestion that students begin to forge meetings with the workers that are affected by low wages. Through the help of some alumni who have been involved, he recruits an individual who speaks Spanish and who is passionate about organizing and encouraging the workers. Through Taylor's influence the group lays out a process chart and six-week plan (provided as Exhibit 6.1) to present a set of specific action steps to the university's administration. The plan includes organizing a hunger strike among the student body should that level of escalation be needed.

While the organization is mostly in favor of Taylor's plan, some believe the hunger strike will send a message that the group is too radical and not willing to negotiate with campus administrators. They are particularly wary of any plan that might involve violating a university regulation or endangering their fellow students' health. The group decides that they all must work closely and on multiple fronts in order to impress upon the university administration the seriousness of their intent to see this issue change on campus. They will continue to discuss the merits of the hunger strike aspect of the plan.

EXHIBIT 6.1 Process Chart for the Living Wage Campaign

Overall Goal

For the University to raise wages of service workers to a living wage

Subgoals

+ Continue to encourage involvement of service workers
+ Build base of students involved in the Living Wage Campaign
+ Spread information about the Living Wage Campaign to students, staff, faculty, and university officials
+ Present "Living Wage Proposal" to university administration

Actions Already Agreed Upon

+ Tabling outside of the Student Union
+ Students making announcements to their classes
+ Presentation of "Living Wage Proposal" to university officials
+ Two teach-ins where we ask university members to spend a Friday morning learning about the issues of poverty, the current pay rates of service workers on our campus, and the need for a living wage
+ Peaceful protest outside of the union

+ Article(s) in the campus newspaper about the Living Wage Campaign and the "Living Wage Proposal"

Potential Actions Requiring Further Discussion
Hunger strike?

Six-Week Plan of Action Steps

Week One
+ Set up meeting with service workers
+ Decide on a slogan or catchphrase for the cause
+ Compile information to have covered during the teach-in and identify a person(s) to work on the curriculum and begin organizing the logistics
+ Reserve the space outside of the union for a peaceful protest during week 5

Week Two
+ Contact university officials to set up a meeting
+ Outreach within university classes—organization members making announcements within their classes to get more students involved
+ Contact the campus newspaper to set up an interview

(Continued)

EXHIBIT 6.1 Process Chart for the Living Wage Campaign (Continued)

Week Three

+ Tabling outside of the union
+ More announcements in classes
+ Editorial sent into the campus newspaper

Week Four

+ Teach-in
+ Presentation to university's administration

Week Five

+ Peaceful protest
+ Teach-in

Week Six

+ Second meeting with university's administration
+ Hunger strike?

Think About It

+ What elements of Collaboration are present in this part of the case study? How is the group sharing power and responsibility? How is it capitalizing on multiple perspectives within and outside of the group?

+ What would it look for the group to have a win-win approach to their disagreement about the hunger strike? What criteria are important to each side?

+ How did the process chart and six-week plan facilitate collaboration? Is anything missing from the plan?

+ Sometimes, the most effective approach to making change is to work within existing structures, reporting lines, and policies. Other times it is those policies and structures that need to change, so it is more effective to circumvent them. How will this group know when it is time to do the latter?

Zoom In: Clear Haziness

In this case, you are the photography editor of the campus paper, *The Weekly*, where a tradition of hazing new members of the photography staff has been uncovered. Collaboration should empower self and others through trust in order to facilitate the division of labor. Based on what you know about *The Weekly's* photography staff, was this happening? How might the actions of the senior photographers undermine the potential for collaboration?

References

Brown, J., Isaacs, D., & World Café Community. (2005). *The world café: Shaping our future through conversations that matter.* San Francisco: Berrett-Koehler.

Chrislip, D. D., & Larson, C. E. (1994). *Collaborative leadership.* San Francisco: Jossey-Bass.

Covey, S. R. (2004). *The seven habits of highly effective people: Powerful lessons in personal change.* New York: Free Press.

Crum, T. F. (1987). *The magic of conflict: Turning a life of work into a work of art.* New York: Touchstone.

Higher Education Research Institute [HERI]. (1996). *A social change model of leadership development* (Version III). Los Angeles: University of California Los Angeles, Higher Education Research Institute.

Johnson, D. W., & Johnson, F. P. (1994). *Joining together: Group theory and group skills* (5th ed.). Boston: Allyn & Bacon.

Johnson, D. W., & Johnson, F. P. (2006). *Joining together: Group theory and skills* (9th ed.). Boston: Allyn & Bacon.

Johnson, D. W., Maruyama, G., Johnson, R., Nelson, D., & Skon, L. (1981). Effects of cooperative, competitive and individualistic goal structures on achievement: A meta-analysis. *Psychological Bulletin, 89,* 47–62.

Jones, S. R., & McEwen, M. K. (2000). A conceptual model of multiple dimensions of identity. *Journal of College Student Development, 41,* 405–414.

Kohn, A. (1986). *No contest: The case against competition.* Boston: Houghton Mifflin.

Kolb, D. A. (1981). Learning styles and disciplinary differences. In A. W. Chickering & Associates (Eds.), *The modern American college: Responding to the new realities of diverse students and a changing society* (pp. 232–255). San Francisco: Jossey Bass.

Komives, S. R., Lucas, N., & McMahon, T. R. (1998). *Exploring leadership: For college students who what to make a difference.* San Francisco: Jossey-Bass.

Komives, S. R., Lucas, N., & McMahon, T. R. (2007). *Exploring leadership: For college students who what to make a difference* (2nd ed.). San Francisco: Jossey-Bass.

Lucas, S. E. (2004). *The art of public speaking.* New York: McGraw-Hill.

Robertson, D. C., & Lubic, B. J. (2001). Spheres of confluence: Non-hierarchical leadership in action. In C. L. Outcalt, S. K. Faris, & K. N. McMahon (Eds.), *Developing non-hierarchical leadership on campus: Case studies and best practices in higher education* (pp. 90–98). Westport, CT: Greenwood.

Rogers, C. R. (1961). *On becoming a person: A therapist's view of psychotherapy.* Boston: Houghton Mifflin.

Rosenberg, M. B. (1999). *Nonviolent communication: A language of compassion.* Encinitas, CA: PuddleDancer Press.

Straus, D. (2002). *How to make collaborations work: Powerful ways to build consensus, solve problems, and make decisions.* San Francisco: Berrett-Koehler.

Smith, D. G., and Associates. (1997). *Diversity works: The emerging picture of how students benefit.* Washington, DC: Association of American Colleges and Universities.

COMMON PURPOSE

Alex Teh

A single arrow is easily broken, but not ten in a bundle.
Japanese proverb

College students are often part of many groups—student organizations, sports teams, the staff at their office, or project groups in class. Think about specific groups you belong to as you examine the concepts in this chapter. Why do those groups exist? What draws people into a particular group? What kinds of things is the group hoping to accomplish?

The answers to those questions are the very reasons that groups (particularly those we discuss in relation to leadership and social change) form and survive. Classes and groups within them exist in order to foster learning about a certain topic. Many student organizations form to create a community for students with similar views or interests. Staff members at an office were hired to bring their expertise to implement the office functions. Common Purpose involves *working with others* in group settings; what it means to be a group comes from the things that link group members to one another. One of the most unifying of those links is the purpose that drives the group. In other words, good groups should be able to ask and answer the question: Why are we here and what are we doing? What is our shared or common purpose?

CHAPTER OVERVIEW

This chapter examines three key components of Common Purpose: its occurrence within *groups*, its presence in *shared vision, aims,* and *values,* and its role in *working with others.* Each component is intertwined with the others—just as each of the C's within the Social Change Model (SCM) works with and is influenced by the rest—and the components of Common Purpose cannot be separated completely from each other. The interactions between these components must be kept in mind when exploring what it means to be a part of a group, what it means to share a vision and values, and how people work with others to articulate a group's common purpose.

WHAT IS COMMON PURPOSE?

What Is a Group?

When thinking about the definition of common purpose, it is important to know exactly what a "group" means. This is particularly important, since a group can take on any number of

>  The ensemble (HERI, 1996) wrote:
>
> Common Purpose means to work with others within a shared set of aims and values. Having these shared aims facilitates the group's ability to engage in collective analysis of the issues at hand and the task to be undertaken. Common Purpose is best achieved when all members of the group share in the vision and participate actively in articulating the purpose and goals of the group's work. (p. 55)

specific names—*committee, council, team, club,* or any number of others—or, like a group of friends, not have a tangible name at all. In the context of leadership, though, groups are more than just people who are in the same place at the same time. In this context, groups are considered to be "three or more people 'interacting and communicating interpersonally over time in order to reach a goal'" (Komives, Lucas, & McMahon, 2007, p. 216).

Teams are specific types of groups, and it often helps to examine literature on teams in order to better understand groups in general. Johnson and Johnson (1994) identify a team not

Think about a group you have been a part of. What did it look like? How big was it? How did it work? Does it match any of the examples presented here?

necessarily in terms of a number of people, but instead as "a set of interpersonal interactions structured to achieve established goals" (p. 503). Katzenbach and Smith (1986) provide a classic and commonly cited definition, writing that "a team is a small number of people with complementary skills who are committed to a common purpose, performance goals, and approach for which they hold themselves mutually accountable" (p. 45).

There are some common themes that run through all these group definitions. First, groups contain more than just a single person. Each definition mentioned either specifies a minimum number of people or indicates interactions that must necessarily include more than one person. Second, all of the definitions assert that the group has a purpose or a goal that it strives to achieve. Finally, each of the three definitions indicates some sort of interaction, cooperation, or commitment among group members to achieve the group's goal (see Chapter Six on Collaboration).

The three parts of this definition of a group may sound familiar. Revisit the components of the definition of Common Purpose listed previously. It is obvious that Common Purpose is very closely aligned with the way in which groups are defined and identified. With a clearer idea of what is meant when talking about a "group," the meaning of having a shared vision or goal can be examined.

What Are Shared Visions, Aims, and Values?

The visions, aims, and values that are central to any group comprise the most general idea of Common Purpose. While

Think again about a group you belong to or even the institution where you are a student. Does it have written statements about its purpose, vision, aims, and values? What are they? Where did they come from? If they do not formally exist, what do you think they might be? How do you know that?

it is important to remember this is only one component of Common Purpose, it is equally important to examine fully the vision and goals of any group and where they came from.

Common Purpose addresses three main questions about a group:

1. What is the ideal future for this organization? (What is its *vision?*)

2. Why does this organization exist? (What are its *aims?*)

3. How do we agree to treat ourselves and others as we pursue our mission and vision? (What are our *values?*) (Komives et al., 2007)

Groups should be able to answer these three questions if they are to have a sense of Common Purpose, and it is often these very elements of Common Purpose that will continue to motivate a group when it hits a rough spot. No matter what relational or external problems arise, a group with a well-articulated, meaningful, and relevant Common Purpose will always have something linking its members together. They have a compelling reason to come together.

Having a vision is an important aspect of Common Purpose. The business world offers an excellent model to examine how shared vision differs from aims or goals. In business, the common goal can be quite simple: companies generally exist to create profit for owners and shareholders and to produce an excellent product for the community. The group's vision, however, is different from its purpose or goals. Kotter (1995) points out that the lack of a good, unifying vision is often the downfall of otherwise successful companies. He says, "A vision says something that clarifies the direction in which an organization needs to move" (p. 63). A vision should go beyond numbers and logistical information, and instead provide a clear picture of the future that will inspire and motivate everyone associated with an organization. For example, think of 3M and its vision of bringing together ingenuity and responsiveness to help people be successful, or Southwest Airlines and its commitment to their employees and to caring about service to customers.

The aims of certain groups can clarify the differences between them. For one sports team, the common purpose may be to compete well and win games. For another, the common purpose may be to continually build skills and teamwork, a goal that can be met regardless of who wins each game. For yet another team, the common purpose might be to meet people and have fun social time. A common purpose clarifies why the group exists and what it is trying to achieve. Having Common Purpose gives group members a feeling of confidence that everyone is in agreement about where the group is headed. It provides clarity about the group's priorities and values and helps to generate a high level of trust among group members and with other members of the community.

Common values are another critical part of Common Purpose and are often the least discussed among group members. However, since values often address how members treat each other and how the group aims will be pursued, a member whose own values and reasons for belonging to a particular group do not fit with the group's values will likely not enjoy the group. For example, one group might place a high value on organization, efficiency, and respect for how busy members are with other commitments. A second group might value social relationships and being able to have a laugh along with getting work done. The two group meetings would operate quite differently. A member from the second group might interpret the first group's efficiency as cold and lacking in fun, unless members from the first group were able to articulate that this behavior is rooted in a desire to show respect for others. An important leadership skill is recognizing indicators of group values and facilitating explicit conversations about them—is this really how the group wants to be or have things just evolved this way without anyone consciously thinking about it?

A clear mission, vision, and set of core values are central to understanding your group's purpose. The things your group is working toward can often serve as unifying factors during rough times. Common Purpose provides clarity when the group has too many projects and needs to make priorities and choices and serves as a tool for periodically refocusing efforts. But where exactly does the Common Purpose come from? If it is best achieved through a shared process among group members, how is that facilitated? How do those ideas come into being, anyway?

Personalized and Socialized Vision

For a group's purpose to truly be a Common Purpose, it must belong to the group and be supported by individual members. Two approaches to establishing a group's aims are personalized vision and socialized vision (Howell, 1988). Personalized vision is created when the "person in charge" comes up with a dream or a plan on their own, then passes that vision on to those in the group. An inspired personalized vision can serve

MONKEYS ON YOUR BACK

Oncken and Wass (1974) wrote a classic description of management styles suited for the business world. Their article offers a helpful metaphor that we can use to think about the process of creating a Common Purpose. They identify the various tasks and time- and energy-consuming activities that occur within an organization as metaphorical monkeys that ride on the backs of whichever workers are responsible for their "care and feeding." For most people in conventional organizations, the goal is to get the monkey off one's back, either by finishing the project or by putting it on someone else. Some monkeys are quickly taken care of and go their own way. Others require a bit more attention and may reside on someone's back for quite some time. Still others are passed from person to person, along with all the responsibilities associated with that monkey. Within a student's context, these monkeys could be things like papers and exams, cleaning up your apartment or residence hall room, or your duties within a student organization.

The point is that, in this organization, the people involved are not working together on tasks. They are operating independently, either taking care of their own monkeys or passing them along to someone else. In a process-oriented group with a Common Purpose, all group members are invested in the tasks that drive the group toward its vision and goals. In an organization with Common Purpose, each task is viewed as a vehicle toward meeting Common Purpose. When all members are invested in a group's Common Purpose, they remain committed to the group, its mission, and its vision.

to recruit people to join a worthwhile effort. The first day of a typical college class often represents this approach. The instructor provides a detailed syllabus that includes everything that instructor thinks you should learn and a schedule that describes exactly how and when you should learn it over the course of a semester. It is likely that some students benefit greatly from the structure and guidance provided by the instructor's vision, but other students may feel forced into that structure and regret not being able to influence or shape the vision (Komives et al., 2007).

 Charles Snelling, a Business Management and Pre-Law student at DePaul University, saw a need for the student leaders of the Black student organizations on campus to come together to discuss issues they all shared. He convinced the executive board members of many of these organizations to form a caucus, meeting each month for a six-month period and having conversations around several key topics: Black male involvement in their organizations and within campus leadership, the role of fraternities and sororities within the campus community, and collaborations among various organizations. Organizations involved in the caucus co-hosted a "UNITY Barbecue" to promote their mutual support for each other's goals. More than 100 students attended. Charles reflected, "The caucus was a true test of our support for each other."

On the other hand, socialized vision is constructed when group members contribute to building the group's aims and purposes. This approach recognizes people's tendency to support and remain invested in what they have helped to create. This does not necessarily mean that each person's personal vision is incorporated in the group vision, but rather that everyone is involved in developing the group vision (Komives et al., 2007). It may be that some parts of the group vision are very different from parts of your personal vision, but through the socialized vision process group members are allowed to set priorities and have a say in the parts of the group vision to which each of them is best suited to contribute.

Returning to the classroom example, what if this time the instructor walks in on the first day with an idea of what he or she thinks the class should learn about that particular subject and presents the syllabus as a general idea of how he or she thinks learning might occur. At this point, what if the instructor asks the class what they think would work for them and engages everyone in a discussion about what important topics should be covered, what kinds of assignments might best facilitate learning, and how the class will work over the course of the semester. Of course, the course may still cover some of the topics the students did not think were too interesting, and not all of the assignments may be exactly matched with each student's personal learning style, but this class is geared much more toward how everyone will interact as a group. In this scenario, it may be that the motivation of students in the class will be quite high, since everyone has had a part in designing what the class will be like.

Can you think of examples of personalized and socialized vision in the groups you belong to? Is there a connection between the approach to creating purpose and the members' commitment to the group and its efforts? When might personalized vision be more effective or appropriate?

These two classroom scenarios demonstrate the difference between a personalized vision and a socialized vision. The value Common Purpose reflects how important it is that the purpose is fully embraced by all members of a group, and not just the positional leader. While an inspired personalized vision can sometimes draw people to a worthwhile effort, allowing the group to collaborate and develop a shared mission, vision, and purpose will create greater levels of investment and commitment to their Common Purpose. Commitment to the shared vision means that members will fulfill their responsibilities to the group, share resources with the group, and support other group members both because they expect them to do the same and because they are invested in the greater goals. It is not just the purpose itself, but the process of developing that purpose that is central to the Social Change Model of Leadership Development (HERI, 1996).

How Do We Work Together?
Groups must transparently practice intentional processes that lead to building Common Purpose. How the group makes

 A civic engagement course at the Georgia Institute of Technology involves students studying issues of sustainable development in the third world, and eventually traveling to a developing country (or within Atlanta in one iteration of the course) to work on development projects there. This course was the hard-fought dream of a number of people on campus, but the original idea was conceived and pushed along by students. It was this initiative that inspired Anu Parvatiyar to run for and serve as the president of the student body at Georgia Tech. Anu observed that being student body president made it easier to push the administration to adopt and support service learning or civic engagement courses on campus.

decisions and how the group maintains a shared vision are central to working together effectively.

Decision Making

Whether a group will adhere to a personalized vision or create its own socialized vision, it will at some point need to resolve exactly what that vision will be. There are several ways in which groups make decisions. Some groups put everything to a vote, allowing the majority to rule the process. Others seek to build consensus, and still others place a great deal of faith in their positional leaders to make decisions for the group.

In most cases, whether or not a group has a formal, positional leader, it is important to recognize that more and more group members expect to be involved in group decision making (Komives et al., 2007). It is always advisable to engage in some amount of meaningful dialogue and listening within groups. Johnson and Johnson (2006) describe six ways in which groups typically make decisions:

1. Decision by authority without discussion: a single positional leader makes a final decision without consulting group members

2. Decision by authority after discussion: the positional leader consults group members for their perspectives and ideas, but ultimately makes the final decision

3. Expert member: the final decision is made by the group member who has the most knowledge or experience related to the issue or problem

4. Average member's opinions: the decision is based on what is presumed to be the opinion of the most typical member

5. Majority control: the decision is based upon the opinion held by the majority of the group's members

6. Minority control: the decision is made by a few key members often when the group is dealing with time pressures

7. Consensus: group members continue to discuss and persuade each other until everyone agrees (or those who do not agree are willing to commit to the decision)

Each of these methods is valid in certain contexts, depending, for example, on the type of decision and the amount of time available to make it. Komives et al. (2007) suggest that for a decision as important as the group's purpose and shared values, groups should use consensus when possible.

A consensus does not necessarily imply that everyone is satisfied with the decision or that even most group members believe that the best decision has been reached. A consensus is present, though, when all team members have had the opportunity to voice their concerns and are comfortable enough with the decision to support its implementation (Rayner, 1996). Make no mistake: consensus is not always an easy

Four guidelines for reaching consensus within a group:

1. Clearly define the issue facing the team
2. Focus on similarities between positions
3. Ensure that there is adequate time for discussion
4. Avoid conflict-reducing tendencies. (e.g., voting) (Rayner, 1996, p. 76)

What kinds of matters should you seek consensus on? How can you facilitate a discussion about purpose and shared values in the organizations you belong to? Do you anticipate opinions to differ widely? How could a consensus discussion be facilitated?

thing to achieve. Groups must have a decent amount of time and be skilled at active listening, compromising, handling controversy, and collaborative discussion in order to move toward consensus (Komives et al., 2007).

In developing Common Purpose, some groups find it useful to schedule a retreat to create a formal mission statement or statement of core values. The climate in other types of groups may not lend itself to such a formal process, but this does not mean they should give up on having a conversation about the group's common purpose. The clever use of icebreakers can kick off a conversation about why the group exists. Creating metaphors can be particularly useful. For example, imagine asking a group's members, "If this group were a consumer product, what would it be?" A response like "a cassette tape player" might indicate feelings that the group's purpose has lost it relevance whereas a response like "an artist's camera, because it captures the true reality of what is happening on campus and brings it to people's awareness" conveys quite a different message. Sometimes conversations about marketing and publicity can be Common Purpose discussions in disguise. Members are motivated to make decisions about what they want others to know about the group and what its purposes are. Carefully facilitated, decisions about what slogan to put on the group's T-shirt can start a meaningful dialogue about what the shirts will convey about the group's purpose and values.

Challenges in Creating and Maintaining Common Purpose
Often, the kind of interaction necessary to develop Common Purpose in a group is an excellent vehicle for the group

to learn how to work together. Going through the process of engaging in dialogue about individual experiences, balancing the perspectives of multiple group members, and making tough choices is a valuable learning experience for all members. It is the responsibility of good leaders and members to help facilitate this process in a way that encourages the group to reflect on how it worked together to foster ongoing improvement of collaborative work. The group will emerge from the process of creating common purpose better equipped to handle the next challenge that comes its way. In essence, the development of a group's common purpose is one of the main ways in which a group learns about itself. Making that development a good experience is the responsibility of all group members.

Along with partners in a community organization, Robertson and Lubic (2001) cotaught an SCM-based course at San Diego State University dedicated to interventions in smoking and underage drinking. At the end of the semester, Janet, one of the college students in the course observed, "We did not maximize what we learned from the class. There were times when some of the Seven C's were used, but they were not reinforced as much as they should have been. One disappointment was when we did not follow one of the most important concepts as a group—Common Purpose. Although we had brainstormed ideas during our first meeting, our decision of the solution was not made together." Robertson and Lubic observed, "Learning, then, occurs by way of success and failure, but most importantly, it is negotiated through *experience*" (p. 97).

The ensemble identified two main types of dilemmas that can arise when trying to establish Common Purpose within a group (HERI, 1996). First, if a person has a personalized vision, they may have a difficult time enrolling or engaging others in that vision. In many cases, this problem arises because the person who first has the idea is not flexible enough to allow others' ideas and suggestions to change the original idea. On the other hand, a group that attempts to create a socialized vision, collaborating to develop a truly shared common purpose, can often find itself paralyzed, unable to efficiently or effectively define its own purpose while working as a group. In these situations, the process of developing a shared vision from scratch may have proven too daunting a task, either because the competing interests of group members were hard to reconcile or the group's general focus itself made refining a common purpose difficult.

In addition to the two problems the ensemble presents, it is likely that a third dilemma poses a problem for some groups. Those groups with regularly revolving memberships can face the question of how to keep their vision and common purpose alive and meaningful as old members leave and new members join. This dilemma is likely prevalent among groups of college students. Given that college students usually leave their institutions after some amount of time, many groups and organizations on campus exist well before and after any one group of students is a part of them. It is likely that these groups have preexisting purposes and at some point underwent the process of developing a common purpose. Student leaders should ask themselves how the purpose of each group they belong to applies to them and how they, as group members, can influence and maintain a group's vision. Intentional activities that ask new members why they want to join this group, acquaint new members with the current vision, and create time to discuss any discrepancies will let new members know their views matter to the future of the group and keep the group renewed and vibrant with these new ideas (Komives et al., 2007).

 Think about a student organization or other student-based group that you are a part of. Where did its shared vision come from? In what ways did you connect or not connect with it? If you had the chance, how would you suggest altering that group's vision? How can new members learn about the group's vision and be involved in shaping the group's future? How often is the shared vision revisited? Who is part of that process?

CONNECTION TO THE OTHER C'S

The Common Purpose element is central to the Social Change Model's approach to leadership and leadership development. In many ways, it is the common thread that links the three sets of values: individual, group, and community (HERI, 1996). Common Purpose is identified as a group value, but for it to be authentic to group members, each individual must connect on some level with the goals of the group.

The ensemble argues that Common Purpose is "predicated on the three individual values" of Consciousness of Self, Congruence, and Commitment (HERI, 1996, p. 57). Working toward a group's Common Purpose will give group members insight into themselves, make them more self-aware, and challenge them to be congruent. A clear sense of common purpose can also help renew people's energy around their commitments.

Of course, Common Purpose is closely linked to the other group values: Collaboration and Controversy with Civility. It may make sense to argue that a group must be collaborative in order to develop a shared vision or purpose, but the connection between these two elements works both ways. While Collaboration certainly aids in developing Common Purpose, a well-developed common purpose can provide the basis for collaborative work within the group. Very much along those lines, the differences that are bound to exist between group members demand an ability to have Controversy with Civility within the group while its purpose is being developed, but Common Purpose again serves as a stabilizer and unifying force that makes Controversy with Civility possible.

CONCLUSION

The Social Change Model of Leadership Development revolves around the idea that leadership is a collaborative, values-based process. Common Purpose is one of three values essential to leadership at the group level. A group's ability to develop and sustain a Common Purpose is based on their intentional collaborative processes that connect individual members together to shape the group's goals and future.

DISCUSSION QUESTIONS

1. Why is Common Purpose an important leadership value?

2. Think about a group you are part of. Does it have a common purpose? If so, how would you describe the way in which that group arrived at its common purpose? If not, what could you do to begin that process?

3. A student once observed that a group would never come to agree on a common purpose if it could not work collaboratively. Do you think this is true? Why or why not?

4. Imagine you are part of a group and cannot tell what its mission or vision is. What evidence or indicators might give you a clue? What questions would you ask to find out?

5. Thinking about your own experience, what is the difference between embracing a predefined vision and participating in the formulation of that vision with others?

JOURNAL PROBES

On Becoming
Preeminent psychologist Carl Rogers (1961) said that people are always in a process of *becoming*. The first two journal

probes are intended to help you reflect on how you see your-self becoming a leader for social change.

1. In what ways can you see yourself becoming more effective at reaching Common Purpose with others?

2. Can you remember a time when you thought about a group's purpose (or vision, or goals) differently than you do now? How is your current approach different from your approach then? How would you describe the difference between Common Purpose and goals in your own words?

Learning Through Experience

The ensemble that created the Social Change Model believed the best way to learn to do leadership was through experience and reflection. This involves challenging yourself to have new experiences that test your ability and awareness **and** to spend time thinking about what you have learned from that experience. The remaining journal probes are designed to maximize learning through experience by guiding your reflective journal writing through Kolb's (1981) four processes of experiential learning.

1. **Concrete Experience.** Describe a specific situation when you had an experience that relates to developing a Common Purpose as it has been described here. Did the group have a Common Purpose or did it not? What happened? What details stand out to you? Describe briefly the situation, what you did and how you felt.

2. **Reflective Observation.** Why did this situation have the outcome it did? What caused the situation to happen in the first place? What responses from yourself and others worked in this situation? Why was that effective? What did not work? Why?

3. **Abstract Conceptualization.** What lessons can you draw from this specific experience that could apply more generally? Given both your reflections and the information in this chapter, what would you do if a similar situation presented itself? What general guidelines would you create for handling future situations like this?

4. **Active Experimentation.** What opportunities might you seek out that would give you the chance to apply what you have learned here? How might you test the lessons or guidelines you created in #3 to see if they work?

APPLYING THE CASE STUDIES

Go back to Chapter Three for more context on each of these case studies. Apply the material covered in Chapter Seven to these cases.

Zoom In: Starving for Attention

In this case, Taylor has become involved in an organization that is challenging the university to pay its service workers a wage that better reflects the cost of living in the area. The more Taylor gets involved with the Living Wage Campaign, the more his attention is captured. He is really excited that the group has a history and a clear direction for the future. He is assigned to working with a group of students on creating a presentation for the Campus Budget Committee meeting that will be in two weeks. At this meeting, the students hope to make a clear case for why it is not right that service employees are being paid nearly $10 less than a living wage at a university where education about social justice is very important to the faculty, students, and staff. To prepare, he spends one night interviewing housekeepers assigned to the academic buildings. As he hears their stories he realizes new insights into the lives of service employees and how they are treated. The stories of the housekeepers motivate him to understand the larger problem with the living wage issues.

As Taylor meets with his subgroup, he notes that they all have passion for the values of the Living Wage campaign. In some ways, this experience is different for Taylor—whereas earlier he was having trouble communicating with family and friends about his passion with this issue, in this group there seem to be shared values and agreement that university staff are being ill treated. As they move forward in planning, the Campus Budget Committee presentation, they trust each other to complete their various responsibilities.

Think About It

+ Why is Common Purpose important to the success of this campaign?

+ Does this group have a personalized or socialized vision?

+ How might this group benefit from taking the time to create a formal statement of common purpose and shared values? Would this help Taylor and others communicate their passion about the living wage issue to those who do not share it?

Zoom In: Clear Haziness

In this case, you are the photography editor of the campus paper, *The Weekly*, where a tradition of hazing new members of the photography staff has been uncovered. How does Common Purpose affect your view or guide your decision in reaction to this situation? The case study does not mention specific values that *The Weekly* holds, yet being on a college campus, you can assume that there should be values congruent with those of higher education. How might having clear values outlined by *The Weekly* help in this situation and guide your reaction to it? If *The Weekly* does not have group values established, how might a facilitated group discussion about creating a common purpose foster an opportunity for the members to talk about the issues surrounding this incident? Would this be a worthwhile exercise to engage in? Why or why not?

References

Higher Education Research Institute [HERI]. (1996). *A social change model of leadership development* (Version III). Los Angeles: University of California Los Angeles, Higher Education Research Institute.

Howell, J. M. (1988). Two faces of charisma: Socialized and personalized leadership in organizations. In J. A. Conger, R. N. Kanungo, & Associates (Eds.), *Charismatic leadership: The elusive factor in organizational effectiveness* (pp. 213–236). San Francisco: Jossey-Bass.

Johnson, D. W., & Johnson, F. P. (2006). *Joining together: Group theory and group skills* (9th ed.). Boston: Allyn & Bacon.

Katzenbach, J., & Smith, D. (1986). *The wisdom of teams*. Boston: Harvard Business Review Press.

Kolb, D. A. (1981). Learning styles and disciplinary differences. In A. W. Chickering & Associates (Eds.), *The modern American college: Responding to the new realities of diverse students and a changing society* (pp. 232–255). San Francisco: Jossey Bass.

Komives, S. R., Lucas, N., & McMahon, T. R. (2007). *Exploring leadership: For college students who want to make a difference* (2nd ed.). San Francisco: Jossey-Bass.

Kotter, J. P. (1995). Leading change: Why transformation efforts fail. *Harvard Business Review, 73*(2), 59–67.

Oncken, W., Jr., & Wass, D. L. (1974). Management time: Who's got the monkey? *Harvard Business Review, 52*(6), 75–80.

Rayner, S. R. (1996). *Team traps: Survival stories and lessons from team disasters, near-misses, mishaps, and other near-death experiences*. New York: Wiley.

Robertson, D. C., & Lubic, B. J. (2001). Spheres of confluence: Non-hierarchical leadership in action. In C. L. Outcalt, S. K. Faris, & K. N. McMahon (Eds.), *Developing non-hierarchical leadership on campus: Case studies and best practices in higher education* (pp. 90–98) Westport, CT: Greenwood.

Rogers, C. R. (1961). *On becoming a person: A therapist's view of psychotherapy*. Boston: Houghton Mifflin.

8

CONTROVERSY WITH CIVILITY

Cecilio Alvarez

[People] must evolve for all human conflict a method which rejects revenge, aggression, and retaliation.
MARTIN LUTHER KING JR.

A story is told about five gorillas whose cage has a large bunch of bananas hanging above a set of stairs. Before long, a gorilla goes to the stairs and starts to climb toward the bananas. After a few steps, all the gorillas are sprayed with cold water. In a while, another gorilla makes an attempt and gets the same result—all the gorillas are sprayed with cold water. Every time a gorilla attempts to retrieve the bananas, the others are sprayed. Eventually they leave the bananas alone.

In time, one of the original gorillas is removed from the cage and replaced with a new one. The new gorilla sees the bananas and starts to climb the stairs. To his horror, all the other gorillas attack him. After another attempt and attack, he knows that if he tries to climb the stairs he will be assaulted. A few days later, another of the original five gorillas is replaced with a new one. The newcomer goes to the stairs and is attacked. The other newcomer, without knowing why, takes part in the punishment with enthusiasm. Next the third original gorilla is replaced with a new one. The new one goes for the stairs and is attacked as well.

Two of the four gorillas that beat him have no idea why they were not permitted to climb the stairs or why they are participating in the beating of the newest gorilla. Eventually, the fourth and fifth original gorillas are replaced, and each is attacked in turn for trying to go up the stairs. At this point, none of the gorillas have ever been sprayed with cold water for going up the stairs. Nevertheless, none of them will approach the stairs, and all will attack another for trying.

Source unknown

This story demonstrates the results of an organizational culture that does not welcome controversy with civility. While "Why don't we go up and get the bananas?" is an obvious question, none of gorillas is willing to ask it because challenging the status quo in this group is met with negative consequences. While an organizational culture that avoids conflict may seem like a great idea to people who are uncomfortable with it, not letting people question the way things have always been done or refusing to acknowledge differing points of view diminishes the group and what it is able to accomplish. The goal of Controversy with Civility is to create a culture in the group that welcomes controversy. The best way to do that is for all members to learn to handle it with civility.

Many people have at times felt caught up in the heat of an argument. Some feel tense, their chests tighten and their bodies stiffen as they raise their voices. Sometimes it feels like they had not taken a breath until the whole situation was over. Other times people experience a sinking feeling and are afraid they will cry, so they just walk away or give in. Some are so uncomfortable with conflict that when a difficult group member makes an absurd comment, they and everyone else stay silent and ignore it. Do any of these seem familiar? Is it possible, with all of these strong emotions, to focus on what the other person was communicating? Is it possible to explain what the argument or issue was fundamentally about, or be aware of how one's own response might be interpreted?

Chances are that in the "heat" of an argument, people remember little to nothing about such an unpleasant experience. Important energy and time are spent on an elaborate show of words and emotions or in giving in to avoid more confrontation that renders participants ineffective in solving a problem. Although it is clear that these approaches to problem solving will be unsuccessful, how can individuals know that they are able to handle difficult situations? Will they get caught in the heat of an argument, engaging in either flight or fight, or will they be able to effectively manage disagreements across differences?

Approaching disagreements is something that many people hesitate to do. Many people feel that willingly engaging with others on points of difference renders them vulnerable to any number of consequences. For some, this is reason enough to avoid problems altogether—either giving in to or silencing other people's opinions for fear of or resistance to what is often an exhausting process, at best. Although this alternative may seem favorable, it also has implications for essential interpersonal relationships and behaviors. People need to decide if they will step away from disagreements, escalate the argument, or challenge themselves to draw meaning from these difficult situations.

CHAPTER OVERVIEW

The ability to manage controversy with civility is critical in the social change process. Efforts to affect change are strongly rooted in collaboration. Understanding controversy—how it occurs and how to identify it—is just as important. The first part of this chapter helps the reader understand this C as a value of the Social Change Model for Leadership Development (SCM) and the important distinction between conflict and Controversy with Civility. This chapter also presents the positive value of controversy and how disagreements in groups form across differences. The last part of the chapter asks readers to reflect on their own personal values, attitudes, and behaviors when engaging with others across different perspectives. Knowing oneself when engaging in disagreements and knowing the skills one can use to manage disputes effectively are necessary in becoming a positive social change agent.

The Social Change Model of Leadership Development Guidebook (Higher Education Research Institute [HERI], 1996) best explains the definition of controversy with civility in the following:

Although much of the organizational literature labels the disagreement and controversy which inevitably occurs within any problem-solving group as "conflict," we want to emphasize that there is a subtle distinction in terminology that needs to be stressed. In the Social Change Model for Leadership Development, **controversy** refers to the disagreements and disputes which arise when those holding contrasting perspectives and opinions are encouraged to share their views with the other group members. By committing themselves to understand the nature of the disagreement and to seek a satisfactory resolution "with civility," the group provides a "safe" environment for acting with **congruence** and for enhancing **knowledge of self and of others.** Group members can respect and value the diversity represented in their team and find **common purpose**

(Continued)

by identifying those issues that are truly important to the group. In this trusting atmosphere individuals will find it easier to **collaborate**, to strengthen their personal **commitment**, and to reach beyond their individual agendas to create positive change for the betterment of others (citizenship). Controversy, in short, is viewed as an inevitable part of group interaction which can reinforce the other values in the Model if it occurs in an atmosphere of civility. (p. 60)

DISTINGUISHING CONTROVERSY FROM CONFLICT

A primary advantage of working in groups rather than alone is to benefit from other people's ideas. People differ in how they perceive situations, how they think through problems, and how they creatively form solutions. It is inevitable then, that in a group of people, differences of opinion will emerge regarding what the group should do and how it should do it. While dealing with these differences takes time and willingness to listen to different perspectives, it is critical to making the most of the knowledge and talent that exists in the group.

It is important to distinguish controversy from conflict. A conflict has opposing sides, two different positions on an idea. People align with one side or the other and debate whose side is right. Visually, conflict draws a line, with people taking a position on one side or the other. A controversy, on the other hand, also involves differing opinions about an idea; however, positions on the issue are not staked out, with one person hoping to "win" over the other. Rather than aligning with one side or another, controversy draws everyone into a circle around the idea, to discuss their different perspectives on it. While conflict is aimed at one side winning over the other side, the goal of controversy is for everyone to understand the issue from multiple points of view, in order to make a better decision. Controversy reflects a thoughtful and considered difference of opinion.

The Importance of Civility

It is difficult to handle controversy and perhaps harder still to do so with true civility. From the time children begin to understand their relationship to others—as siblings, as kids on a school playground—they are socialized to avoid conflict. For some, "No fighting" and "Be nice" are messages that shaped our behaviors. For others, getting what they want by fighting reinforces the use of power and the disregard of others. How many individuals interpret and approach conflict may be traced back to these early messages. People may have learned that they can either be strictly right or wrong; that one person's point of view is more valid than another's; and perhaps that disagreement is synonymous with fighting. It is no surprise, then, that many would want to avoid speaking up when they disagree. This is the message that has been learned and one that has consistently been reinforced through many life experiences.

Civility however, is more complex than just "not fighting" and "being nice." Civility certainly does not require that a person stay quiet when he or she disagrees, pretending that all is well when it is not. Instead, it means learning how both to voice disagreement and to respond to disagreement from others in a way that respects other points of view. In "The Virtues of Leadership," Thomas J. Sergiovanni (2005) describes civility as a virtue "that embraces diversity, encourages tolerance, and legitimizes controversy. Civility builds frameworks within which people can cooperate despite their divergent views and interests" (p. 117).

As much as civility may be thought of as a great character trait, it is also an attitude, a behavior, and, in the Social Change Model, it is a value. It requires the belief that there is not just one "right" point of view, but that everyone will see an issue slightly differently, depending on his or her background and previous experiences. Civility does not require the group to agree with every opinion that is raised, but each opinion should be listened to with respect and taken under consideration while considering the issue or making the decision. Chapter Six on Collaboration described how important respectful listening is in collaboration.

In effect, Controversy with Civility challenges group participants to discuss diverse opinions and perspectives, while maintaining respect for those sharing other views. Without regard for respect or consideration of others' ideas, group members can quickly lose themselves in the "heat" of an argument, preferring to "win" or give up and "lose" rather than truly understand the issue and solve the problem. By creating an environment in which various opinions are valued, a group can promote constructive discourse in order to negotiate a favorable outcome.

Promoting Controversy and Civility

Controversy with civility is not an episodic phenomenon, but an ongoing one. To have this value does not mean that when the occasional conflict arises, it should be handled merely by "being nice" to each other. To truly understand controversy with civility means to create a sustained culture within the organization in which people's different points of view and different ways of thinking about problems are respected and utilized for the betterment of the group. Healthy groups help controversies surface so the group can deal with all divergent views en route to making a sound decision. So how is this accomplished? The following are three ways of thinking about the combination of controversy and civility.

One approach is to mistakenly try to **maintain civility by avoiding controversy**. For example, organization officers might withhold information about plans or decisions being made so other members do not have the opportunity to voice dissent. The established norm in these groups is to either agree or be silent. Members who question the established way of doing things are treated as though they are either not smart enough to understand, that it is not their business, or they are disloyal to the group. The other members exchange annoyed glances and roll their eyes because this person "just doesn't get how things are done around here." It does not take long in such a group for voicing a disagreement of any kind to feel too risky. Consider the story of the gorillas at the start of the chapter.

Think about how a culture has been created around conflict. Think also about how a group could create a culture in the organization where disagreement is civil, and normal and expected, so people do not hesitate to disagree for fear others will not respond well.

A second approach **embraces controversy, but without civility**. In this group, members are not afraid of voicing opinions but are not able to do so in a way that respects other views. A different opinion is often attributed to lack of intellect or to a character flaw rather than to a difference in experience or perspective. Those with different opinions dismiss others' views as just wrong or not worthy of comment. Sometimes this occurs during meetings, with members becoming defensive or reacting in anger without thinking of consequences. It also occurs behind the scenes, with members forming opposing sides and planning takeovers. Ideas are linked to people, so disagreeing with an idea may mean wanting to remove the person who backs that idea from power. When opposing viewpoints reach a stalemate, the organization may even divide into two separate organizations. In some cases, two organizations with nearly identical purposes exist side by side for so long that no one remembers why they separated in the first place.

Finally, a third approach is to **promote controversy with civility.** In this approach, group members are able to trust that others will not react negatively to being disagreed with. Rather than becoming defensive of their position, group members express appreciation for those with the courage to speak up and offer a perspective that has not been explored yet. Those with unique perspective or different ways of thinking through problems are valued for helping the group consider all the angles before making a decision. This does not mean every person's argument is considered valid—reasoning based on credible evidence should always prevail—but all perspectives are given the consideration they are due.

To promote an organizational culture that values controversy with civility requires several elements that will be expanded upon here: awareness of one's own worldview, awareness of others, building trust, identifying the roots of controversy, and fostering dialogue.

Awareness of One's Own Worldview

The perspectives one brings to relationships in a group or perspectives on what are important goals for the group to pursue come from one's own context influenced by one's gender view, racial or ethnic view, religion, and other cultural context and heritage. The same is certainly true for others. Recognizing that individuals may have different worldviews enables one to be open to explore personal assumptions and understand the assumptions of others.

In visual art, "negative space" refers to the space between or around objects. A classic example of negative space is Rubin's vase, an optical illusion in which the outlines of two faces are positioned opposite of one another. The resulting space between the outlines, the negative space, tricks the brain into visualizing an image of a vase. Thus, one is left to question whether the image represents two faces or a vase.

This classic illusion highlights an important element in beginning to understand oneself in the midst of controversy. The brain, in this example, is conflicted by perceiving two different images—two faces and a vase. Although human thinking is much more complex than distinguishing between two images, it is tied to the perception of an event. This perception with which individuals approach any situation is known as *worldview*.

A person's worldview, or frame of reference, defines something much more complex than one's opinion or perspective on a situation. In Adlerian therapy, a type of counseling therapy, the client's frame of reference is known as his or her "subjective reality" (Corey, 2005). "This 'subjective reality' includes the individual's perceptions, thoughts, feelings, values, beliefs, convictions, and conclusions" (p. 96). In essence, this means that the set of one's collective life experiences influences the way in which one makes meaning of events in one's life. For example, people might think about the last time they worked in a group. How would they describe their role and the role of others in the group? Were there things they enjoyed about the group? Were there things that frustrated them about the group? If they had the experience of working in a group before then, the way in which they approached their most recent experience was in some ways shaped and influenced by what they had learned about working in groups prior to that experience. In other words, they may have tried to take on a similar or different role, depending on their previous group experiences. Moreover, they may have tried to adapt their experience to reflect the things they had enjoyed and avoid the things that had frustrated them with other groups. Similarly, the way people approach controversy is framed within a set of what they have learned and experienced. These frames are as complex as our thinking itself but nonetheless can teach us about the way in which we perceive controversy.

 What are the things that make you who you are? How would you define yourself to others? Take the time to think about the many dimensions of your identity that have shaped the person that you are today. How have these factors influenced your thoughts, values, and beliefs?

Awareness of Other Worldviews

The ensemble felt that "effectively resolving opposing views and opinions requires an understanding of the individuals involved: their assumptions, their values, and their goals"

(HERI, 1996, p. 61). Each individual brings his or her own worldview and understanding of the environment to any given situation. "Cultural differences, how power and authority are understood, and the specific socio-cultural context of the disagreement must also be considered to gain insight and resolution of the controversy" (p. 61).

 In order for controversy with civility to exist as a group process value, a significant understanding of both individual and group values must occur. (HERI, 1996, p. 61)

Just as one approaches any situation from a frame of reference that has been informed by all of the ways in which their experiences have shaped them, other members of the group do the same. This is, essentially, what makes groups dynamic: the bringing together of diverse thoughts, beliefs, and values, that have been informed by different experiences. Take, for example, a student government organization at a university comprised by the different representatives from each of the colleges or schools within the university. Each representative looks after the interests of his or her college and contributes a perspective shaped by the values that are important to that college. As a representative in the organization, however, the representative is responsible for understanding the interests and values of those with whom he or she "shares the table."

Exploring Leadership (Komives, Lucas, & McMahon, 2007) states that "groups are made up of great diversity. Even if members are all of one sex or one race or one major, there are great differences in personality, learning preferences, and experiences" (p. 153). The ways in which people in groups are different from others are extensive. As a result, individuals must recognize, account for, and seek to understand these differences in working through controversy. By acknowledging the ethnic, cultural, gender, and international diversity that exists within groups, they can move forward through controversy and strengthen our common purpose.

In the last reflection, you identified the ways in which specific dimensions of your identity have influenced and shaped your thoughts, beliefs, and values. What do you think you would find if you compared your responses to those of your two closest friends?

Trusting the People and the Process
Having the confidence to voice an opinion that is different from the rest of the group requires trust. Trust may be characterized by the degree to which group members have confidence that a person can be relied upon to behave in a predictable way. Group members must be able to trust that while others may not share their opinion, they will respect

that it comes from a person with a valid perspective and will take it into consideration.

Kouzes and Posner (1987) identified several important things one can do to foster trust in an organization. A few of these include:

1. **Use the word *we*.** When discussing the group's goals and accomplishments, remember that no one person does the group's work alone. Be clear that the ideas and the credit for success belong to the whole group rather than a single person.

2. **Encourage interactions.** When people are isolated from each other, it is difficult to build trust. Schedule regular meetings that include opportunities for people to interact, not just hear announcements.

3. **Create a climate of predictability.** In order to build trust, group members need to do what they say they will do. Follow through on commitments and keep promises. Reward honesty, even when it brings bad news.

4. **Involve everyone in planning and problem solving.** Avoid making decisions behind closed doors.

5. **Trust others.** When members risk opening up to each other, sharing what they value and what they hope for, they demonstrate willingness to trust each other.

In addition to trusting others, engaging in controversy with civility requires trusting the process. Encouraging dissent and differing opinions means a loss of control over where the group is going. This can feel risky and creates a certain degree of vulnerability. It is important to trust that the process of sharing multiple perspectives and working through differences will help the group arrive at a better decision. Trusting the process means realizing that when controversy emerges, it is not a sign that something has gone wrong with the group. Rather it is a sign that the process is working and multiple points of view are ferreting out potential problems or helping the group to be more inclusive.

Identifying the Root of Controversy

Although controversy can be simplified to mean the sharing of "a difference of opinion," the definition used by the Social Change Model of Leadership Development emphasizes "the process in which individuals holding contrasting perspectives in a group are encouraged to engage with one another across these differences" (HERI, 1996, p. 60). Dissonance in controversy is much like dissonance in music, when a group of musical notes create an unsettling sound.

According to Festinger (as cited in Matz & Wood, 2005), *dissonance* is a psychological discomfort or an aversive drive state that people are motivated to reduce, just as they are motivated to reduce hunger. Most people are quick to want to resolve disagreements, and perhaps even avoid them, without thinking about or understanding how they occur. "Festinger's original dissonance theory did not specify the origins of cognitive inconsistency beyond the general notion that inconsistency arises when one cognitive element does not follow from another, as occurs when others in a group disagree" (Matz & Wood, p. 23). In effect, people attribute dissonance to a "difference of opinion," rather than attempt to understand how various elements of human interaction may shape disagreements. Controversy, therefore, can occur from a number of difficult situations that may arise from the group process. Consider the following reasons and number of ways that controversy may occur (see Exhibit 8.1).

Controversy that results from the differences in values and ideas that members have should be recognized as a normal and healthy part of groups being groups. However, controversy that results from a lack of decision-making processes, unresolved prior disagreements, or other explanations in Exhibit 8.1 should be dealt with. Groups should establish a process to bring controversies into the conversation in civil and productive ways.

Dialogue

Dialogue skills may be the critical answer to many leadership problems in group settings. David Bohm (2004) describes dialogue as coming to a shared meaning or new understanding. He contrasts dialogue and debate in several ways:

+ A debate has opposing sides, each trying to show the other is wrong.

+ A dialogue engages each differing point of view in order for everyone to understand the issue better.

- The goal of a debate is to win the argument.

- The goal of dialogue is for everyone to come to a shared understanding of the issue, one that takes all perspectives into account.

- Individuals engaged in debate defend their positions and challenge the opposition.

- Individuals in dialogue are open to examining what underlies their assumptions. They consider how the way they

 At a small, private, liberal arts university in Oregon, students felt compelled to challenge the university's action (or lack thereof) toward addressing social justice issues on campus. For years, incidents occurred on campus that were left unaddressed: inappropriate off-campus theme parties, racially biased incidents on campus, homophobic remarks on athletic teams, and so on. Students organized under the guise of "Concerned Students for Social Justice" (CSSJ) to address the campus and its administration. They held rallies, forums, and talked with their peers about making positive social change on campus. Although they were met with hostility, inaction, and otherwise negative remarks, the CSSJ continues to work toward engaging in difficult dialogues to create change on their campus.

EXHIBIT 8.1 Explanations for Controversy

Lack of Communication	Failure to share ideas and feelings allows others in the group to make assumptions. People form their interpretation about what they think the other person or persons will say, or anticipate how they will respond. People tend to focus on the negative out of fear for what they do not know. They grow distrusting and defensive against what they believe is going on, not what they have communicated with others about and know is true.
Difference in Values	Every individual holds attitudes, beliefs, and opinions that are different from others. These individual perspectives have been informed by different experiences. When people are unable to recognize and respect these value differences, controversy forms in an attempt to do things "the right way."
Lack of Effective Decision Making	Differences exist in the ways in which group members approach making decisions. If members limit themselves to assigning one person to "be in charge," they lose their ability to collaborate and account for different ideas and perspectives. Controversy ensues when they feel left out of the decision-making process and are unable to contribute valuable insight.
Discrepancies in Role Expectations	Members in groups are often responsible for carrying different roles. These roles involve expectations and responsibilities that are essential to healthy group functioning. When members of a group are unclear about these responsibilities, they impose expectations on others who may or may not be responsible for such things. When these expectations are not met, they can fall into a "blame game" over who was supposed to do what.
Change That Causes Disequilibrium	Harmony is important in many group settings. Although people like feeling safe and secure in the status quo, they must inevitably face changes in a group. When changes are unclear—when one does not understand them or see how change will occur—one grows distrusting and fearful.
Unresolved Prior Disagreements	Avoiding disagreements and harboring negative feelings or attitudes against another person or group of people is detrimental to the group process. Controversy arises out of an inability to face and manage disagreements across differences because those disagreements will surely resurface.

Source: Adapted from LEADS, Kansas State University (2001), p 2.

think about problems leads them to the opinions they have. Other people's thinking is used to improve understanding of the issue.

Being able to dialogue is perhaps the most important skill in achieving controversy with civility. Many college campuses are now using a process called Intergroup Dialogue to engage students in learning across difference. While they exist for a specific purpose, often to engage students in learning about diversity, their design can be adapted to help other types of groups learn to use the dialogue process. Intergroup Dialogues often use a four-stage design:

Stage 1:   The group members get to know each other and build relationships, sometimes through intentional team-building activities. The group learns about the concept of dialogue.

Stage 2:   Members of the group learn about each other's backgrounds, experiences, and values. They focus on building trust and respect for each other. This stage lays a foundation for the dialogue to come, as members learn about each other's assumptions.

Stage 3:   Group members engage in dialogue about controversial topics. Participants voice their perspectives and learn about other points of view. Understanding the issue is emphasized, and defending any one position as "right" or "wrong" is discouraged. The stage 3 dialogue leads to the whole group having a better understanding of the issue.

Stage 4:   Based on the whole group's improved understanding, the group creates an action plan. (Zúñiga, Nagada, & Sevig as cited in Zuniga, Nagda, Chesler, & Cytron-Walker, 2007, p. 7)

 Think back to a time in which you have had to manage controversy between two individuals. Identify what the problem was and then think about some of the ways in which you could have used the skills and tools mentioned earlier in the chapter to sustain communication, raise consciousness, and bridge differences. What kinds of questions could you have asked? What observations could you have made? What type of creative activities could you have used?

CONNECTION TO THE OTHER C'S

As has been mentioned in previous chapters, all of the C's are linked such that improving effectiveness in one C will positively affect one's ability to do the other C's, and vice versa. It is no less true with Controversy with Civility. Working with others through differences of opinion, values, or ideas provides opportunities to examine one's individual values. Experiences with controversy are opportunities to practice being Conscious, Congruent with values, and Committed to the group even when the going is not easy.

Controversy with Civility also influences the other group C's. A group's ability to Collaborate and come to Common Purpose can be taken to the next level by learning to welcome differences of opinion and work through them with civility. Finally, Congruence with values is at the heart of Citizenship, whether it be in the local community or globally. As an active community member working toward change, one will inevitably encounter controversy. Maintaining civility means being socially responsible and working across differences for the betterment of a community.

CONCLUSION

As one of the Seven C's, Controversy with Civility acknowledges that disagreements are inherent in a process that strongly emphasizes and encourages collaboration. At the same time, the process of managing controversy with civility is set apart from traditional conflict management approaches in that it focuses on working through disagreements across differences. By recognizing how disagreements occur, understanding oneself and others, maintaining a civil approach, and using effective skills to resolve disputes, one can continue on as a social change agent in effectively working across differences.

DISCUSSION QUESTIONS

1. How is Controversy with Civility a different approach than the ways in which you have approached or experienced conflict management in student organizations or other groups?

2. An important element in managing controversy with civility is understanding how you feel about and approach controversy. Think about two different occurrences in which you have experienced disagreement with another individual or group, one that you feel was resolved positively and the other that was resolved less favorably. (Note: Less favorably does not indicate that you "lost" in a disagreement.)

   a. How did you feel throughout each of these instances?

   b. Who were the key individuals or groups involved?

   c. How was controversy managed? What was the process in reaching resolve?

   d. What would you have changed in either case?

   e. How might these experiences have benefited from an approach of controversy with civility?

3. What are some of the connections that you have made and reflected on between Controversy with Civility and the other C's of the Social Change Model?

JOURNAL PROBES

On Becoming

Preeminent psychologist Carl Rogers (1961) said that people are always in a process of *becoming*. The first two journal probes are intended to help you reflect on how you see yourself becoming a leader for social change.

1. How aware are you of becoming more effective at handling Controversy with Civility?

2. Can you remember a time when you approached controversy differently than you do now? How is your current approach different from your approach then?

Learning Through Experience

The ensemble that created the Social Change Model believed the best way to learn to do leadership was through experience and reflection. This involves challenging yourself to have new experiences that test your ability and awareness **and** to spend time thinking about what you have learned from that experience. The remaining journal probes are designed to maximize learning through experience by guiding your reflective journal writing through Kolb's (1981) four processes of experiential learning.

1. **Concrete Experience.** Describe a specific situation when you had an experience that relates to Controversy with Civility as it has been described here. What happened? What details stand out to you? Describe briefly the situation, what you did and how you felt.

2. **Reflective Observation.** Why did this situation have the outcome it did? What caused the situation to happen in the first place? What responses from yourself and others worked in this situation? Why was that effective? What did not work? Why?

3. **Abstract Conceptualization.** What lessons can you draw from this specific experience that could apply more generally? Given both your reflections and the information in this chapter, what would you do if a similar situation presented itself? What general guidelines would you create for handling future situations like this?

4. **Active Experimentation.** What opportunities might you seek out that would give you the chance to apply what you have learned here? How might you test the lessons or guidelines you created in #3 to see if they work?

APPLYING THE CASE STUDIES

Go back to Chapter Three for more context on each of these case studies. Apply the material covered in Chapter Eight to these cases.

Zoom In: Starving for Attention

In this case, Taylor has become involved in an organization that is challenging the university to pay its service workers a wage that better reflects the cost of living in the area. In addition to suggesting the group meet with campus workers who are affected by low wages, Taylor has suggested the organization plan a hunger strike as a backup plan, in case the university administration ignores their message.

Though many in the group were excited about Taylor's bold plan to hold the administration to a strict timeline of complying with change around issues of the living wage on campus, not all were happy with Taylor's approach. After the group had worked through a plan, some began voicing their concerns that the campus would not understand the purposes behind the hunger strike because the group was doing not enough proactive education. One member wrote an e-mail to Dan, the president, that she could not participate in a hunger strike because it was just too extreme and she was scared about her health and the health of others. Another wrote Dan that he would not be coming to more meetings, that this direction was too radical.

As organization leaders begin hearing about these negative feelings, they convene a meeting to talk about it. Dan shares, "I'm worried about the negative grumblings I've heard about and I think we need to address it." Larissa, the education and outreach coordinator, replies, "We all believe in the values of the campaign—that's why we're here. However, I've also spoken to a number of group members who are concerned that we are moving forward too quickly and that the campus is not going to understand the conviction behind the campaign if we rush our plan." Taylor says, "Well forget them, we have to do something bold or nothing will change!"

After a long discussion, the leadership team agrees that any disagreements needed to be aired openly. They decide to review the values behind the campaign and plan a meeting for later in the week with all group members to discuss the dis-agreements. They are hoping to have all perspectives heard and create a new plan if necessary.

Think About It

+ Using this case as an example, how is Controversy with Civility different from compromise?

+ Why would it be more difficult for the leadership team to facilitate the type of meeting they are planning if they did not have shared values already established?

+ How do members' perspectives on appropriate methods of getting attention differ and where do those differences come from?

+ Which of the explanations of controversy described in this chapter apply here?

+ If you were on the leadership team, how would you go about planning the upcoming meeting? How would you structure the discussion to encourage a dialogue rather than a debate?

+ What creative solutions might come out of the meeting that the leadership team is planning to facilitate?

Zoom In: Clear Haziness

In this case, you are the photography editor of the campus paper, *The Weekly*, where a tradition of hazing new members of the photography staff has been uncovered. Imagine that you go to *The Weekly*'s executive board, and everyone agrees with you and your perspective on how to react to the situation. Now, imagine that you go to the executive board and none agree with your reaction to the situation. Still, the most realistic possibility is that some will agree with you and some will not. Think about those three situations separately. How might you react to them differently? Which of the explanations of controversy described in this chapter apply here? How might you go about fostering a dialogue about the issue, rather than a debate?

References

Bohm, D. (2004). *On dialogue*. New York: Rutledge Classics.

Corey, G. (2005). *Theory and practice of counseling and psychotherapy* (7th ed.). Belmont, CA: Brooks/Cole.

Higher Education Research Institute [HERI]. (1996). *A social change model of leadership development* (Version III). Los Angeles: University of California Los Angeles, Higher Education Research Institute.

Kolb, D. A. (1981). Learning styles and disciplinary differences. In A. W. Chickering & Associates (Eds.), *The modern American college: Responding to the new realities of diverse students and a changing society* (pp. 232–255). San Francisco: Jossey Bass.

Komives, S. R., Lucas, N., & McMahon, T. R. (2007). *Exploring leadership: For college students who want to make a difference* (2nd ed.). San Francisco: Jossey-Bass.

Kouzes, J. M., & Posner, B. Z. (1987). *The leadership challenge: How to get extraordinary things done in organizations.* San Francisco: Jossey-Bass.

Matz, D. C., & Wood, W. (2005). Cognitive dissonance in groups: The consequences of disagreement. *Journal of Personality and Social Psychology, 88*(1), 22–37.

Rogers, C. R. (1961). *On becoming a person: A therapist's view of psychotherapy.* Boston: Houghton Mifflin.

Sergiovanni, T. J. (2005). The virtues of leadership. *Educational Forum, 69*(2), 112–119.

Zuniga, X., Nagda, B. Chesler, M., & Cytron-Walker, A. (2007). *Intergroup dialogue in higher education: Meaningful learning about social justice.* ASHE Higher Education Report, 32(no. 4). San Francisco: Wiley Periodicals.

PART 4

Individual Values

Those of us inspirited by the call to make a difference in the world have no choice but to take the journey of self-discovery.

DENNIS ROBERTS

Although leadership is a process that takes places among people working together toward positive change, individuals have a responsibility to expand their personal capacity to engage in this collaborative leadership. This journey into self-awareness is essential both to be able to relate authentically to others in group settings and to make the personal commitments essential to working toward positive change.

Learning and personal development are a lifelong process. Most people can look back to ways they were when they were younger and realize they have developed more complexity in their thinking, understand themselves in deeper ways, and value the interdependence in their relationships. Psychologist Robert Kegan (1994) describes the interaction of cognitive, intrapersonal, and interpersonal development as a stage of consciousness. A stage of consciousness shifts when one is able to look back on oneself at an earlier time and realize how one is now different in attitudes, beliefs, and skills from that time. The thoughtful assessment promoted in this book is intended to enrich a *mindfulness* about self and self in the context others. This mindfulness describes the process of "becoming" presented in the Preface of the book.

In Part Four, the Social Change Model (SCM) examines leadership development from the individual perspective or level. The ensemble asked, "What personal qualities are we attempting to foster and develop in those who participate in a leadership development program? What personal qualities are most supportive of group functioning and positive social change?" (Higher Education Research Institute [HERI], 1996, p. 19). The three values explored in Part Four are Consciousness of Self, Congruence, and Commitment.

References

Higher Education Research Institute [HERI]. (1996). *A social change model of leadership development* (Version III). Los Angeles: University of California Los Angeles, Higher Education Research Institute.

Kegan, R. (1994). *In over our heads: The mental demands of modern life.* Cambridge, MA: Harvard University Press.

9

CONSCIOUSNESS OF SELF

Justin Fincher

*I want, by understanding myself, to understand others. I
want to be all that I am capable of becoming.*
KATHERINE MANSFIELD

Knowing oneself is the foundational bedrock of the journey into deeper leadership. "Knowing yourself makes
you more effective in working with others. It gives you insight
into how your behavior affects them positively or negatively.
It affords you a better understanding of yourself as a stimulus
for influencing others" (Lee & King, 2001, p. 72).

CHAPTER OVERVIEW

This chapter describes several aspects of the self that people can become more aware of, such as being aware of one's
guiding values, personal style, skills, and aspirations. Several

> A sophomore student in the Southwestern College (Kansas) leadership program was the director of a freshman orientation project that involved the entire freshman class working on home improvement projects in the community surrounding the college campus. He reflected, "At first I was doing this project and going to do it well because I didn't want to be embarrassed in front of my team; then I started to do it because I didn't want to let you (the program director) down; then I started to realize that I was doing this project and I didn't want to let myself down; finally I got it—I started doing the project so I wouldn't let down the people I was trying to help."

practices to help one become more self-aware are explored, including reflection and seeking feedback from others. Finally, the chapter explores the topic of mindfulness, a critical leadership skill.

DEFINING CONSCIOUSNESS OF SELF

Consciousness of Self refers to people's awareness of their own personality traits, values, and strengths, as well as their ability to be self-observers who are mindful of their actions, feelings, and beliefs. It involves not only knowing who they are in general, but also being aware of themselves in their current state—how the environment and other people are affecting them and vice versa. Having consciousness of self does not imply an end point at which one can say, "I've done it. I know myself." Rather, adopting a way of living that continually informs the person about who he or she is and what is most important marks achievement in this C.

The ensemble that developed the Social Change Model (HERI, 1996) clarified that Consciousness of Self:

implies an awareness and an acknowledgement of those relatively stable aspects of the self that go to make up what we call "personality": talents, interests, aspirations, values, concerns, self-concept, limitations, and dreams. Second, self-awareness implies "mindfulness," an ability and a propensity to be an accurate observer of your current actions and state of mind. (p. 31)

Some might mistakenly confuse consciousness of self with being self-conscious. People who are self-conscious are afraid to act as they naturally would because they are worried about what everyone else thinks about them. Consciousness of self is quite different. People who are conscious of themselves know where their values come from; they know what they are good at and what they are not. This results in the confidence to act authentically, because their validation as a good and worthy person comes from inside, from self-approval, not from the approval of others.

BENEFITS OF CONSCIOUSNESS OF SELF FOR LEADERSHIP

Knowing oneself and accurately observing the self in interaction with others is critical to effectiveness when working with others. A recent study examined how college students come to identify themselves as leaders (Komives, Owen, Longerbeam, Mainella, & Osteen, 2005). One of the key findings of the study was that developing self-awareness is a critical aspect of learning to see oneself as a leader. Self-awareness affected this process along five dimensions: (1) deepening self-awareness; (2) building self-confidence; (3) establishing interpersonal efficacy; (4) applying new skills; and (5) expanding motivation.

The researchers found that students experienced a *deepening self-awareness* as they came to be aware of how they worked with others. In the beginning, students defined themselves by how others seemed to see them. The skills or personality traits they were conscious of were those that had been pointed out to them by a parent, teacher, or friend. As they had opportunities to work with others and gain experience, their understanding of who they were began to come from their own inner sense of identity. They also became increasingly aware of how their gender and cultural groups affected group interactions.

As students became more aware of their skills, personality attributes, and values, they began *building self-confidence* in their abilities to take on new responsibilities and challenges within their groups. The confidence that comes from this self-awareness is important to leadership effectiveness. Self-confident individuals tend to "take on unpopular issues, stand up for their values, and not need peer affirmation" (Komives et al., 2005, p. 600). Self-aware individuals are also able to focus on their strengths while understanding their limitations, protecting against overconfidence. Without an accurate perception of one's limitations, leaders can get deep into a task or situation and not realize quickly enough that they are not prepared fully for the task and need assistance.

Self-awareness also affected the students' belief in their ability to work well with other people, or their *interpersonal efficacy*. For example, some cultures value building relationships and trust before turning their attention to the task at hand. A student who is aware of having learned this approach from her culture is able to temper her frustration when working in a group that is more focused on getting the task done first. This concept connects back to the opening quote of the chapter by Katherine Mansfield: "I want, by understanding myself, to understand others. I want to be all that I am capable of becoming."

Students with an awareness of their weaknesses were better equipped to challenge themselves to *apply new skills* and improve themselves through practice. A student who realizes he is not the best listener can begin to actively seek out opportunities to develop this skill and apply it in different settings. By the same token, students who are aware of their strengths can consider new ways contribute their abilities to benefit the groups of which they are a part. A student who is complimented by a professor about how well she is able to organize projects into manageable parts may realize that is just what her community service organization needs to get the community cleanup project to finally come to fruition.

Students in the study who became increasingly aware of their values had an *expanding motivation* to get involved and address the issues that were most important to them. For example, a student may become aware of how deeply she admires her mother's struggle to immigrate to the United States in order to give her children a better education. That awareness could provide the motivation for the student to become tirelessly involved in groups that support recent immigrants, providing English tutoring, helping to navigate the citizenship process, and other related issues.

 What are some strengths and skills that you contribute to groups that you work with? How can you enhance the areas that you currently see as limitations to further develop your leadership abilities? What motivates you to want to make a change? How do you act on that motivation?

ASPECTS OF INDIVIDUAL IDENTITY

There are many factors that shape the ways in which each individual is unique from others. The following section of the chapter explores those that were specifically identified by the ensemble who created the Social Change Model: (1) values and principles; (2) personal style; (3) talents, skills, and specialized knowledge; and (4) aspirations and dreams.

Values and Principles

Values and principles represent the priorities that guide how people live their lives, how they decide what is most important, when to take a stand, and how they know what they are and are not willing to do in order to reach a goal. Sometimes it can be difficult for people to identify their values in the abstract, but when put in a particular situation they know when something is "just not right."

One way to help identify values and principles is to think about where they come from. The following are just a few examples of sources of values and principles to consider.

Culture. People of a particular culture often share at least a few values in common. For example, the dominant culture in the United States tends to value self-reliance, freedom of choice, and a strong work ethic. It also holds some arguably less positive values, such as materialism and conspicuous consumption. Ethnic cultures in the United States share some cultural values with their fellow Americans but often have other values that are distinct. For example, some of these cultures maintain strong ties to the past. Children are taught to learn from the group's history, and particular reverence is given to the wisdom of older family members. In some cultures, people value the needs of the group over the needs of the individual, and would look down upon someone who lived with independence, seeing them as not having an appropriate regard for others (Bordas, 2007). These are just a few examples of how people's values are influenced by the cultures of which they are a part. Cultural values can shape not only behavior, but also the way one perceives the world and interprets events.

Faith. For people who grew up with a particular spiritual tradition, its messages about how to treat others and how to live a good life are taught from such a young age that it might be difficult to be aware of any other way to be. People who are drawn to a particular religious group as adults often chose that tradition because they find the values and principles communicated there to be congruent with their own values.

Family. One way to identify one's personal values is to think about the behavior that is held up as an ideal in one's family. One might consider, what traditions does the family maintain and what values do those traditions communicate? What stories about ancestors or grandparents are passed down to children and what values or principles do they reflect? What sayings were common in the family? Examples might be, "Just do your best and forget about the rest," or "There is no room for second place," or "A failure to plan is a plan to fail." Advice and proverbs are often repeated by parents again and again to help children learn to share the same values as the parents and family.

Generational Peers. Peer groups like the Baby Boomers, Generation X, and the Millennials share historical experiences that have shaped how they interpret events and what they believe is most important. For example, one value often associated with the Millennials (people born after 1980) is community and connectedness with others. They tend to be joiners rather than going at it alone, and they are often quite committed to the groups and institutions of which they are a part. They enjoy being able to always be connected to friends and family via technology, such as cell phones and instant messaging, options that didn't exist for earlier generations of college students (DeBard, 2004).

Personal Style

Personal style refers to many different aspects of personality. For example, some people are outgoing and talkative, even thinking out loud, while others listen, observe, and share their thoughts only after having given them careful consideration. Some people prefer to carefully schedule their time, planning to complete major projects in advance of deadlines. Others prefer spontaneity to a schedule and have learned to adapt to whatever comes along. Personal style includes hundreds of descriptors, like *timid, aggressive, organized, adaptable, optimistic, competitive, easygoing, patient, reserved,* or *goofy.* Being aware of one's own style is useful for understanding interactions with others, particularly with those whose style is different from one's own.

Leadership styles refer to those traits that relate to how a person behaves when in a position of leadership. Some lead through a hands-off approach, letting the group self-organize. Others prefer to control the direction of the group. Some tend to focus on the task or problem the group is working on, others focus on supporting group members and making sure everyone feels included so they can contribute to the group's success. Some are naturally inspirational and are good at motivating people. Others motivate by being a role model, getting their hands dirty right alongside everyone else. Many leadership theorists believe there is no one right style, but each has strengths and weaknesses depending on the situation and task at hand (Northouse, 2007).

While some people prefer to work with others who are similar to them in style, every personality brings some benefit. Sometimes an aspect of the self that one person perceives as a weakness is viewed as a strength by others—and vice versa. Sometimes a person's greatest flaw is actually a positive style that has just gone too far.

Talents, Skills, and Specialized Knowledge

It is possible for people to be so accustomed to having the ability to do something that they forget that not everyone can do it. The ability to persuade others, organize big projects, delegate tasks, keep track of budgets, cheer someone up, or be a good listener are all useful skills that are worth cultivating.

Some approach consideration of talents and skills from a negative perspective—listing areas to improve or skills that need to be learned in order to be effective. While improving on weaknesses is always useful, this approach ignores the usefulness of cultivating one's natural strengths. Focusing on one's strengths allows a person to both hone them further and think about new contexts in which they can be applied: "Each person's greatest room for growth is in the areas of his or her greatest strength" (Buckingham & Clifton, 2001, p. 8).

Clifton and Nelson (1992) recommend several strategies to identify one's strengths. Some of these include examining successes to determine what particular skills resulted in a positive outcome, and paying attention to tasks that are easily learned in order to determine what strengths are involved in doing it well.

Aspirations and Dreams

Some people have a specific picture of what they want to be doing in five, ten, or twenty-five years. Others do not have a time-dated plan, but they could name several things they would like to do someday. Aspirations include both personal and career-related goals, and they affect how people choose to invest their time in the present. It is important to spend at least some time considering how one defines success. How does one know what is ultimately most important?

An emerging approach to leadership draws connections between spirituality and leadership. This approach highlights two key needs for people working in groups: having a sense of *calling* and a need for *social connection* or membership. Calling refers to having a sense that one's work is meaningful, that it is important that the work is accomplished because of its value for others (Fry, 2003). This model certainly applies to those searching for a career-related calling: How will one's work satisfy the need to make a difference? However, it can be much broader than that, including other areas in which people consider what kind of involvement they want to have. The concept of having a calling means simply that people need to feel that they matter, that their time spent living was of value in some way. Reflecting on what one's calling might be is certainly an act of Consciousness of Self.

OTHERS' PERCEPTIONS OF US

One aspect of self-awareness that a person cannot reflect on alone is learning how one is seen by others. Obviously it is valuable to have a sense of one's personal style, but it is equally important to know how other people would describe it, based on their interpretations of the behaviors they see. Psychologists Joseph Luft and Harry Ingham developed a now-classic graphic called "The Johari window" that sheds light on this issue (Luft, 1970). (See Exhibit 9.1.) These domains examine information and the degree to what is known to the self and known by others.

EXHIBIT 9.1 Johari Window

	Known to Self	Unknown to Self
Known by Others	I **Open** or **Public**	II **Blind Spot**
Unknown by Others	III **Hidden** or **Private**	IV **Unknown** or **Undiscovered**

Source: Luft, J. (1970).

Quadrant I (*open*) includes information known to self and known to others. For example, Chris is a Yankees fan, loves being a parent, and is not a good public speaker. This is information that both he and everyone else knows about him. Quadrant II (*unaware*) contains information known to others but not self. The classic version of this document in the exhibit uses the term "blind" but we recommend you discuss this as "unaware." Chris's roommate has noticed that when Chris is tired from having being up all night, he often snaps at his friends and is irritated by things that normally do not bother him. Chris is not aware that lack of sleep leads him to behave differently than normal. Quadrant III (*hidden*) contains information known to self but not to others. Chris's cousin is autistic, which is why he is so devoted to volunteering with children with disabilities. This is information he has not shared with people at college however, so his friends do not know the source of his motivation to be a volunteer. Finally Quadrant IV (*unknown*) contains information known neither to self nor to others. Although Chris was raised in a family that practiced Catholicism, he has not been to mass while at college. He has not spent any time thinking about why that might be nor about what it means about his faith and beliefs. Neither Chris nor anyone else knows why he has not been motivated to attend mass. A goal of Consciousness of Self would be to decrease the number of things in Quadrants II and IV, and increase the number of items in Quadrants I and III.

How might you draw the sizes of the boxes in your own Johari window? What self-disclosure might make more of your hidden motives known to others? How might trusted friends give you feedback so you can understand your *blind* and *unknown* quadrants more clearly and thereby expand your *open* box? Why might reducing your hidden area affect your ability to lead effectively?

TAKING TIME TO BECOME CONSCIOUS OF SELF

As has been mentioned, Consciousness of Self is not an end point, but a journey. People do not achieve a state of self-awareness. Rather, they achieve a way of life that continually informs how they see themselves. Peter Senge (1990), creator of a popular approach to organizational effectiveness called the *learning organization*, emphasized the importance of being in an ongoing state of self-awareness, which involves "continually clarifying what is important to us . . .continually learning how to see current reality more clearly" (p. 141).

It is difficult with today's busy lifestyles to take time to stop and think about issues of self-awareness or the lessons that life's experiences are teaching. Western culture places value on *doing*. It is considered a mark of excellence to be always doing, always achieving something. If one is not doing, then he or she is wasting time (Rogers, 2005). Increasingly, simply doing one thing is no longer enough. People find themselves multitasking in order to do even more in the same amount of time. Many students can simultaneously write a paper, eat dinner, and chat with a friend. But this constant busyness does not lend itself to Consciousness of Self.

A lifestyle that fosters an ongoing practice of developing self-awareness needs to include a retreat from all the doing. It would include some point in the day to shake oneself lose of the daily grind, to unplug and enjoy some rare silence. It might even involve going somewhere different from one's typical route—anything that allows a person to step away from daily routines and reflect on bigger questions. Not "What should I do next?" but "Who am I? How would I describe myself? What values am I living by? Why am I here?"

While some may think this sounds like daydreaming or wasting time, it can lead to both greater effectiveness and more clarity about what all the "doing" is for. Kabat-Zinn (2005) said:

> You actually become more alive now. This is what stopping can do. There is nothing passive about it. And when you decide to go, it's a different kind of going because you stopped. The stopping actually makes the going more vivid, richer, more textured. It helps keep all the things we worry about and feel inadequate about in perspective. (p. 12)

 Try taking time daily to check in with yourself to see how you're doing. Instead of thinking about what you need to do next, think about what you are learning about yourself. Considering how you've spent the day today, what value seems to be most important to you? Is the way you are living getting you closer to the person you want to be?

BECOMING CONSCIOUS OF SELF

Becoming self-aware and mindful requires conscious intentional action. While people who have developed a way of life that continually informs their self-awareness do so in many different ways, these practices nearly always include (1) a practice of reflection, (2) openness to feedback, and (3) learning about the self through assessment.

Reflection

Reflection refers to thinking back about an experience in a way that helps one learn from it. It can be compared to looking in the mirror and studying oneself to see what is really there. There are many forms of reflection, including writing in a journal, talking with group members and friends, or simply quietly thinking on one's own. Something as simple as taking a minute after a difficult conversation with a roommate to cool one's emotions and collect thoughts can be a useful way to reflect on how the conversation went. Reflection can help people learn about themselves in many different ways; for example, it can:

+ Help them become more aware of how they tend to behave with others

+ Foster exploration of how their values and background influence that behavior

+ Challenge them to consider whether approaches that worked in one context will apply in another (if it helped resolve a roommate conflict, would it work in a student organization meeting?)

+ Challenge them to look at the same situation from someone else's perspective

+ Identify how their own personality, cultural worldview, or skills affect what they notice, how they interpret a situation, and how they choose to act

+ Spur new ideas about how to approach a future situation differently

+ Identify new skills or approaches that they could intentionally try to learn or improve

Having an ongoing practice of reflection can uncover trends in one's own behavior and serve as a reminder of the challenging tasks that have already been conquered.

What if you were to take a task that you complete on a daily basis, like walking to class, and use that time as an intentional reflection period? As you walk across campus, think about a task that you completed that day, someone you interacted with, or even something that made you upset or angry. Once you have thought of something, focus on your own reaction to this situation and focus on the dimensions of your values and beliefs that may be involved in that reaction. What can you learn about yourself from this experience? Would you do anything differently if it happened again?

Feedback

Reflection is an internal process that is crucial for individuals to enhance their Consciousness of Self. It can be equally important to get direct feedback about one's performance and behaviors. Feedback is a process of collecting external information from other sources in order to provide a better, more descriptive picture of one's strengths and weaknesses. Both positive and negative feedback can be helpful, but negative feedback can easily take a toll on one's self-confidence and motivation. In order to make the best of feedback, it is useful to approach it in a way that is open and integrative.

People who are sincerely *open* to feedback take advantage of opportunities to get it. In fact, they seek out feedback rather than waiting for others to come forward with it. They show they are genuinely interested in what others have to say. Rather than pushing away compliments, they offer a gracious "Thank you" and look for further details. For example, if someone makes a very general comment about their "excellent leadership" they might inquire further, "What do you mean? What did I do here that was useful for you?" Likewise, they are open to negative feedback, without getting defensive. Even if they do not agree with the feedback they are hearing, they listen without interrupting, knowing there will be time later to reflect on whether the feedback is accurate or useful. It is important to allow those giving the feedback to feel heard.

Being open and sincere about hearing feedback from others does not imply that a person should agree with all the feedback they are given. *Integrating* the advice of others with one's own way of thinking is a challenge that often involves reflection on one's experience in light of given feedback. Sometimes negative feedback may come from an incorrect interpretation of events. Other times, it may be the result of anger that is more reflective of the feedback giver's own issues than on the leader's behavior. Whether that interpretation is incorrect or simply different from the leader's own perspective is an excellent topic for reflection.

Assessments

Many survey-style instruments exist to help expand one's self-awareness, particularly in areas of personal style. While many of these types of assessments are available on the Internet, it is often preferable to have a qualified professional review the results of the assessment in order to fully understand its meaning. Most colleges and universities offer at least some personal assessments through the counseling center, career center, or leadership development program. The following are a few assessments that are often used in campus leadership development programs:

- Myers-Briggs Type Indicator: www.mbticomplete.com
- True Colors: www.truecolors.org
- The Leadership Practices Inventory: www.lpionline.com/
- ANSIR: ansir.com
- StrengthsQuest: www.strengthsquest.com/

MINDFULNESS

Up to now, this chapter has focused on self-awareness, or "acknowledgment of those relatively stable aspects of the self that go to make up what we call 'personality'" (HERI, p. 31). The other half of the definition of Consciousness of Self is mindfulness, "an ability . . . to be an accurate observer of your **current** actions and state of mind" (HERI, p. 31, emphasis added). People who are mindful can simultaneously act and be observers of themselves acting.

Different from being reflective of the past week or thinking about how to solve a problem, mindfulness is being observant of oneself in the present moment. It is also about being specific about what one is doing, thinking, and feeling. For example, it is not enough to say, "Right now I am talking to my friend." It is, "Right now I'm listening to my friend talk about her problems. I'm feeling pretty annoyed. I guess I'm wishing she'd listen to my problems for once." Or, "Right now I'm listening to my friend talk about her problems and I'm proud of how well I'm really listening to her. It feels good to be able to be here for her." Awareness of one's own mental state makes it possible to be more effective in interactions with others.

Mindfulness is about waking up from a life on automatic pilot and starting to pay attention to what is happening. College life can be characterized as going directly from doing one thing to planning the next thing to do. Many students run from one task to the next without being aware of how they feel. It is possible for a person to be in a bad mood all day, but not realize it until he finds himself yelling at a roommate. It is important to learn to recognize when one has unacknowledged stress, just as it is important to be aware of when one is feeling good in order to identify those things that provide personal fulfillment. Many procrastinators find that by being mindful they can identify and overcome the things that prevent them from getting their work done. Once they are aware that they are putting off doing their work, they can ask themselves, "What is it about this project I'm afraid of?" and respond appropriately to the answers they discover (such as fear of failure, or fear of feeling incompetent if it turns out they are unable to learn how to do the task).

Kabat-Zinn (2005) refers to people's constant actions and thoughts as being driven by unconscious impulses rather than undertaken in awareness. He compares these thoughts and impulses to a river or waterfall, running uncontrollably

 Next time you are in a frustrating conversation, or are feeling restless and distracted in a class, or are feeling excited and hopeful in a meeting, try being mindful. Observe yourself at that specific moment. What are you doing? Are you alert, tired, or sharply focused to the situation? Are you truly listening? What is your emotional state? See if you can find words to describe your feelings precisely. Are you reacting to the situation or acting out of conscious thought?

such that a person gets caught up in it and carried away. Learning to be mindful is like consciously deciding to step out of that river and instead sit by its bank and observe it. Where are all of these feelings and impulses to act in certain ways coming from? Where are they going?

Mindfulness in Leadership

Being mindful makes it possible to work more effectively with others. It allows group members to recognize when they are being emotionally reactive to others rather than operating from their own principles and values. Covey (2004) describes these people in this way: "Their behavior is a product of their own conscious choice, based on values, rather than a product of their conditions" (p. 71). Many of us know people whom Covey describes as *reactive*. Their emotions and actions follow directly from the conditions around them. "If the weather is good, they feel good. . . . When people treat them well, they feel well; when people don't, they become defensive or protective" (pp. 71–72). Mindful leaders are still affected by others and by the situation, but they are able to consciously choose how they will respond. The very recognition that their response is a choice and not an inevitable result of the circumstances is at the heart of mindfulness. Covey would say that we cannot choose what happens to us, but we can choose how we respond.

The following hypothetical scenario illustrates what mindfulness can look like in a leadership context. Gerri is the president of the Math Honors Society. One of her goals was for the organization to start a volunteer math tutoring program in a nearby high school. As the group discusses it, Gerri brings up a conversation she had with one of the teachers about the group focusing on tutoring girls, to help build their confidence with math and counteract the false social messages about math being harder for girls. Another member named John raises several objections to that idea, many of them valid. As the group continues to discuss the idea, John gets increasingly agitated, interrupting others and raising his voice. Gerri tries to focus the conversation, reminding them that while the group has its goals, what the teacher wants for her students should be taken into account. John responds to Gerri bitterly, "If you already have the project all planned out then you shouldn't waste everyone's time pretending to get input."

While being mindful happens quickly, the following is an example of the kinds of things that Geri might be thinking:

- **Observation of current emotional state.** I am really mad all of a sudden and really embarrassed. I can't believe he just insulted my leadership in front of everyone. I'm feeling vindictive too, he has clearly been trying to steer this conversation, what a hypocrite to say I'm not including others' input!

- **Observation of the situation.** Even though we were disagreeing, I didn't really get mad until that last comment. Why did it particularly get under my skin? Hmmm, up to then we were discussing the issue, but that last comment was attacking *me*. Why would John suddenly go after me instead of making an argument for tutoring girls and boys? Is he feeling threatened by me? Why?

◆ **Observation of own behavior.** [Replays the meeting again in her head, observing how she behaved through it.] Maybe it's possible that John and others interpreted my comment about having talked to the teacher already as trying to control the group too much. I need to calm this conversation down and get us all to talk about what's really bothering us. Maybe this outburst doesn't have anything to do with the tutoring program.

This example illustrates several important outcomes of mindful leadership. First, without attending to her feelings and behaviors in the moment, Gerri might have responded with an equally personal attack on John. Mindfulness makes it possible for the leader to more clearly understand the situation and craft a more productive response to it than responding emotionally. Second, mindfulness protects leaders against defining themselves based on other people's projections of them. Eleanor Roosevelt said, "No one can hurt you without your consent." Gerri can choose to let John's comment damage her perception of herself as a good president, or she can choose to believe that John's comment was distorted by his anger at the current situation. This does not mean that Gerri never responds to feedback from others—she did take a moment to observe that perhaps she needs to be less controlling—but that is quite different from defining herself as a "bad president" in response to John's feedback. Third, in this example, mindfulness made it possible for Gerri to understand John a little better. When people become frustrated with others, they often oversimplify the situation, assuming the other person is just a difficult or unreasonable person. In truth, most people are reasonable if one stops and makes the effort to understand their perspective on the issue.

CONSCIOUSNESS OF SELF IN IMPLEMENTING THE VALUES OF THE SCM

Each reader should assess his or her own readiness to engage in social change and to engage with others in socially responsible ways in all group experiences. St. Norbert College in Wisconsin used the SCM with both college students and in designing outreach leadership development programs for high school students. They found a number of students struggling to grasp the foundations of the SCM.

> Some are unable to articulate their values or share
> them with the group. One group of affluent high school
> students was unable to generate a list of societal issues
> that might be addressed by leadership. Another train-
> ing participant stated, "We have a good life here. Why
> do we need to change it?" These students struggled
> through the training, finding no meaning or purpose in
> it. (Langdon & Mathias, 2001, p. 142)

The educators observed that for many of these students, their "'readiness' for social change appeared to be correlated with their awareness of and direct experience with social ills" (p. 142). On the other hand, for many of the participants the values in the SCM were readily embraced and affirmed their own deeply held values. One college student shared, "I have been waiting all my life for these words [the core values of the SCM] to come together" (p. 142).

How aware are you of social change issues? What new consciousness of yourself have you developed to learn to lead within the SCM framework? How have you challenged yourself to work more effectively with others in group settings?

Outcalt, Faris, and McMahon (2001) share the story of undergraduate Sarah Hansen after she experienced the University of California Los Angeles Bruin Leaders program on the SCM. Sarah wrote:

The seminars that made me look at how I lived my life and how I operated in groups . . . were the most influential. And the messages parlayed at the seminars did not seem to take effect in my life until the C's that were most estranged from me became more and more blatantly obvious. My weaknesses were brought to my attention, and I was able to confront them head-on. And in the process, I came to understand myself better, learn what I wanted, and discover what it was that I wanted from myself and from the people around me. (p. 223)

Sarah reflected further on what she gained from learning about the SCM in this nonhierarchical leadership program:

I learned to speak freely with people who otherwise would have scared me silent. I realized that my contributions were valued and should not be muffled by fancy titles. I learned to assert myself and to be confident in myself, which was something that I thought I had mastered before. I did what I thought was impossible: I honed my leadership skills. As a result, I observe myself being more assertive and self-confident, yet aware of the circumstance and myself. I am less intimidated by positions and titles and have developed strong relationships with professors and TAs [teaching assistants]. (p. 223)

Sarah concluded, "I feel like I have truly evolved to become a more stable, cognizant, and happy individual" (p. 223).

CONNECTION TO THE OTHER C'S

Learning to use the social change model of leadership is an ongoing process of continual improvement, with gains in any particular C resulting in increased capacity to do the other C's. Having Consciousness of Self affects the ability to be Congruent and Committed. As people become more mindful of their behavior and more conscious of their values, principles, and preferred ways of being, they cannot help but be more aware of times when their actions are not Congruent with their inner truth. Self-awareness and occasional reflection on what is most important creates a sense of renewal to Commitment.

Consciousness of Self also positively affects the group C's. Groups can foster a more authentic Common Purpose when participants are clear about their personal goals and values for the group. When individuals are knowledgeable of the skills and perspectives they can contribute and are aware of how their personal style affects interactions with others, the group's ability to do Collaboration is greatly enhanced. When individuals in groups are able to practice mindfulness, their ability to monitor their emotional state in the moment makes Controversy with Civility a real possibility. Finally, students' efforts to be of service to their communities through Citizenship are more powerful when the work is an authentic reflection of the individual's personal values and convictions.

CONCLUSION

Social change typically does not happen at the individual level, yet individuals are involved in every aspect of societal change.

Feedback and reflection offer ways to develop a deeper understanding of how you understand your abilities, skills, and personal knowledge. With this stronger understanding, you can more effectively collaborate with others who have a similar purpose. Since the process of social change is values based, Chapter Ten discusses how to live in congruence with the values that were examined in this chapter.

DISCUSSION QUESTIONS

1. What are the personal values that guide how you interact in groups? How do you approach citizenship in your communities?

2. What strengths does your personal style bring to working in groups? In what ways does your style sometimes make group work challenging?

3. What form of reflection (for example, journaling, quiet time for thought, a discussion partner or group) would be most realistic for you to take up as a regular practice of examining who you are?

4. Do you seek feedback? How do you react when others give you feedback?

5. How would the group values of Collaboration, Common Purpose, and Controversy with Civility work differently if everyone in the group were able to practice mindfulness?

JOURNAL PROBES

On Becoming

Preeminent psychologist Carl Rogers (1961) said that people are always in a process of *becoming*. The first two journal probes are intended to help you reflect on how you see yourself becoming a leader for social change.

1. How are you becoming more conscious of self? Are you aware of being more mindful as well as more self-aware?

2. Can you remember a time when you had different values, personal style, skills, or aspirations than you do now?

Learning Through Experience

The ensemble that created the Social Change Model believed the best way to learn to do leadership was through experience and reflection. This involves challenging yourself to have new experiences that test your ability and awareness **and** to spend time thinking about what you have learned from that experience. The remaining journal probes are designed to maximize learning through experience by guiding your reflective journal writing through Kolb's (1981) four processes of experiential learning.

1. **Concrete Experience.** Describe a specific situation when you had an experience that changed or reinforced how you saw yourself. How were you defining yourself? What were

your values? Alternatively, describe a situation when you were able to be mindful. What happened? What details stand out to you? Briefly describe the situation, what you did, and how you felt.

2. **Reflective Observation.** Why did this situation have the outcome it did? What caused the situation to happen in the first place? What responses from yourself and others worked in this situation? Why was that effective? What did not work? Why?

3. **Abstract Conceptualization.** What lessons can you draw from this specific experience that could apply more generally? Given both your reflections and the information in this chapter, what would you do if a similar situation presented itself? What general guidelines would you create for handling future situations like this?

4. **Active Experimentation.** What opportunities might you seek out that would give you the chance to apply what you have learned here? How might you test the lessons or guidelines you created in #3 to see if they work?

APPLYING THE CASE STUDIES

Go back to Chapter Three for more context on each of these case studies. Apply the material covered in Chapter Nine to these cases.

Zoom In: Starving for Attention

In this case, Taylor has become involved in an organization that is challenging the university to pay its service workers a wage that better reflects the cost of living in the area. In addition to suggesting the group meet with campus workers who are affected by low wages, Taylor has suggested the organization plan a hunger strike as a backup plan, in case the university administration ignores their message.

Initially, Taylor is frustrated with the setback of having to discuss why members are disagreeing in the group about the direction of their plan. The meeting challenges Taylor to articulate why he designed the timeline for the administration in the way he did.

In reflecting on the meeting with some group members over dinner, one of Taylor's friends comments that "it was so cool to see that each side totally wants the same thing—a living wage—yet each person approaches that in a different way." This got Taylor thinking about his own beliefs and values, attitudes and emotions toward this issue. He started thinking about the frequent interactions he had been having with service staff around the university that other students on the campaign had not had. He considers how these interactions have shaped his values and sense of urgency in ways that differ from students who have only been learning about the living wage from books and lectures. While it is frustrating that the others students don't share his sense of urgency, he can see now that he would feel the way the other students do had he not had his own personal experiences.

Think About It

+ How can Taylor's awareness of his values and how he came to have them help him to be more effective in working with students who disagree with him?

+ How is his experience with the Living Wage Campaign shaping Taylor's beliefs?

+ How are Taylor's beliefs shaping the Living Wage Campaign?

Zoom In: Clear Haziness

In this case, you are the photography editor of the campus paper, *The Weekly*, where a tradition of hazing new members of the photography staff has been uncovered. Your values and style affect how you lead this group whether you are able to articulate them or not. Think about the beliefs, values, attitudes, and emotions that motivate you. How might they be challenged if you were in the position of this photography editor? How might you become more aware of your beliefs, values, attitudes, and emotions through reacting to this situation? Imagine going through this situation with a minimal sense of self versus reacting to this situation with a very established consciousness of self. How would both of these scenarios look different? What values or beliefs are being enacted by the senior photographers? How aware are they of those values?

References

Bordas, J. (2007). *Salsa, soul, and spirit: Leadership for a multicultural age.* San Francisco: Berrett-Koehler.

Buckingham, M., & Clifton, D. O. (2001). *Now, discover your strengths.* New York: Free Press.

Clifton, D. O., & Nelson, P. (1992). *Soar with your strengths.* New York: Delacorte.

Covey, S. R. (2004). *The 7 habits of highly effective people.* New York: Simon & Schuster.

DeBard, B.(2004). Millennials coming to college. In M. Coomes & B. Debard (Eds.), *Serving the millennial generation* (New Directions for Student Services no. 106, pp. 33–45). San Francisco: Jossey Bass.

Fry, L. W. (2003). Toward a theory of spiritual leadership. *Leadership Quarterly, 14,* 693–727.

Higher Education Research Institute [HERI]. (1996). *A social change model of leadership development* (Version III). Los Angeles: University of California Los Angeles, Higher Education Research Institute.

Kabat-Zinn, J. (2005). *Wherever you go there you are: Mindfulness meditation in everyday life.* New York: Hyperion.

Kolb, D. A. (1981). Learning styles and disciplinary differences. In A. W. Chickering & Associates (Eds.), *The modern American college: Responding to the new realities of diverse students and a changing society* (pp. 232–255). San Francisco: Jossey Bass.

Komives, S. R., Owen, J. E., Longerbeam, S., Mainella, F. C., & Osteen, L. (2005). Developing a leadership identity: A grounded theory. *Journal of College Student Development, 46,* 593–611.

Langdon, E. A., & Mathias, N. B. (2001). Designing experiential training sessions for the social change model of leadership development. In C. L. Outcalt, S. K. Faris, & K. N. McMahon (Eds.). *Developing non-hierarchical leadership on campus: Case studies and best practices in higher education* (pp. 139–147). Westport, CT: Greenwood.

Lee, R. J., & King, S. N. (2001). *Discovering the leader in you: A guide to realizing your personal leadership potential.* San Francisco: Jossey-Bass.

Luft, J. (1970) *Group processes: An introduction to group dynamics* (2nd ed.). Palo Alto, CA: National Press Books.

Outcalt, C. L., Faris, S. K., & McMahon, K. N. (2001). (Eds.). *Developing non-hierarchical leadership on campus: Case studies and best practices in higher education.* Westport, CT: Greenwood.

Northouse, P. G. (2007). *Leadership theory and practice* (4th ed.). Thousand Oaks, CA: Sage

Rogers, C. R. (1961). *On becoming a person: A therapist's view of psychotherapy.* Boston: Houghton Mifflin.

Rogers, J. (2005). Spirituality and leadership: The confluence of inner work and right action. *Concepts & Connections, 13*(2), 1–3.

Senge, P. M. (1990). *The fifth discipline.* New York: Doubleday/Currency.

CONGRUENCE

Tricia R. Shalka

> *Happiness is when what you think, what you say and*
> *what you do are in harmony.*
> MAHATMA GANDHI

Consider the harmony Gandhi is referring to in this quote. For congruent leaders, change agents, and citizens, what they do is an authentic reflection of who they are and what they believe. Their inner world of values, principles, and priorities matches their outer world through their decisions and actions, including the way they treat others. Leaders who are not congruent put on a façade. They act in ways that they think others want to see or that will make them more popular rather than in ways that represent who they really are.

Clearly, Congruence is very closely connected to Consciousness of Self. The work of being a person of congruence begins with the work of understanding oneself. This chapter represents the next step: making one's actions match that understanding of self. It is an easy concept to understand, but much more difficult to put into daily practice.

The ensemble that created the social change model defined congruence this way:

> Congruence refers to thinking, feeling, and behaving with consistency, genuineness, authenticity, and honesty toward others. Congruent persons are those whose actions are consistent with their most deeply held beliefs and convictions. Clearly, personal congruence and consciousness of self are interdependent.
>
> Developing a clear consciousness of self is a critical element in being congruent. Being clear about your values, beliefs, strengths, and limitations is especially important. It is, therefore, imperative to understand your most deeply felt values and beliefs before congruence can consciously develop. (Higher Education Research Institute [HERI], 1996, p. 36)

CHAPTER OVERVIEW

This chapter begins by describing what it means to be congruent with one's personal values. Some of the challenges that come with being a person of Congruence are considered. Finally, the role of congruent individuals within groups is explored.

KNOWING THE SELF

Being able to clearly articulate one's values and priorities is critical to leadership, but it is not enough. Congruence means acting in ways that reflect those values and priorities. One way that people act with congruence is by being sure that the things they claim are most important to them are the things that get most of their time and energy. If a student says that his or her education is a priority, then congruent action means resisting the temptation to spend the afternoon playing video games and instead investing that time in writing a research paper that is great rather than "good enough." Another way to act with congruence is to be guided by values in interactions with other people. Those who believe everyone should be treated equally will be as polite to the short-tempered neighbor as they are to the professor who is deciding whether to give them a B+ or an A. Other ways people act with congruence include keeping promises and admitting mistakes. Certain situations can make congruence with values more difficult than others. Being aware of the types of situations that make it more difficult to be congruent is an excellent way to continue to become more conscious of self.

The more people are aware of their personal values and philosophies, the more they are able to understand their own motivations to act. For example, a student who realizes that she values trying to understand different viewpoints may suddenly understand why she so cherished her time studying abroad. This experience provided opportunities to continually learn to see the world through another culture's lens. With this new awareness, she will be better equipped to find even more ways to practice this value, including exploring career options.

In their study of more than 200 change agents from diverse backgrounds and interests, Porras, Emery, and Thompson (2007) found that success in the long term has less to do with some of the stereotypical responses to success, such as honing in on the best idea or finding the best organizational structure to operate from, than it does with individuals understanding what is personally meaningful to them. "At some point in their lives, all of them found themselves on a collision course with a kind of need that generated a relentless, passionate conviction to change the way things are for the long run, often despite how society might judge them" (p. 4). What was consistent with all of these identified change agents was their personal commitment to work for the causes and purposes that were congruent with their fundamental core being.

Being congruent is not only something that anyone can do, it is something that everyone must do. The sorority member who challenges her sisters not to attend a party with a racist theme at their neighboring fraternity is being congruent with her values. An athlete who believes being involved in sports has been an invaluable experience might be a volunteer soccer coach for the Special Olympics to provide similar opportunities to others. The student who suggests a game of cards rather than a beer-chugging contest is being congruent with values around responsible drinking.

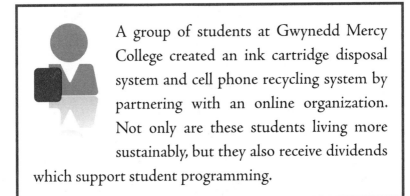

A group of students at Gwynedd Mercy College created an ink cartridge disposal system and cell phone recycling system by partnering with an online organization. Not only are these students living more sustainably, but they also receive dividends which support student programming.

As a person's awareness of core values grows, the desire to act consistently with those values grows as well. Assessing what matters and why it matters is fundamental to becoming a person of congruence. What one will and will not stand for are worth reflecting upon, as it will help determine the ways in which values and actions can meet. One's words and actions hold tremendous power in reflecting inner motivations. Nobel Peace Prize winner Kofi Annan articulated, "To live is to choose. But

Would someone who just met you be able to identify your values by observing your behavior? Do others see you as you see yourself? Does the amount of daily time and energy you allocate to school, family, community or your own personal growth reflect how much you value each of those things? In what situations is it hard to be congruent with values?

to choose well, you must know who you are and what you stand for, where you want to go and why you want to get there."

Congruent Content and Processes

A deep understanding of personal values leads to an awareness that provides the means of obtaining personal goals that are congruent with personal values. Rost (1993) refers to this as applying ethics to both the content and the process. *Content* refers to whether one's end goal or purpose is acceptable given one's morals and values. *Process* refers to how one goes about reaching that purpose, and often receives less attention than content. Is it enough for a leader's goal to be consistent with his personal values if he reaches it by being deceitful, aggressive, and dismissive to those who disagree? If the leader claims to be an inclusive decision maker it certainly would not be a congruent approach.

Mahatma Gandhi is widely regarded as an example of a leader whose content and processes were congruent with his beliefs. Gandhi helped the people of India attain independence from Great Britain by promoting a widespread practice of non-cooperation and nonviolent resistance (Isaacs, Alexander, Law, & Martin, 2000). Rather than resorting to using the violence and coercion their oppressors used, Gandhi inspired the peasants and farmers of India to resist using means that were incongruent with their cultural and spiritual values. The success of the people of India to fight power through nonviolent means inspired many other movements worldwide, including the civil rights movement in the United States.

Gandhi's life is a particularly extraordinary example of congruence, and it was something in which he deeply believed. In fact, despite his tireless efforts to inspire Indians to use nonviolent resistance, he was also quoted as saying, "It is better to be violent, if there is violence in our hearts, than to put on the cloak of nonviolence to cover impotence." This quote implies that Gandhi valued each person's congruence even more than he valued his method of nonviolent resistance.

Gandhi's ability to maintain his principles in the face of challenge was formed through smaller-scale challenges in his youth. For example, throughout his schooling, Gandhi struggled in his English courses, eventually mastering the language only after considerable strain and effort (Payne, 1969). One day his teacher gave his class several English vocabulary words to spell. When Gandhi was unable to properly spell the word *kettle* his teacher suggested that he should copy it from the student beside him. Although Gandhi bent to the teacher's authority, he was disturbed by the suggestion that he should use another student's work, violating his own moral code. He concluded his teacher was wrong, and the memory of that moment stayed with him for years (Payne).

What would it look like in the life of a college student to not only take action on issues that matter, but to take action in a way that is congruent with one's principles? Challenging campus administrators to respond to the needs of a particular group of students may be an end goal that is congruent with a student's values, but what about the means to reach that goal? Students need to ask themselves: What am I willing and not willing to do in order to be heard? Is it okay to break university policy? Is publicly embarrassing a campus official a strategy I'm willing to use? As a leader, will I use deceptive tactics in order to get what I want, or will I be transparent about my goals and open to learning about the administrators' perspective on the issue?

> Think back to when the content of a goal has seemed so important to you that you were willing to have a less than congruent process to reach it. Had you given the situation more thought and time, and perhaps included others in your pursuit of the goal, how could you have had congruent processes as well as content?

The Courage to Act Congruently

To be a person of congruence requires constant work. It is a continual process of being aware of one's intentions, actions, and motives. It requires that people challenge themselves to do the right thing even when it is not convenient. It may mean standing up to one's own friends, risking popularity, or putting oneself in serious danger of feeling foolish. It also requires being reflective of those experiences, in a way that is brutally honest about what went right and what went wrong. As Sarah Ban Breathnach (1995) reminds us, "When we live our lives authentically, we discover our true place in the world for the first time. But this self-knowledge is not easily acquired. It takes tenacity and daring to travel the darkest interior of one's self."

The lives of leaders are not meant to always be easy. People will be tested throughout their lives, but that should not keep them from trying to find a way to make their actions match their values. Elie Wiesel, a Holocaust survivor, has spent much of his life writing and talking about the horrific circumstances inflicted on millions of Jewish people under Nazi rule. Bearing witness to such an unimaginable trauma as the Holocaust is a sacred task with incredible difficulties attached. Wiesel acknowledges the impossibility of trying to communicate such horrors to those who have not experienced them personally, but he also feels compelled by something deep within him to try, regardless. "Could the wall be scaled? Could the reader be brought to the other side? I knew the answer to be No, and yet I also knew that No had to become Yes" (Wiesel, 1990, p. 15).

Porras, Emery, and Thompson (2007) describe a concept they call the "Mandela Effect," "when you can create enduring success not because you are perfect or lucky but because you have the courage to do what matters to you" (p. 2). The Mandela Effect derives its name from Nelson Mandela, who led the sometimes violent struggle against apartheid in South Africa. Following his release from 27 years in prison, he convinced those involved in the anti-apartheid movement to change from a hostile approach to one of reconciliation and healing. This was not easy. It was a risky proposition and took great political skill to convince his followers to change tactics. Rather than continue the anger that was tearing the country apart, his ability to convince the African National Congress to negotiate with South Africa's White elite resulted in the first multiracial democracy in South Africa. The lesson of the Mandela Effect is that the power to create lasting change results, in part, from a person's deepest values being reflected in his actions.

There is so much to be done in this world for those who would be change agents, one might wonder, "Where do I start?" For many, the answer to that question is, "Be congruent." Be congruent in small ways, every day, even when no one is looking, or, even when everyone is looking. As Harriet Beecher Stowe aptly noted, "To be really great in little things, to be truly noble and heroic in the insipid details of everyday life, is a virtue so rare as to be worthy of canonization" (cited in Ban Breathnach, 1995). People become courageous the same way they become congruent: by doing it. Every small act of courage makes the next act easier to do.

Taylor Wessels and Kate Baker, students at Miami University in Ohio, worked to make their campus more accessible for people with mobility disabilities by exploring student seating at hockey games and redesigning the campus tour route. As a result of their advocacy efforts, the two students are now part of a campus-wide committee examining accessibility issues for the entire community.

The Courage to Realize One's Potential

Congruence requires courage in part because of the risk taking involved in standing up for what one believes in. In some ways, however, it requires another kind of courage—the courage to believe in one's capabilities and potential. Sometimes, when people tell themselves they are not good enough or worthy enough to be the ones who stand up for what is right, they are acting from a lack of courage to be what they are capable of. In some ways, they are taking the easy way out, rather than acting on their true strength and potential. Marianne Williamson is an author and former head pastor of the Renaissance Unity Interfaith Spiritual Fellowship. Some of her writings address the issue of summoning the courage to believe in our abilities to be change agents. In her book, *A Return to Love: Reflections on the Principles of a Course in Miracles* (1996), Williamson articulates the level of courage it can take to overcome the fear of allowing our outer life to reflect the power of which our inner life is aware:

> Our deepest fear is not that we are inadequate. Our
> deepest fear is that we are powerful beyond measure.
> It is our light, not our darkness, that most frightens us.
> We ask ourselves, Who am I to be brilliant, gorgeous,
> talented, fabulous? Actually, who are you *not* to be? You
> are a child of God. Your playing small doesn't serve the
> world. There's nothing enlightened about shrinking so
> that other people won't feel insecure around you. We
> are all meant to shine, as children do. We were born to

make manifest the glory of God that is within us. It's not just in some of us; it's in everyone. And as we let our own light shine, we unconsciously give other people permission to do the same. As we're liberated from our own fear, our presence automatically liberates others. (pp. 190–191).

All people have the potential to shape their surroundings. Sometimes it is easier to look to others to do the right thing—perhaps to the elected leaders or to the outgoing, popular, or well-spoken leaders. However, true leadership comes from anywhere in the organization, and from any kind of personality. True leadership happens whenever an individual makes the decision to act congruently with the intention of making positive change (Komives et al., 2005; Sanborn, 2006). What is needed isn't popularity or charm, but a sense of core purpose and values and the courage to take action that is consistent with those.

Whether in big ways or in small ways, becoming a social change leader happens when people recognize that the thing that moves them is worth acting upon no matter the level of difficulty that may be associated. As Kouzes and Posner (2002) articulate, "Leadership begins with something that grabs hold of you and won't let go" (p. 52). *Discovering* what that "something" is constitutes the journey of Consciousness of Self. *Taking action* on that identified "something" is the journey of Congruence. *Sustaining* that action is the work of Commitment (see Chapter Eleven).

CONGRUENCE AND AUTHENTIC LEADERSHIP

Among the emerging approaches to leadership this decade is one that has been labeled "authentic leadership." The concept is grounded in the Greek philosophy, "To thine own self be true" (Avolio & Gardner, 2005). The theory itself focuses on many of the same concepts discussed here. Specifically, the theory concentrates on the development of individuals (both leaders and followers) who "are 'in tune' with their basic nature and clearly and accurately see themselves and their lives. Because fully functioning persons are unencumbered by others' expectations for them, they can make more sound personal choices" (Avolio & Gardner, pp. 319–329).

Chapter Nine, on Consciousness of Self, described not only the importance of awareness of one's values and principles, but also awareness of one's strengths, skills, personality, and leadership style. Authentic leadership speaks to leadership that is congruent with these aspects of the self as well as being congruent with one's values and principles. Leaders who are inauthentic act as they believe others expect them to act rather than being true to the person they already are. For example, although a student may be aware that she has a more introverted personality, she may think that others do not believe an introvert can do leadership. So, she does not think about the strengths that introversion can bring to leadership, such as the ability to truly listen to others without interrupting and a tendency to think things through carefully before speaking, rather than "thinking out loud." Instead she puts all her energy into trying to get others to think she is an extrovert. The group is not able to benefit from her true strengths, and since her attempt at extroversion is not real, the group does not benefit from the strengths that real extroverts bring to groups either.

According to Avolio and Gardner (2005), authentic leaders know both their strengths and their personalities and are aware of the benefits these things bring to the groups they are in. Authentic leaders know how they think through issues as well as how they feel about them, and their actions fall in line with their own ethical code. In their relationships with others, authentic leaders are transparent about their intentions, values, and priorities. They do not attempt to hide their stance on an issue until a popular opinion emerges. While they are open to questioning their assumptions and learning from the

Leading congruently means believing that who you are is enough—that the personality, values, strengths, and skills that you bring to the table are unique to you and will be useful to the group. While it is certainly a positive thing to try to add new skills and learn to see situations from different perspectives, trying to give others the impression that you are someone you're not is not productive. Think of a time when you tried to create the impression that you had a different personality or perspective than you really do. What situation prompted you to behave that way?

perspectives of others, they have enough strength in their own convictions to avoid hopping onto whatever bandwagon is trendy at the time.

Congruence and Character

Leading authentically is an ultimate example of character. Character is intricately connected to congruence. As Rushworth Kidder (1998) reminds us, "Character . . . is what you are in the dark, when no one's looking" (p. 181). Like congruence, character is composed of values and behavior (Kidder), as well as being true to oneself.

General Norman Schwarzkopf maintained that 95 percent of the failures in leadership in the twentieth century could be attributed to failures in character (Covey, 1998). It is easy to be enticed into thinking that leadership fails because of specific skills that are either not used or are used incorrectly. Schwarzkopf's observation, though, is an important one. As has been discussed in previous chapters, leadership is much deeper than a simple list of skills. In part, the ability to be a change agent comes through the alignment of one's values and behavior.

Character encompasses the expression of a person's uniqueness but also one's connection to a collective whole. Vartan Gregorian, a former president of Brown University, explains the Armenian word *nekaragir* as being similar to the English word *character*. According to Gregorian (1998),

> *Nekaragir* is the embodiment of one's own uniqueness as an individual: it embraces one's dignity, honor, and

independence and one's commitment to a corpus of
moral and social values that forge ties among individuals, families, ancestors, generations, and society and
that affirm our common humanity on the one hand
and our uniqueness on the other. (p. 109).

Implicit within Gregorian's quote is that character is the expression of one's core values with the understanding that they are
purposeful only in relation to others. "Character is one's commitment to a value system that transcends individual limitations and universalizes us" (Gregorian, p. 110). What matters
to each individual is important. What is perhaps even more
important is that person's ability to implement those core values in ways that acknowledge interdependence in this world.

BEING CONGRUENT IN GROUPS

Acting congruently may be tested when engaging with peers in
group settings. Being congruent when working with a group
presents an important challenge: what to do when one's own
values and principles are in conflict with the direction the
group is heading? As Paul Gam (2001) articulates, navigating
personal truths alongside the truths of others is an important
journey in the life of a leader:

Does it matter that I am right according to my own
truth? The answer is yes in that it is the source of my

strength and renewal to stay the course. It is my com-
pass and engine. However, the answer is also no, not if
I want to be a truly effective leader. When I chose to be
a leader, I thought I was electing an elevated stage of
influence and privilege. Little did I realize I was actually
forgoing an even playing field, and taking on an inferior
position. To be a true leader, it is insufficient only to
be right. It is not just those who share my truth whom
I aim to lead. It is all the others who do not share the
same needs or desires. To lead, I must see through their
eyes and walk in their shoes. I must recognize their
truths as if they were my very own. (p. 91)

The Social Change Model ensemble identified the need
to balance one's own values with the need to be inclusive of
other people's perspectives and values: "What of those times
when your values and beliefs are at odds with the ebb and flow
of the group, when your heart tells you that the group is heading in a wrong direction? How do you balance your need to be
congruent with your need to be a collaborative partner in the
decision-making process?" (HERI, 1996, p. 37).

Consider a prestigious honor society that is conducting
its annual new member selection process. One member, Shira,
observes that the applicants who know current members personally seem to be the only students who are being selected
for membership. She feels that students who move in different
social circles than the honor society officers should have an
equal chance at being selected for membership. She interrupts

the selection process and suggests a way to track applications by a number rather than by the applicant names, in order to make the selection anonymous and therefore based on the credentials on the application.

In this example, the group's process was in conflict with Shira's own values. In other cases, a congruent group member might be called upon to hold the group accountable to its own values. For example, the students in a community service organization who are planning a new service project may get into a debate about whether to host a carnival for a local elementary school or do a playground cleanup day including painting over graffiti on the school building. As the group begins to lean toward the carnival idea, talking about how fun it would be, José reminds everyone that the school principal talked about the mess in the playground as a real problem, adding:

> When we formed this group, we agreed that one of
> our guiding principles would always be that what the
> community needed would always dictate the work we
> would do. I know a carnival would be more fun to do,
> and you all know I hate painting. But are we here for
> the community or for ourselves?

Another issue related to being congruent in groups involves responding to group values that differ from one's own. For example, some people, because of either cultural background or individual personality preferences, may value starting meetings exactly on time. They feel it shows respect for members who are juggling busy schedules. Other people

Paige Haber was a member of the Arizona Blue Chip Program, a four-year leadership program at the University of Arizona. One of the core values that attracted Paige to the Blue Chip program is its focus on community service. Hoping to put that value into action, Paige talked with others about creating a service day for Blue Chip Program participants that would address needs in the greater Tucson community. The students identified relevant service projects, and hosted the first All Blue Chip Service Day with more than 125 student volunteers and 20 service sites. Even though Paige and her peers have graduated, in the Spring of 2008 the program hosted the fifth annual All Blue Chip Service Day.

may value a flexible starting time, to take advantage of the informal conversations that can occur while the group waits for everyone to arrive. The key in working with others and trying to be a person of congruence is in thinking broadly about values and intentions. As Komives, Lucas, and McMahon (2007) note, "Even when things are not what they ought to be, each of us can practice a personal philosophy of being the kind of person, leader, or participant we value" (p. 31).

Adaptive Leadership

Ronald Heifetz (1994) teaches leadership at the Kennedy School of Government at Harvard University. His approach to leadership focuses on helping people in organizations to be aware of when the group is being incongruent, and to help them learn how to "address conflicts in the values people hold, or to diminish the gap between the values people stand for and the reality they face" (p. 22). This approach to leadership is called *adaptive*, which is a term he uses to highlight the comparison between effective groups and the ability of organisms in nature to adapt to new situations. His example is the light-colored peppered moth that lived in England prior to the Industrial Revolution. On a lichen-covered tree trunk, this moth was practically invisible. The polluted air of the Industrial Revolution killed the lichens however, and the bare tree trunks underneath were quite dark. In time, through evolution, the peppered moths adapted to this new environment, and eventually they became darker in order to blend once again into the tree trunk. Heifetz describes organizations as needing to be similarly adaptive. Ways of operating that once worked may no longer be the most effective.

Consider as an example, a student advisory board that determines whether new student groups should be approved for recognition or not. The campus regulations state that student groups must have twenty members to be recognized by the institution. At issue is a new organization for Muslim women that has not been able to gain a full twenty members. Some members of the advisory board feel they should take it upon themselves to challenge the campus regulation. One member states, "For myself, I have gained so much from being able to connect with others like me through Black Student

Union. I think other students should have that opportunity too." Another member points out that the campus claims to value both diversity and helping all students feel welcome and at home, but this regulation would seem to run counter to that claim. "This new organization is particularly needed because there aren't many Muslim women on this campus. That in itself makes it harder for them to recruit enough members to qualify for recognition." Two members argue in favor of upholding the membership rule. They are concerned that by making exceptions, the group would be inserting subjectivity into a process that is meant to be objective. "An objective process is our only way to protect against some populations being given special favors or preferential treatment." Most board members, however, feel the meeting has already gone over its scheduled time. They feel that the regulation exists, and it is the board's role to determine if the applications meet the rule.

This example illustrates the many issues involved in adaptive leadership. How should the group reconcile the value of objectivity with the value of opportunities for interest groups with too few members? One board member was transparent about her personal values and experience playing a role in how she considered the problem, and another member pointed out the college's potentially conflicting values. Most of the board members respond the way many people do; they want to continue with normal operating procedures without questioning whether those procedures are appropriate given new circumstances. Heifetz (1994) describes this tendency to avoid addressing the incongruence as "work avoidance" (p. 37). Many people are resistant to having to do the work of dealing with the conflict and anxiety associated with a long-term struggle over competing values, particularly when a clear solution does not seem possible. Work avoidance can take many different forms: "Holding onto past assumptions, blaming authority, scapegoating, externalizing the enemy, denying the problem, jumping to conclusions, or finding a distracting issue may restore stability and feel less stressful than facing and taking responsibility for a complex challenge" (p. 37). Work avoidance is often subconscious rather than deliberate. In Heifetz's approach, the very essence of leadership is to identify when a group is being incongruent with either its own values or those of its environment, and helping that group face the incongruity head on.

CONNECTION TO THE OTHER C'S

Just as learning to do the other C's of the social change model enables a person to be Congruent, Congruence increases effectiveness in the other C's. Having Congruence in situations when one's values and principles are questioned improves Consciousness of Self. It also reinforces one's resolve to continue with Commitment.

The group C's are also positively affected by Congruence. Groups can foster more authentic Collaboration, Common

Purpose, and Controversy with Civility when participants are Congruent with their values and challenge others to be Congruent as well. Finally, Congruence with one's own values makes it possible to be more effective as a Citizen, particularly as one encounters others whose values differ.

CONCLUSION

Living one's values is an evolving process. At times, being a person of Congruence means standing alone for what one knows deep down must be done. There may very well be times when acting with congruence will not be the popular choice and when it will mean taking risks with which others will not agree. But, there are both internal and external rewards for those who are able to exhibit congruence. A sense of congruence with their fundamental beliefs gives people the courage to say, "I really don't think that joke is funny," or "Yes, I will help you. That project is important to me," or "No, I can't do that. I have to focus on a family issue right now," or "I cannot vote for this activity. It is demeaning to many people and is not worthy of our organization." There is a Hasidic saying: "Everyone should carefully observe which way his heart draws him, and then choose that way with all his strength." Making this choice is embracing congruence, which, as has been discussed here, is a fundamental part of being a leader and a change agent in everyday life.

DISCUSSION QUESTIONS

1. How do you build trust and credibility with yourself and with others? How does this look different if you are new to a group versus working with people you have collaborated with for an extended period of time?

2. How can the personal values of individual group members contribute to or be transformed into shared group values?

3. Is it possible to always be a person of congruence? In what kinds of situations is it more difficult?

4. How do you deal with an impasse? If several members in a group draw a "line in the sand," how do you help to move the group forward without group members feeling like they have to sacrifice their core values?

5. Suppose you begin to realize that your fundamental values are in stark opposition to those you are working with. How far should you bend for the good of the group? What is the threshold at which you should walk away from the group or project?

6. Can core values change? Are they fixed or flexible? Are values relative or absolute?

JOURNAL PROBES

On Becoming

Preeminent psychologist Carl Rogers (1961) said that people are always in a process of *becoming*. The first two journal probes are intended to help you reflect on how you see yourself becoming a leader for social change.

1. What has helped you become more congruent?

2. Can you remember a time when it was less important to you to be congruent than it is now? Is your situation different now or is it you that is different?

Learning Through Experience

The ensemble that created the Social Change Model believed the best way to learn to do leadership was through experience and reflection. This involves challenging yourself to have new experiences that test your ability and awareness **and** to spend time thinking about what you have learned from that experience. The remaining journal probes are designed to maximize learning through experience by guiding your reflective journal writing through Kolb's (1981) four processes of experiential learning.

1. **Concrete Experience.** Describe a specific situation when you had an experience that relates to being congruent as it has been described here. Were you congruent in a situation where it was difficult? Did you fail to be congruent? What happened? What details stand out to you? Describe briefly the situation, what you did and how you felt.

2. **Reflective Observation.** Why did this situation have the outcome it did? What caused the situation to happen in the first place? What responses from yourself and others

worked in this situation? Why was that effective? What did not work? Why?

3. **Abstract Conceptualization.** What lessons can you draw from this specific experience that could apply more generally? Given both your reflections and the information in this chapter, what would you do if a similar situation presented itself? What general guidelines would you create for handling future situations like this?

4. **Active Experimentation.** What opportunities might you seek out that would give you the chance to apply what you have learned here? How might you test the lessons or guidelines you created in #3 to see if they work?

APPLYING THE CASE STUDIES

Go back to Chapter Three for more context on each of these case studies. Apply the material covered in Chapter Ten to these cases.

Zoom In: Starving for Attention

In this case, Taylor has become involved in an organization that is challenging the university to pay its service workers a wage that better reflects the cost of living in the area. In addition to suggesting the group meet with campus workers who are affected by low wages, Taylor has suggested the organization plan a hunger strike as a backup plan, in case the university administration ignores their message.

The day has arrived for the organization to have their long-anticipated meeting with the university administration. The president of the group, Dan, presents to the administration the goals and values of their campaign. The budget implications of increasing the staff's pay to a living wage are presented as well. Finally, Taylor is to present the conclusion and the timeline the campaign is willing to give the administration to respond to the presented information. Instead of being overly critical, Taylor thoughtfully challenges the administration to act on their stated values. He reminds them that the university's mission statement emphasizes that the institution uphold and promote justice for all people in society. "In fact," says Taylor, "this administration often speaks publicly about their desire to see all students graduate and become change agents in the world. Well, I guess many of us here are just getting started a little early."

Taylor acknowledges in his conclusion that neither students nor administration are perfect and he understands why the payment structure may have been set up the way it was in the first place. However, he emphasizes his hope that now that it has been brought to their attention, this administration will remedy the inconsistency swiftly.

Think About It

+ Will Taylor's point about the university's incongruence with its values resonate with the campus administration?

+ What areas of institutional incongruence do you observe on your own campus?

Zoom In: Clear Haziness

In this case, you are the photography editor of the campus paper, *The Weekly*, where a tradition of hazing new members of the photography staff has been uncovered. Are the senior photographers acting incongruently in this case study? If so, how? As the photography editor, how would your acting congruently or incongruently affect the outcome of the situation? Would the change issue even be addressed if you choose not to act with congruence? Why or why not?

References

Avolio, B. J., & Gardner, W. L. (2005). Authentic leadership development: Getting to the root of positive forms of leadership. *The Leadership Quarterly (16)*, 315–338.

Ban Breathnach, S. (1995). *Simple abundance: A daybook of comfort and joy.* New York: Warner Books.

Covey, S. R. (1998). Growing great children. In M. S. Josephson & W. Hanson (Eds.), *The power of character: Prominent Americans talk about life, family, work, values, and more* (pp. 99–106). San Francisco: Jossey-Bass.

Gam, P. J. (2001). Recognizing others' truths. In W. K. Kellogg Foundation, *Leading from the heart: The passion to make a difference* (pp. 89–93). Battle Creek, MI: W. K. Kellogg Foundation.

Gregorian, V. (1998). Our moral DNA. In M. S. Josephson & W. Hanson (Eds.), *The power of character: Prominent Americans talk about life, family, work, values, and more* (pp. 109–115). San Francisco: Jossey-Bass.

Heifetz, R. A. (1994). *Leadership without easy answers.* Cambridge, MA: Harvard University Press.

Higher Education Research Institute [HERI]. (1996). *A social change model of leadership development* (Version III). Los Angeles: University of California Los Angeles, Higher Education Research Institute.

Isaacs, A., Alexander, F., Law, J., & Martin, E. (Eds.). (2000). *A dictionary of world history.* Oxford, UK: Oxford University Press.

Kidder, R. M. (1998). The eagle and the knapsack. In M. S. Josephson & W. Hanson (Eds.), *The power of character: Prominent Americans talk about life, family, work, values, and more* (pp. 181–198). San Francisco: Jossey-Bass.

Kolb, D. A. (1981). Learning styles and disciplinary differences. In A. W. Chickering & Associates (Eds.), *The modern American college: Responding to the new realities of diverse students and a changing society* (pp. 232–255). San Francisco: Jossey Bass.

Komives, S. R., Lucas, N., & McMahon, T. M. (2007). *Exploring leadership* (2nd ed.). San Francisco: Jossey-Bass.

Komives, S. R., Owen, J. E., Longerbeam, S., Mainella, F. C., & Osteen, L. (2005). Developing a leadership identity: A grounded theory. *Journal of College Student Development,46,* 593–611.

Kouzes, J. M., & Posner, B. Z. (2002). *The leadership challenge* (3rd ed.). San Francisco: Jossey-Bass.

Payne, R. (1969). *The life and death of Mahatma Gandhi.* New York: E. P. Dutton.

Porras, J., Emery, S., & Thompson, M. (2007). *Success built to last: Creating a life that matters.* Upper Saddle River, NJ: Wharton School Publishing.

Rogers, C. R. (1961). *On becoming a person: A therapist's view of psychotherapy.* Boston: Houghton Mifflin.

Rost, J. (1993). *Leadership for the twenty-first century.* Westport, CT: Praeger.

Sanborn, M. (2006). *You don't need a title to be a leader: How anyone, anywhere can make a positive difference.* Colorado Springs, CO: Waterbrook.

Wiesel, E. (1990). *From the kingdom of memory: Reminiscences.* New York: Summit.

Williamson, M. (1996). *A return to love: Reflections on the principles of a course in miracles.* New York: HarperPerennial.

COMMITMENT

Ashlee M. Kerkhoff and Daniel T. Ostick

Individual commitment to a group effort—that is what makes a team work, a company work, a society work, a civilization work.

VINCE LOMBARDI

I'm doing what I think I was put on this earth to do. And I'm really grateful to have something that I'm passionate about and that I think is profoundly important.

MARIAN WRIGHT EDELMAN

Commitment, the final individual C, pulls together the concepts of Consciousness of Self and Congruence and drives the group effort. In a sense, Commitment serves as the anchor for change, for without it all of the other C's cannot be integrated. The ensemble agreed that "some degree of commitment is essential to accomplish change" (Higher Education Research Institute [HERI], 1996, p. 40). In order for change to occur, one must commit to seeing personal values contributing to the collective effort through action.

CHAPTER OVERVIEW

This chapter explains the concept of Commitment and its role in the Social Change Model (SCM) of Leadership. It concludes with how to identify and sustain commitments and questions for reflection to explore personal commitments.

THE MEANING OF COMMITMENT

At the very core of Commitment is the individual and his or her innate passion or desire. This internal passion drives Commitment and requires active engagement.

 The ensemble defined commitment as:

Commitment implies intensity and duration. It requires a significant involvement and investment of one's self in the activity and its intended consequences. It is the energy that drives the collective effort and brings it to fruition. (HERI, 1996, p. 40)

True commitment comes from within and can be seen by intensity and desire. It does not feel forced or unnatural; rather, the desire to commit to something is compelled by intrinsic motivation, as if it could not be any other way. Commitment is the passion within that compels one to act to achieve a certain outcome. This individual commitment supplies the drive to advance the collective effort.

> Commitment requires a level of intensity and duration in relation to a person, idea, or activity. It requires a significant involvement and investment of self in the object of commitment and in the intended outcomes. It is the energy that drives the collective effort . . . and is essential to accomplishing change. It is the heart, the profound passion that drives one to action. (Astin, 1996, p. 6)

True commitment lies in one's deep, internal passions and motivations. A commitment is an intense desire and necessity to one's being. It sustains through challenges and is the motivation behind actions and seeing something to the end. This passion is not necessarily something that should or ought to be done, but rather something that needs to be done because of a personal drive to act. Authentic passion and commitment are not about having to do something because of some external pressure. It is about wanting and having to do something because one will not allow oneself *not* to do something. In *Common Fire: Lives of Commitment in a Complex World*, Parks Daloz, Keen, Keen, and Daloz Parks (1996) describe this urge as the double negative, as if one must respond to something internal and it would be a greater risk not to do something than to do something. "It's as simple as 'you can't *not* do it'" (Parks Daloz et al., p. 197). Commitment is not a sacrifice; it is a deep sense of fulfillment that seems essential and natural to one's being.

Having said that, it is important to know that commitment can be developed and can grow or fade over time. Everyone is capable of commitment and likely expresses the deep commitment explained here in one way or another. Commitment is "the quality that motivates the individual and supplies the energy and passion to sustain the collective effort" (Astin & Astin, 2000, p. 14). For societal change to happen, individuals must first see this quality of commitment as part of their being. Commitment can be seen as a competency that needs to be developed, and in developing this competency, "people not only affect their own level of commitment . . . but also affect the people around them" (Jaffe, Scott, & Tobe, 1994, p. 19). Commitment can be seen as the fuel that powers organizational drive.

THE ORIGINS OF COMMITMENT

> *Can you lead without knowing what you stand for? Yes,*
> *but you won't make lasting or far-reaching change. Values*
> *underlie the motivation of all great leadership.*
> ROBIN GERBER

For commitment to be authentic it must come from within, from motivation that is intrinsic in nature. While some energy may come from external factors and supports, energy really is sustained with an individual's own motivation and will. Think about it—is an individual more apt to devote herself to something if someone forces her or if she is acting on her own volition? There must be some sort of internalized passion that sustains an individual and motivates him or her to continue on.

Finding Personal Passion for Leadership

As Gerber (2002) suggested, "Finding your leadership passion or mission means being true to your nature. It means finding your 'certain thing'" (p. 88). Commitment that is truly authentic in nature builds congruence between values and actions. In Gerber's book, *Leadership the Eleanor Roosevelt Way*, the author offers eight lessons to finding leadership passion:

- Finding your leadership passion will depend on clarifying your values. Values motivate great leadership, underpin the actions that you take to build your leadership, and lead to lasting and transforming change.
- Leaders act within their environment. Every act of leadership based on your mission builds your capacity for making change on a larger and more transforming scale.
- Leaders can learn to develop their achievement motivation. This "need to achieve" means always challenging yourself, working to the highest standards, and overcoming obstacles in your way.
- Take the phrase "I can't" out of your vocabulary. Nobody succeeds by expecting to fail.

+ Take the word "should" out of your vocabulary. Act on your authentic wants and needs, not on those that are imposed by others.
+ Find like-minded people who share your passion. Learn from each other, and teach each other.
+ Finding your leadership passion will give you the perseverance, strength, and conviction to meet your goals.
+ Never give up your quest to find your leadership passion. (p. 104)

Finding this passion is an ongoing process, but it can help clarify values and commitment in a place where one finds deep personal gladness intersecting with a larger reality (Parks Daloz et al., 1996). This can be a very powerful experience that helps give direction and energy to an individual's commitments. "When you start living your leadership passion you will be swept forward . . . with the energy that comes from acting on authentic feelings and beliefs. You will carry a touchstone that gives you patience, persistence, conviction, and strength" (Gerber, p. 102). This process of discovering one's leadership passion can deepen commitment. As an individual develops a greater consciousness of self, he or she examines those deeply held convictions and takes strong examination of personal beliefs. Identifying that internal passion is a first step in being fully committed, and that passion can be intensified by action.

The Influence of Personal Experiences

For some, this passion and commitment is developed from personal experiences. Students who grew up in poverty may find a passion for helping others. A student who lost important family members at a young age may develop a commitment to mentoring others or tutoring children. A student who immigrated to the United States may use his or her personal experiences to advocate for new immigration laws. A student with a talent for music may find immense joy in promoting the arts in the local community, while a student with an inspiring and supportive teacher in high school may want to develop a mentor program that passes these lessons on to others. Looking

During her freshman year at the University of Wisconsin, Katrina Mijal participated in her very first alternative break trip to the Gulf Coast, where she helped rebuild homes damaged by the hurricanes in 2005. She did not know then how that trip would change her life in so many positive ways in the years to follow. She ended up taking a job offer at Wisconsin, where she now works to plan alternative break trips for other students. Katrina shares, "This job has taught me so much and it has also challenged me to become something I never saw myself as before: a leader."

back and reflecting upon struggles, successes, and important life events can provide clarity and focus to personal passion and help direct efforts to areas of personal importance.

Talking with others about one's passions and ideas for change, perhaps in a leadership course, can lead to strengthening commitments and linking with others for change. At the University of Southern California, Kyle had such an experience (Cherrey, Garbuio, & Isgar, 2001):

> In his first year, Kyle was involved in the Emerging Leadership Program. He utilized this experience to springboard into a plethora of co-curricular activities. Kyle was asked to represent the student's perspective on a variety of university initiatives including "Your Portfolio." During his junior year he approached the coordinator of the USC Volunteer Center about the feasibility of creating a Homelessness/Spirituality Alternative Spring Break Program. The Dean of Religious Life had also approached this same coordinator about a similar idea. The coordinator introduced Kyle to the Dean of Religious Life. They conducted a week of intense activities with the migrant worker community in the Monterey Bay area and continued the project back in Los Angeles with the Dome Village Project. (p. 116)

Individuals at the Emerging Leadership Program observed that "Kyle's leadership ability was challenged throughout this entire process. This experience encouraged him to question his values and beliefs constantly" (p. 116). Having shared his interests and passions with others, Kyle learned to follow through on his commitments and to find others to bring them to fruition.

External Factors That Influence Commitment

Though commitment originates within, it is important to recognize those external factors that can help support an individual's commitment or leadership passion. "No one can force a person to commit to something, but organizations and colleagues can create and support an environment that resonates with each individual's heart and passions" (Astin, 1996, p. 6). People can provide encouragement and support that gives an individual increased motivation. By having a supportive environment and being surrounded by others who share similar passions, individuals are encouraged in their own personal commitment. Additionally, affirmation and validation from a supportive environment can matter greatly in sustaining an individual's commitment (Parks Daloz et al., 1996).

Having a supportive environment can provide a strong vehicle for advancing commitment and the collective effort; however, other factors may just as equally drive an individual's commitment level. Such external factors, like financial incentives, recognition for work well done, and status also need to be identified as personal motivators for some individuals. Facing adversity or being challenged in one's passion can also deepen commitment. Debating with someone who shares a dissenting viewpoint or falling short on a goal, as examples, can be motivators that drive one to further develop that passion and recommit to a cause. Though challenges may be barriers or lead to questioning one's commitments, they can also give motivation to reignite the fire, reexamine one's passions, and reenergize. Identifying the range of external motivators that drive personal passion will help direct and sustain commitment.

To What Can People Be Committed?

Commitment and passion can take different forms depending on the individual and the context of the commitment. People can be committed to a wide variety of things, and one can demonstrate that commitment in many different ways. In fact, the passion that drives commitment can be directed toward many different things including people, ideas, and activities (Astin, 1996). While some may see commitment solely as involvement in on-campus clubs and organizations, there are many more ways to demonstrate one's commitment. Regardless of how one demonstrates his or her commitment, the importance of commitment lies in the content and focus of the commitment (Parks Daloz et al., 1996).

Ideas, beliefs, and values drive commitment. As Chapter Ten (Congruence) addresses, an individual must act in ways that align with personal beliefs and attitudes. In this way, people are able to be authentic and honest with others. Beliefs and values can focus around many areas that affect how people think, feel, and act. Family values, spirituality, or religion are often the source for people's most deeply held beliefs. A person also may have passion for a particular cause that reflects political or social beliefs. These causes could range from commitment to the rights of students on a college campus to a stance on abortion or the war in Iraq. Education may also be a cause to which one is committed, which could be as broad as issues of access to education to commitment to a particular academic discipline, such as a major concentration.

Oftentimes, commitment takes form through involvement in activities that relate to a person's values or beliefs. On a college campus, activities frequently take the form of clubs or cocurricular activities, service organizations, academic disciplines, athletics, or fine arts. Commitment can also be seen in larger organizations, such as a university or place of employment. Depending on the activity, one's values, and how one prioritizes those values, an individual may have varying levels of commitment to each of his or her involvements. This type of commitment may be seen as a deep loyalty to a mission of an activity or organization that leads a person to act on its behalf.

Parks Daloz et al. (1996) posit that there is another kind of commitment toward the common good, which may or may not overlap with some of the previously mentioned areas of commitment. Commitment that rests in the common good focuses primarily on how one can be a part of something larger than oneself. Committing to the common good means making a concerted effort to understand how one's individual experiences have an impact on the larger global community. People who are committed to the common good understand

John and Cheston Bailon grew up on a Navajo reservation in Shiprock, New Mexico. Soon after enrolling at Arizona State University, they decided to enlist in the Marine Corps and served in Operation Iraqi Freedom III in Al Anbar Province. Upon returning to ASU, John and Cheston were selected as Tillman Scholars and fulfilled their *Leadership Through Action*™ project, centered on their passion for their community and Native American culture. They saw that there were substantial problems on the reservation, including drugs, alcohol abuse, social issues, and the need for mentoring programs to help guide children toward a happy and healthy future. Since they began their work with the Dine (Navajo) reservation, they have worked with twelve at-risk students currently enrolled in high school. They have plans for the group to visit college campuses in the spring of 2009 with hopes of all twelve enrolling in college the following fall.

the complex interconnectedness of people and their individual behaviors and decisions. While this type of commitment may seem difficult to grasp or beyond an individual's reach, it can also be looked at as the Social Change Model's focus on the collective effort. The reality is that many, if not most, of our individual actions in some way have an impact on those around us. The recognition of being a part of a larger community can help deepen individual commitments, no longer acting on behalf of oneself, but rather understanding that personal actions influence the experiences of others.

COMMITMENT IN GROUPS

[One]'s mind, once stretched by a new idea, never regains its original dimension.
OLIVER WENDELL HOLMES

As quoted at the beginning of the chapter, Vince Lombardi, a celebrated American football coach, understood that the group effort comes from individual commitment. The combined energy of individuals is what provides a driving force for the productive functioning of a group. Banding together with others to form a collective commitment to a cause can strengthen efforts. Individuals who share similar passions, Commitments, and a Common Purpose are better able to see Collaboration at its best.

> Students at the University of Vermont employed strategic, well-coordinated activism through a silent, yet dramatic protest of the board of trustees to successfully get gender identity and expression included into the university's nondiscrimination statement.

In an ideal world, all groups would operate in such productive ways. However, as mentioned earlier, people have different levels of commitment and may demonstrate that in various ways. Though a group may share a common purpose, each individual has the power to affect the functioning of that group. If one member is not fully devoted to the group's intended outcomes, the other members of the group can feel that in group performance. Group members must be devoted not only to maintaining that internal motivation, but also to following through on tasks necessary to the group's operation. For example, a group member who is not present for group meetings hinders the productivity of the group, in that the individual is unable to contribute his or her energy and perspective to the effort. This can also be seen when a group member does not follow through on assigned tasks. Faltering commitment from one group member then puts added strain or work on other group members and can slow productivity and energy necessary to accomplish group goals.

An individual's level of commitment not only has an effect on group outcomes, but the group or object of commitment can also reinforce an individual's commitment. Positive experiences within a group can reinforce individual commitment and spur motivation. If a person in a group feels needed or that he or she can make a positive contribution, he or she is more likely to be committed to the efforts of the group. Success or positive change rewards commitment and can deepen it further.

Likewise, an unsupportive or unhealthy group environment can impede an individual's commitment and service to the group. While there may have been initial internal motivation that led an individual to serve, unsupportive environments may force an individual to question his or her service to that group. These types of situations pose a challenge to individuals who are deeply committed, because they may lead to a choice between remaining loyal to the group or taking care of their own needs.

IDENTIFYING COMMITMENT

So how can it be determined if true commitment is present? First, there must be intensity and a significant involvement and investment of oneself. This investment will likely be focused on one's strongest held beliefs or leadership passion. Having significant involvement may take considerable effort and time on the part of an individual, but this in turn can affect the collective effort and outcome. To identify commitment, one must have fully examined those internal motivators that have led to involvement. Further examination of those involvements can lend insight to the level of investment and commitment an individual has.

Quality Over Quantity

To be deeply committed, an individual must be able to fully realize internal passions and the actions needed to drive a collective effort. Deep commitment implies full, personal investment in a group's purpose and goals. In order to have deep commitment, it is important to examine all of one's involvements and the level of commitment needed and desired for each. In college, involvement can take many forms and it can be difficult to prioritize involvements and how to devote one's time. Though it may be tempting to be involved with many activities, being involved with a large number of activities can in fact decrease one's ability to be fully committed, as an individual's energy is spread thin. Too often, students look for more clubs and organizations to put on their résumés. But while a long list may be impressive to some, those involvements lack meaning and depth if students are unable to connect their experiences to their own personal values and motivation. If students cannot articulate experiences about what they have learned, how they have contributed, and how their goals are aligned with that of the group, then what value is this group providing to the individual? What value is the individual providing to the group? Individual commitment provides the significant involvement and investment of one's energy to answer these questions and provide fulfilling experiences.

SUSTAINING COMMITMENT

> *Perseverance is not a long race; it is many short races one after another.*
> WALTER ELLIOTT

Because of the intensity that is required of commitment, it can be challenging to sustain commitment over time. Overcommitment and conflicting commitments may affect achievement of outcomes. College students tend to have many conflicting commitments; demands on their time can be overwhelming. Demands often come from many sources during the college years, including academic coursework, employment, family or relationships, and activities. Though there is not always an easy solution to handling conflicting commitments, self-awareness and congruence are especially helpful in prioritizing and considering what is most personally important.

One of the personal challenges of strong commitment is burnout. Burnout can be considered a type of depression, conveying a "general sense of futility and hopelessness, a paralysis of word and deed—as if there is no point in talking or persisting with one's activities" (Coles, 1993, p. 137). Burnout can be battled partially through a reframing of its origins, recognizing that authenticity of commitment drives its sustainability. "It's not that we sustain a commitment; it's more that [we] are sustained by the commitment" (Parks Daloz et al., 1996, p. 196). Taking time to reexamine intrinsic motivators can provide a renewed sense of energy as the values and beliefs behind commitment present themselves once again.

Balanced self-renewal is crucial to sustaining commitment to values and organizations. Covey (1989), in *The 7 Habits of Highly Effective People*, refers to the principle of "sharpening the saw," an analogy of exercising and attending to the physical, mental, social and emotional, and spiritual dimensions of our nature. An individual's saw can be sharpened through exercise and nutrition, reading and journaling, offering service or empathy to others, and taking time for personal reflection. Each dimension influences and interacts with the others. "Any dimension that is neglected will create negative force field resistance that pushes against effectiveness and growth" (p. 303). Taking time for self-care can be crucial for sustaining the level of investment required for commitment.

Consider the student who has found her personal passion working with autistic children and has decided to begin a student organization dedicated to education, outreach, and advocacy. The student has profound commitment shaped by personal experience with autism within her family and hopes to engage other students in her pursuits. Her initial forays into advertising for members and generating interest have fallen flat. Her studies are demanding, and her part-time job does not leave a lot of room for outside activities. The idea of getting this organization up and running seems daunting, and every two steps forward are paired with a step back. It is easy to see how commitment could wane for this student. Commitment might be renewed and sustained by finding time to clear her head through exercise, taking time to remember where her passion comes from through visits or talks with family, taking personal time to volunteer in the community, and reframing each small success as a step in the right direction. Renewal and the sustainability of commitment take effort and do not happen unless the individual commits to sharpening her saw.

CONNECTION TO THE OTHER C'S

While the previous chapters have shown that the other C's build the capacity to have Commitment, having Commitment also enhances how people experience the other C's. Being committed to something, deeply and over time, helps people understand their values and personal style more deeply. Similarly, as unforeseen challenges come along, having Commitment puts one's ability to be Congruent to the test. Consciousness of Self emphasizes the importance of self-awareness. In order to be committed to something, an individual must first understand what it is that is motivating him or her. Further, because Commitment can only be fully realized with action, people must not only have an awareness of their values and beliefs, but they must also act in ways that demonstrate those values as part of who they are. And while commitment ultimately contributes to the collective effort, there is an element of commitment to the self that is crucial. (For a deeper discussion on the importance of gaining self-awareness, see Chapter Nine, Consciousness of Self.)

The group C's also clearly benefit from individual Commitment. When individuals are committed to each other through both success and challenges, their Collaborations, Common Purposes, and ability to handle Controversy with Civility are challenged again and again. The group can reach a point where it has been through so much together, and members know how to work together so well, that the group C's can be understood at a more complex level. The group values can go beyond having meaning in terms of one-time cases, like having a collaborative meeting, or working through one tough controversy. Long-term commitment means knowing what it feels like to be collaborative all year, and to have Common Purposes that get passed down from graduating seniors to first-year students. There is no way to understand the other C's at that level without having Commitment.

Finally, it is by demonstrating Commitment that a person can build the trusting relationships in the community that are needed to have active, effective Citizenship. Citizenship requires individuals to be deeply committed to the greater good. Commitment is sometimes the one element that makes the difference between a good idea that goes nowhere, and one that actually happens, and makes a real difference for one's campus, local community, state, country, or planet.

CONCLUSION

Commitment implies action—using personal passion and internal motivations to initiate some kind of change. Commitment strongly affects change because it drives action, which means that any individual can be a part of change. "Change starts with one person seeing a possibility and taking action on it. We must each look within ourselves for the wisdom, vision, the ability, and the motivation to change" (Jaffe, Scott, & Tobe, 1994, p. 252). When individuals find their leadership passion and are authentic in their commitments, they can find common purpose with others and create effective change. Though it may seem as though one individual cannot make a large impact, expressing individual commitment is the first step to moving others to create change. As Margaret Mead once said, "Never doubt that a small group of thoughtful, committed citizens can change the world; indeed, it's the only thing that ever has."

DISCUSSION QUESTIONS

Take a moment to consider your own personal commitments. How do you make meaning of your responses?

1. In general, what motivates you? (Helping others, recognition, money, making an impact, and so on.)

2. Where do your passions lie? What topics or social issues get you excited?

3. Think of times in your life when you have felt most focused, energized, or satisfied. What brought you this feeling? Are there themes that run across these examples (that is, all involve children, all involve working in groups, all resulted in large-scale change, all allowed me to display my creativity)?

4. If there was one job you would do for free, what would that be? What about the job is more important than pay to you?

5. When has your personal commitment and passion been influenced by other individuals or by a group? What lessons do you take from this?

6. When has your personal commitment led others to find purpose or passion toward a goal or cause?

7. What causes you to burn out or lose hope and direction? Are there themes across these examples?

8. What do you do to combat burnout? What actions have you taken to reflect upon your purpose?

JOURNAL PROBES

On Becoming

Preeminent psychologist Carl Rogers (1961) said that people are always in a process of *becoming*. The first two journal probes are intended to help you reflect on how you see yourself becoming a leader for social change.

1. How do you see yourself becoming more committed to the things that are important to you?

2. Can you remember a time when it was less important to you to have Commitment than it is now? How do you account for the difference?

Learning Through Experience

The ensemble that created the Social Change Model believed the best way to learn to do leadership was through experience

and reflection. This involves challenging yourself to have new experiences that test your ability and awareness **and** to spend time thinking about what you have learned from that experience. The remaining journal probes are designed to maximize learning through experience by guiding your reflective journal writing through Kolb's (1981) four processes of experiential learning.

1. **Concrete Experience.** Describe a specific situation when you had an experience that relates to commitment as it has been described here. Did you maintain commitment? Did you experience burnout or other obstacles? What happened? What details stand out to you? Describe briefly the situation, what you did and how you felt.

2. **Reflective Observation.** Why did this situation have the outcome it did? What caused the situation to happen in the first place? What responses from yourself and others worked in this situation? Why was that effective? What did not work? Why?

3. **Abstract Conceptualization.** What lessons can you draw from this specific experience that could apply more generally? Given both your reflections and the information in this chapter, what would you do if a similar situation presented itself? What general guidelines would you create for handling future situations like this?

4. **Active Experimentation.** What opportunities might you seek out that would give you the chance to apply what

you have learned here? How might you test the lessons or guidelines you created in #3 to see if they work?

APPLYING THE CASE STUDIES

Go back to Chapter Three for more context on each of these case studies. Apply the material covered in Chapter Eleven to these cases.

Zoom In: Starving for Attention

In this case, Taylor has become involved in an organization that is challenging the university to pay its service workers a wage that better reflects the cost of living in the area. In addition to suggesting the group meet with campus workers who are affected by low wages, Taylor has suggested the organization plan a hunger strike as a backup plan, in case the university administration ignores their message.

Despite organizing an excellent presentation to present at the meeting with the university administration, they have decided that at this time this type of budgetary shift cannot be made without adversely affecting the university's fiscal health. Many in the campaign are frustrated and feel defeated. However, Taylor's passion and energy to make a difference seems to be at an all-time high. He reminds the group that they never thought this would be an easy process and reminds all the members of the relationships they had all forged over the past several months with the various staff that are affected adversely by this policy. Though discouraged, group members feel as if they must go on and do more or they will not be promoting change based on all their resources.

Think About It

+ How does Commitment affect the other C's?

+ Is Commitment an element that primarily impacts change on the individual level or does it impact change more broadly?

+ How might Commitment make a difference in the potential varying outcomes of this campaign?

Zoom In: Clear Haziness

In this case, you are the photography editor of the campus paper, *The Weekly*, where a tradition of hazing new members of the photography staff has been uncovered. You are in the driver's seat to determine how you might react to this situation. In many ways, you could consider ignoring it and little would come of it, yet addressing it would mark the way for true socially responsible leadership that could set a profound example and better the experience of a number of students. How is this element interrelated with the other two elements on the individual level (Congruence and Consciousness of Self)? How might Commitment come from being involved in a situation such as this one?

How could one help others around them gain commitment to a collective effort?

References

Astin, A. W., & Astin, H. S. (2000). *Leadership reconsidered: Engaging higher education in social change*. Battle Creek, MI: W. K. Kellogg Foundation.

Astin, H. S. (1996, July/August). Leadership for social change. *About Campus, 1*(3), 4–10.

Cherrey, C., Garbuio, J. B., & Isgar, R. (2001). Common cause: Different routes. In C. L. Outcalt, S. K. Faris, & K. N. McMahon (Eds.), *Developing non-hierarchical leadership on campus: Case studies and best practices in higher education* (pp. 109–118). Westport, CT: Greenwood.

Coles, R. (1993). *The call of service: A witness to idealism*. Boston: Houghton Mifflin.

Covey, S. R. (1989). *The seven habits of highly effective people: Restoring the character ethic*. New York City: Simon & Schuster.

Gerber, R. (2002). *Leadership the Eleanor Roosevelt way: Timeless strategies from the first lady of courage*. New York City: Penguin.

Higher Education Research Institute [HERI]. (1996). *A social change model of leadership development* (Version III). Los Angeles: University of California Los Angeles, Higher Education Research Institute.

Jaffe, D. T., Scott, C. D., & Tobe, G. R. (1994). *Rekindling commitment: How to revitalize yourself, your work, and your organization*. San Francisco: Jossey-Bass.

Kolb, D. A. (1981). Learning styles and disciplinary differences. In A. W. Chickering & Associates (Eds.), *The modern American college: Responding to the new realities of diverse students and a changing society* (pp. 232–255). San Francisco: Jossey Bass.

Parks Daloz, L. A., Keen, C. H., Keen, J. P., & Daloz Parks, S. (1996). *Common fire: Lives of commitment in a complex world.* Boston: Beacon Press.

Rogers, C. R. (1961). *On becoming a person: A therapist's view of psycho-therapy.* Boston: Houghton Mifflin.

PART 5

Change
Agents

Leadership = conviction in action
DENNIS ROBERTS

Roberts (2007), a member of the Social Change Model (SCM) ensemble and author of *Deeper Learning in Leadership*, believes that "leadership = conviction in action" (p. 98). Putting all the C's together mobilizes individuals to understand themselves and come together in collaborative ways to accomplish social change.

One's commitments to action embody the very leadership the SCM values. Author Jennifer Louden (2008) calls this an "inner approach with outer impact." Indeed, *Leadership Reconsidered* authors (Astin & Astin, 2000) assert:

> Consistent with the notion that leadership is concerned with change, we view the "leader" basically as a **change agent**, i.e. "one who fosters change." Leaders, then, are not necessarily those who merely hold formal "leadership" positions; on the contrary, all people are potential leaders. (p. 8)

Roberts (2007) encourages students to

> start at a place where you can reasonably determine that you will be effective—think big and bold for a better future, constantly check your purposes and those of others on whom you rely, regenerate ideas and resources to continue your progress, and cherish the

opportunity to be a constant student of leadership and your own experience." (p. 129)

Become mindful of yourself engaging with others and hold high expectations that you can make a difference with your actions.

Today's times need new approaches to leadership. Former college president Lorraine Matusak (1996) observed, "Commitment, courage, caring service, collaboration, broad inclusive visionary thinking, and a deep respect for the gifts of others are the key concepts for the new breed of leader needed for the twenty-first century" (p. 12). Deciding that you will do something to make a difference to advance your commitments and that you will work with others in socially responsible ways is to be a change agent.

References

Astin, A. W., & Astin, H. S. (2000). *Leadership reconsidered: Engaging higher education in social change.* Battle Creek, MI: W. K. Kellogg Foundation.

Louden, J. (2008). Retrieved July 11, 2008 from http://www.selfgrowth.com/articles/Louden22.html.

Matusak, L. R. (1996). *Finding your voice: Learning to lead anywhere you want to make a difference.* San Francisco: Jossey-Bass.

Roberts, D. R. (2007). *Deeper learning in leadership: Helping college students find the potential within.* San Francisco: Jossey-Bass.

BECOMING A CHANGE AGENT

Marybeth J. Drechsler and William A. Jones, Jr.

My father always told me to persevere in times of adversity. As an individual and as part of a group, those words were a driving force in my work with the Residence Hall Association (RHA). As a group we were committed to making a difference through our individual talents, and we ensured that administrators heard the student voice. We did so by creating a stronger connection with University staff even if our constituents viewed this action as being compliant. We did this so that when policy changes were made they were made with consideration of the on-campus students' experience.

This connection was due in part to RHA members being on committees or sought out to consult on changes to housing, parking or dining policies, and in part to our own drive to make a difference for current and future residents. There are many opportunities on this campus to be involved which will impact our own lives as well as others. One just needs to step out there with an idea; take a chance, speak up and get involved.

A small group is just the beginning. Keep in mind that from a single person have come some of the greatest changes in our history. However, with a few people you have the ability to expand and reach further; strengthened by numbers and committed to the same effort. All you need is an idea to set the spark and perseverance to keep it afire.
STUDENT IN THE RESIDENCE HALL ASSOCIATION
AT THE UNIVERSITY OF MARYLAND

After learning about the Social Change Model of Leadership Development (SCM), some readers may be wondering, "Am I someone who can make change happen? What can my group do to benefit others? How can I go about creating this kind of leadership process in my group?" The student group context in the RHA example is only one type of environment in which change agents operate.

CHAPTER OVERVIEW

This final chapter challenges readers to ask, How can I apply the social change model as a guide for initiating and sustaining positive social change? This chapter discusses what a change agent is, how to recognize the change agent within oneself, how self-efficacy and empowerment affect how people learn to be change agents, and how people go about becoming change agents through experience and reflection. This chapter serves as a reprise and summary of the content of Chapters

Four through Eleven, much like the reprise in a musical score brings one back to the primary theme of the music.

WHAT IS A CHANGE AGENT?

In chemistry, the term *agent* refers to what the scientist adds to a solution to initiate a chemical reaction. The agent puts a chemical process in motion, transforming substances and making things happen. With this perspective in mind, one can envision a person in this agent role. Such a person assumes leadership responsibilities and serves as a catalyst for a group, stirring people up in an effort to make positive change occur. A chemist would not add just any substance into a solution in order to produce a reaction—that could be harmful or ineffective. In the same way, people who serve as change agents in their organizations or communities also must work in intentional ways to produce the desired effects.

In academic scholarship, management and organizational change theories have shaped the definition of a change agent. While earlier approaches focused on the traits and skills that are needed to foster change, emerging perspectives emphasize the values associated with creating social change. The change agent, from this definition, is a person committed to a dynamic leadership process, lifelong learning, and relationships (Osteen, 2003).

Becoming a change agent starts with recognizing there is a need for change (Higher Education Research Institute [HERI],

1996). The conditions present do not match up with what one believes to be truly important. The ensemble that authored the Social Change Model asserted, "This incongruence provides the impetus or 'calling' to action" (p. 70). For example, a student with Consciousness of Self may start to focus on her passion for the environment. Living on a campus that is largely powered by carbon-based energy may lead her to feel that she is not living in Congruence with her values and solidify her Commitment to creating change on her campus around this issue. Realizing groups can accomplish more than she can alone, she would Collaborate with others, addressing Controversy with Civility in order to take into account multiple perspectives on biofuels, wind and solar energy, and reducing current energy waste through more efficient light bulbs and heating and cooling systems. By reaching a Common Purpose, the group can get to work. Seeing themselves as Citizens of their campus and local community, the group will increase their effectiveness as they build partnerships with other groups in the community.

In order to work with others, change agents must create an atmosphere that is conducive for the Seven C's discussed in this book. Some may think that sounds like someone else's responsibility. Surely creating an environment for Collaboration and Congruence is an administrator's or teacher's job, isn't it? No, it is not. Any student can affect the culture of an organization, including colleges and universities. Change agents are already helping to shape their landscape simply by being aware of how their actions impact others, by including others in the process of change, setting a direction and defining responsibilities, by helping people develop the skills or attain the knowledge they need, by embracing the process of working with others, and by validating the importance of the change project (HERI, 1996).

EMPOWERMENT

A first step to becoming a change agent is to claim the personal empowerment to recognize oneself as a leader. This book and the SCM affirm that leadership is not based on a title; indeed one can be a change agent without being the person with the label of leader. *Self-empowerment is based on the personal awareness that you can be "a" leader even if you are not "the" leader* (Komives, Owen, Longerbeam, Mainella, & Osteen, 2005). One can think about a time when working in a group—whether it was a student group, for a group project, or at work—where the person in the leadership position was not the person actually making the difference within the group. Was it someone else who appeared to be the driving force? What was the source of that person's power? It is important to explore the concept of power and leadership self-efficacy further, as these two concepts can be driving influences on a student's sense of self-worth as a change agent.

The Concept of Power

The concept of power is subtly woven throughout the Social Change Model. Power is involved in understanding how individuals and groups accomplish change, how power differentials influence civic engagement and sense of citizenship, how individuals learn they have influence and are influenced by others, and how collaborative groups share power, particularly in nonhierarchical settings. Power is a complex and multifaceted concept and may best be examined at the end of this book as readers think about turning the SCM values into action as change agents.

Power can be a very positive concept, unless it is used for negative purposes. Power should be defined as the ability to make things happen. The idea of power has been skewed over the years to be synonymous with authority; seen as being held only by the person who holds the title in an organization. This type of power, or "legitimate power," is only one type of power described in the classic work by French and Raven (1959). Differentiating types of power helps one become conscious of the basis of power one exhibits or may be attributed to one. For example, in the French and Raven taxonomy, "expert power" refers to someone who holds advanced-level knowledge in a given area and may have influence or power within a group when using that expertise.

Imagine that the student government association at a school is creating a taskforce to combat illegal file-sharing on campus. One task that the group has to deal with is the selection of a new file-sharing system that provides legal methods of music downloads for students. The member of the committee who has advanced knowledge of the technical components surrounding different types of software and on which tool will

EXHIBIT 12.1 Types of Power

Type	Definition	Example
Referent Power	Power a person gains from the respect of others; a voluntary power bestowed upon you by those around you because of your personal attributes	Andrea is a really hard-working student employee. Whenever you need her she is always there for you as a valuable team member. Because of this trait, whenever Andrea is in need of help, the other team members are eager to become available for her as she was for them.
Legitimate Power	Power gained from a position of authority giving you the right to direct the actions of others	John was elected as the chair of the local residence hall community. Because of his position, the resident director presiding over that community usually turns to him as the voice of the residents.
Expert or Knowledge Power	Power gained from specialized knowledge, skill, or expertise in a given area	Kareem teaches an introductory English class. When he has a question regarding technology in the classroom, he always turns to Laura first as she is very adept at using a computer.
Reward Power	Power that comes from your ability to give something of value (material or otherwise) to someone else	Everyone is always respectful of Ethan, who is the administrative assistant to the director of the center because he controls who gets access to her calendar.
Coercive Power	Power to get others to do things by force, punishment, or threat of punishment	In order for Sarah to receive an A on the assignment, she must follow the teacher's guidelines even if it means she cannot be as creative as she really wants to be.
Connection Power	Power because of your relationship or friendship to a person who is important to someone else	Sometimes a lobbyist for a business will send gifts to the husband of a senator in order to make a positive impression on that government official.

(Continued)

EXHIBIT 12.1 Types of Power (Continued)

Type	Definition	Example
Power by Purpose	Power that is driven by a vision or goal and is characterized by sharing influence and a lessening of personal ego	Julie quickly refocuses the group conversation by appealing to the shared purpose developed by each of the group members.
Perceived Power	Power the person has to influence others	Because the teaching assistant has direct access to the instructor, many students work with him to bring about changes in the course.

Source: Adapted from French and Raven (1959).

provide the best services to the student body for a lower the cost has expert power. There are many different sources of power one can draw from.

Every person who is in relationship with others has some way of influencing others in a positive way. Whether through a skill set or our passion to get something accomplished, each one of us has the ability to make change regardless of if we have a leadership title or not. The person holding the leadership title is not the only person who can influence change. Every member of the group operates from some source of power.

Shared power is the basis of working collaboratively in the SCM. Individuals use their personal power to advance the Common Purpose of the group and realize there is enhanced ability to influence change when working together. When

Jordan Curry, finance major at Arizona State University (ASU), entered the *Leadership Through Action*™ program in the fall of 2006. Focusing on his vision of executing "Basketball Beyond the Barrio," he partnered with another member of the program, Terra Ganem, a sustainability major at ASU, to design a basketball camp for underprivileged kids in elementary school. With nearly 100 kids participating, the Tillman Scholars were able to provide cultural activities, artistic outlets, athletic training, and mentoring relationships to break interracial and cultural barriers for these children. "Basketball Beyond the Barrio" success continues today as it prepares for the third annual camp.

one is in a positional leadership role, this awareness of shared power leads to collaborative, participatory, shared leadership style.

LEADERSHIP SELF-EFFICACY

When individuals believe in their abilities to act as leaders, it is called having a sense of leadership self-efficacy (Bandura, 1995). Leadership self-efficacy has an impact on choices individuals make. If a person has confidence that she can make a difference with a cause or as a leader, she is more likely to get involved. What and how much a person will learn through leadership experiences is influenced by what she believes about her capabilities as a leader (Denzine, 1999). An individual is going to be able to achieve and perform well if she thinks she can do so. In general, the more people believe in their own capabilities, the more likely they will choose to act in leaderly ways, assume leadership roles, and handle the responsibilities of leadership with success.

According to social psychologist Albert Bandura (1995), people develop confidence in their capabilities to accomplish tasks through (1) *mastery experiences* where they are able to practice and to demonstrate skill development; (2) *vicarious experiences*, which involves seeing others like themselves, including peer role models, achieve desirable goals; (3) *social persuasion*, such as when others provide them with support and verbal affirmation of their abilities; and (4) awareness or mindfulness of their *psychological and emotional states* that help the deal with such emotions as anxiety about taking on leadership roles or engaging in challenging tasks.

A concrete mastery experience recently occurred for Sarah, a student who chaired a semiformal dance committee for her student organization. In her role, she had opportunities to coordinate the work of other people, schedule meetings, delegate tasks, and order supplies. Successfully navigating the challenges of dance planning helped Sarah "master" some important leadership skills. Now, imagine the dance committee member Anthony, who watched his chairperson tackle the many responsibilities associated with the event. Since he sees himself as being similar to Sarah in age and ability, Anthony vicariously developed a greater sense of leadership efficacy simply by watching her success. In addition, throughout the planning process, the dance committee members were repeatedly told that they could, indeed, pull off the dance. Their advisor used social persuasion to motivate their efforts by offering positive reinforcement, helping the students reframe past negative experiences, and showing students how their previous successes could help during challenging situations. Finally, the advisor and Sarah closely monitored committee members' emotional reactions or mental states. They provided the students with support with their dance-related tasks, in

Ingrid Easton, a student at Washington & Lee University, became engaged in social change as a result of a course she took on poverty. Through the Bonner Leader program, she received an internship in Washington, D.C., and discovered a program called Campus Kitchen Project, a national initiative that transforms leftover dining hall food into nourishing meals for community residents. Upon returning to W&L from her internship, Ingrid successfully started a chapter of the Campus Kitchen Project that has continued beyond her graduation.

order to help them manage stressful situations, particularly during exam times.

It is important to understand that a personal sense of self-efficacy is developing and that each group member can help others feel like they can "do leadership" for change as well. As people have successful mastery experiences that require them to think and act to manage situations, they build beliefs in their abilities. On the other hand, when people fail before they really learn to believe in themselves, the developing sense of self-efficacy is undermined. In addition, when people see social role models to whom they can relate accomplishing tasks, this may improve their own senses of self-efficacy. Also, encouraging and supportive verbal expressions by others sometimes help people believe they are capable of achieving or accomplishing things. People will try harder to succeed if they are boosted by the beliefs of others in their abilities. Finally, if people feel they can manage stress and other toxic emotions, they are better able to tackle their responsibilities. With these notions in mind, think about how, as a leader, you can use this

Student participants of the LeaderShape Institute at the University of Kansas have seen many of their visions come to reality. A few examples include a multicultural leadership retreat, a collaborative Habitat for Humanity fundraiser, and the building of a new campus recreation center.

information to work with others whether you are in a positional role or serving as an active member in the group.

COLLECTIVE EFFICACY

The Social Change Model emphasizes more than simply the individual's ability to influence change. It focuses on leadership from groups and within communities. In order to work toward change from beyond the personal standpoint, groups of people also must believe in their capacity collectively to influence social change for the common good.

Self-efficacy contributes to perceptions of collective efficacy (Denzine, 1999). A change agent both possesses a sense of personal efficacy for creating social change and an ability to build a sense of efficacy with others. Change agents need strong senses of self-efficacy when working in groups to create social change. "Bandura and Wood . . . observed that change leaders would use their self-efficacy to creatively surmount barriers and constraints. Their self-confidence motivated them, even in the presence of overwhelming difficulty, and they were determined to achieve their goals" (Pearlmutter, 1999, p. 7).

FACILITATING THE CHANGE PROCESS

Change agents are fundamentally responsible for facilitating the change process. As discussed in Chapter Four, change can be difficult for some people, so it is important to understand

The effectiveness of the group working together for change is evident in an example from the University of Nevada Las Vegas (Martin, 2001):

> While implementing the SCM is a continuous process, some visible benefits of adopting a non-hierarchical approach to leadership have been immediately evident at UNLV. . . . University officials have noticed that the way in which students approach issues of concern has changed. More and more, students reported that they see themselves in a partnership with the university administration. Rather than merely complaining about particular campus policies, many students attempted to work with other students and staff to make a change. For example, a student on the Task Force for an Inclusive and Just Campus Environment recently spearheaded the formation of the Public Safety Advisory Board to give students a voice regarding the policies and practices of the campus police department. (p. 107)

ways to be open and accepting of change. First, change agents must understand the context within which they are practicing leadership. Who are the people in the organization? How will they best work together and respond to change? Second, effective leadership means understanding, maintaining, and communicating core values of the group in times of change. As you think about being a change agent, be sure to remember what makes your group unique, where it is situated in the bigger system of other campus or community organizations, and what things are important to its members. Exhibit 12.2 describes other perspectives and competencies for change agents.

Change agents can use big picture perspectives to facilitate change within groups. Senge (1990) highlighted that the big picture is particularly relevant within what he called "learning organizations." The SCM advocates for groups and organizations to be dynamic settings where the diverse talents of members work toward change. These are environments "where people continually expand their capacity to create the results they truly desire, where new and expansive patterns

EXHIBIT 12.2 The Social Change Model Value of Change and Becoming a Change Agent

Value	A Change Agent Should Understand	A Change Agent Should Have	A Change Agent Should Demonstrate
Change	That change is a process Resistance at the community/ society, group, and individual levels Strategies for overcoming resistance	Positive perceptions of change Comfort with ambiguity and transition Self-confidence Patience A willingness to step outside of one's comfort zone	An ability to influence systems The creation of a sense of urgency An ability to articulate a change vision The willingness to take a risk to make a difference

of thinking are nurtured, where collective aspiration is set free, and where people are continually learning how to learn together" (p. 3).

In a learning organization, Senge (1990) put forth that leaders have important tasks that are frequently overlooked. He calls these roles those of *designers, stewards,* and *teachers.* According to Senge, these leaders "are responsible for building organizations where people continually expand their capabilities to understand complexity, clarify vision, and improve shared mental models—that is, they are responsible for learning"(p. 340). From this perspective, guiding and facilitating a change process means taking less authoritarian roles than those recommended by Kotter (1996) in Chapter Four. Those in the designer roles operate behind the scenes, implementing the vision, purpose, and core values (Senge). The steward is one who nurtures and cares for the vision of the organization, keeping its meaning transparent in how the group operates. The teacher "must be able to understand the systemic forces that shape change" (Senge, p. 356) and foster learning about the change for everyone else.

RELATIONSHIPS MATTER TO CHANGE AGENTS

A foundational principle for change agents is the recognition that relationships with other people are very important to the change initiative. Regardless of anyone's position within a group, all group members should consider the ways other people will be included or ways the group has an impact on them. Leadership that aims to create change is communal in its nature, requiring that people act in ways that are purposeful, ethical, empowering, inclusive, and process oriented (Komives, Lucas, & McMahon, 2007). Being ethical in one's decisions and actions, empowering others, including a variety of people and perspectives, and acting with a shared or common purpose are achieved by identifying methods and approaches that best fit each specific group.

INCORPORATING DIVERSE PEOPLE AND PERSPECTIVES

Everyone, at some point in time, has a great idea that would improve the way things within a group function. A lot of time might be spent planning every detail and incorporating various stakeholders; however, when it comes time to implement the change, obstacles arise pertaining to how others view the change. Being able to see the consequences of change from another person's perspective is an important concept in shaping change (Conner, 1992). Each group member may view things differently. Each group member may view things differently as demonstrated in the anecdote from Daryl Conner's *Managing at the Speed of Change*.

DIFFERING FRAMES OF REFERENCE: THE WOLF IN THE CLOSET

When my youngest son, Chase, was four years old, he watched a movie one night that frightened him. For several months, he was convinced that at night when he was alone in his room there was a wolf in the closet. All the explanation and conclusive evidence in the world could not convince him that there wasn't a wolf waiting to pounce on him once it was dark.

My wife and I turned on the lights, we went through the closet by item, and we sealed off the closet doors. Nothing mattered. He was sure that there was a wolf in the closet waiting to attack. No matter how often we invoked the adult reality of the situation, we could not change his perception that the wolf existed.

If we had attempted to manage Chase's fear the way most managers deal with the concerns of those affected by change, the only thing that we would have taught him was that we don't know what we're talking about. The typical approach is to say, "Look, there can't possibly be a wolf in the closet. I'm the dad, and dads know these things".

We resolved the situation by appealing to Chase's perceptions, tackling the problem within his frame of reference – not ours. Chase's godmother bought him a large paper-maché figure of Michelangelo (one of the Teenage Mutant Ninja turtles, of course, not the Renaissance painter and sculptor). With the Ninja Turtle safely guarding the closet, Chase no longer had to worry about the wolf. Any four-year-old knows that there isn't a wolf on the prowl that is a match for Michelangelo.

ON BECOMING A CHANGE AGENT

Leadership educator Laura Osteen (2003) studied students who were recognized as effective change agents. Her research revealed that the process of becoming a change agent involved the dual development of two important processes: *meaningful involvement* and *learning to lead change*. She describes each of these as dual tracks or rails as the "rollercoaster" of change. The first of these tracks is the involvement rail (see Exhibit 12.3).

EXHIBIT 12.3 Top View of the Involvement Category

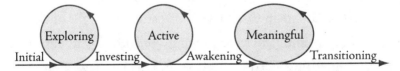

Source: From Osteen, L. (2003). Osteen, L.K. (2003). *Virtual rollercoasters: A grounded theory of undergraduate change agent development* (p. 90). Unpublished Doctoral dissertation. College Park: University of Maryland. ©Laura Osteen, Used with permission.

After getting on the involvement rail, students explored their personal interests and the organizations that fit with those interests. Mark found it important to observe in the initial stages of a transition to campus, "When you first come on . . . you observe for a while and see how things work" (p. 92). Students made decisions of how much time and energy they had to invest in organizations and got active in the select organizations that best fit their goals. The process of being active awakened them to expanding their roles in those organizations and having a meaningful experience with others in the organization toward their shared goals. Osteen observed that for Christine, meaningful involvement was "a combination of recognizing the changes that needed to occur and accepting responsibility for creating them" (p. 104). Christine described this shift as a change from, "'Okay, well somebody should do something about it,' and then, eventually you're like 'I can do something about it.' . . . This transitioning of 'somebody needs to' versus 'I need to'" (pp. 104–105). Eventually the students transitioned out of organizations as their goals changed or they graduated and left campus. In this transitioning process, Ebone was very concerned that the next person "in her shoes" continued support for the change vision.

The students in Osteen's (2003) study thought of change as "forward leaning, forward moving" (p. 108). Jawad described it as "something getting better" and Mark saw change as "enhancement of what the current system is" (p. 104). Osteen observed that "change was larger than their individual self interests" (p. 109). Most students could not imagine changing the entire world, so they "tailored the scope" of their change to their own campus (p. 128).

In becoming change agents, students found they needed to understand the focus of the change and embrace a commitment to change. Once embraced, students realized that change was inevitable and made a conscious choice to incorporate it into their lives. Christine stated, "It (change) just becomes a part of you" (Osteen, 2003, p. 120). In order to implement change, students needed to imagine what things would be like if the change occurred. Exhibit 12.4 illustrates the track of learning to lead change.

Liz saw communications as essential in the implementation stage of the process and that change starts when "someone plants a seed" leading the group to a good discussion. She observed, "Then you go into even arguments, and the process of hashing out" why the change is needed, what it will be, why you want it, and whether it will even work (Osteen, 2003, p. 131). Students knew mistakes were part of the process. Christine found mistakes effecting her confidence level at first, so "you kind of have to bounce back from it" and see that "you've made progress in some capacity" (Osteen, 2003, p. 136). Wisely, Christine reflected, "Now what can I learn from it and how can

EXHIBIT 12.4 Learning to Lead Change

Understanding ▶▶ Embracing ▶▶ Envisioning ▶▶ Implementing ▶▶ Evaluating ▶▶ Cycling

Source: From Osteen, L. (2003). Osteen, L.K. (2003). *Virtual rollercoasters: A grounded theory of undergraduate change agent development* (p. 108). Unpublished Doctoral dissertation. College Park: University of Maryland. ©Laura Osteen, Used with permission.

I do the process again but better this time? A change facilitator is always evolving because they do learn from process to process" (p. 136). These students felt the change process never ends, it just recycles. Rebecca said, "I don't know when [the change cycle] actually began. . . . As long as you realize that you're just somewhere in the continuum and it's a process and it never goes backwards" (p. 137). Exhibit 12.5 shows a top perspective with "five tiers between Involvement and Learning to Lead Change" and is also shown from a side perspective.

Engaging in more and more change activities eventually makes it a habit. Christine clearly saw the cycle of change, when she observed, "You see one thing, then you see another, and then you see another, and you start realizing all the different changes that can be made" (p. 137).

Through involvement in student organizations and the life of the campus, students progressively learned to lead change. Their development as change agents occurred through

How did you explore groups to become involved with when you came to campus? What led you to be more active in a select group? How did the process of being a member of a group lead you to understand and embrace a commitment to work toward change? What strengths did you bring to implementing a change initiative? What are your concerns about transitioning out of your groups?

EXHIBIT 12.5 Leading Change Through Involvement

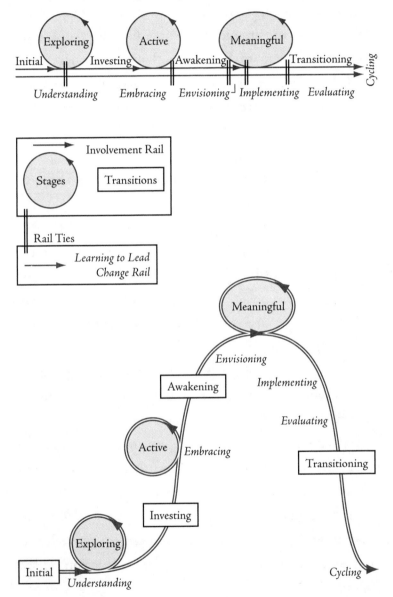

Source: From Osteen, L. (2003). Osteen, L.K. (2003). *Virtual rollercoasters: A grounded theory of undergraduate change agent development* (p. 139). Unpublished Doctoral dissertation. College Park: University of Maryland. ©Laura Osteen, Used with permission

interdependent experiences of meaningful involvement and implementing change. They all acknowledged the challenges of taking risks and frequently failing, noting it took a deep personal investment to face those challenges. These experiences led to a continual process of evaluating and transitioning into future organizations and visions for change.

BECOMING A CHANGE AGENT BY SHARPENING THE C'S

As has been mentioned in each chapter, the Seven C's of the Social Change Model represent leadership values that are in an ongoing state of being sharpened. None of them should be seen as an end goal, but as areas for continual improvement. Alexander Astin, one of the founding members of the ensemble that created the Social Change Model, cautioned against conceptualizing the Seven C's as a checklist (personal communication, 2007). People do not get proficient at one C so that they can move on to working on the next. As each chapter in this book has reinforced, improvement in any C builds the capacity for improvement in the other C's. The ensemble proposed a process of learning leadership that "moves from self-reflection to collaboration and then to more self-reflection, a continuous cycle of reflection followed by active learning that results in increased involvement and action" (HERI, 1996, p. 27).

Another reason the "checklist" perception of the model does not work is that, in practice, the C's are not learned one at a time. This book has described them in separate chapters in order to make their meaning clear. However, through actual experience and reflection, it is easier to understand how the C's reinforce each other all the time. An experience with controversy with civility can make the participants each reconsider their own congruence. A debate about common purpose may need to start by having members clarify how they see themselves as citizens.

Every time a person's experience deepens understanding of a particular C, that understanding in itself increases the person's capacity to understand even more. Professor Michael Coomes describes the phenomenon this way: the greater one's island of knowledge becomes, the greater the shore of wonder will be (personal communication, 1995). The more people know, the more they are exposed to how much more there is out there to know.

EXPERIENCE IS THE BEST TEACHER

The ensemble that created the Social Change Model believed that the best way to learn to be a change agent was through experience and reflection. The experience half of the equation refers to taking action, having the courage to get in there and try—testing out new skills, approaches, tactics, and ways of doing things. Reflection, on the other hand, refers to thinking about what happened, what can be learned from it, and how to go about it next time.

Many times, the idea of reflection conjures up images of solo activities like journaling or reminiscing. However, several members of the ensemble witnessed powerful experiences when students engaged in reflection together. When the members of a group all have access to the vocabulary of the Seven C's, they are able to talk about how they go about being a group using the model as a basis for reflection. For example, one group always allowed time to wrap up each meeting with a group reflection on how the meeting went, for example,

> We had some major controversy this week, and how does everyone feel about whether we did it with civility? Do we all feel our perspectives were given fair consideration? Does the conclusion we reached match our group's mission and our personal values? How could we go about facilitating these discussions in future meetings?

Group reflection can foster growth and learning in the individual and community C's as well as the group C's. When trusting and honest relationships are present, the feedback members can give each other on the individual C's can be invaluable to learning about being more effective in groups. For example, members can help each other identify how they approach problems differently based on personality traits or prior experiences. They can challenge each other on whether they are acting congruently, gently reminding each other when their actions do not seem congruent with the values they have described in the past.

Groups who engage with each other in these ways see themselves as change agents and leaders who are continually in the process of learning how to be more effective. They see each other as valuable resources for learning to be more effective. By engaging with each other, they gain practice in applying the skills of the Social Change Model, they gain role models as they observe each other in action and see what kinds of approaches seem to work, and they receive feedback from each other on their own behaviors. These kinds of opportunities make it possible for change agents to make the most of their leadership experiences. Everyone benefits from relationships like these, and the ensemble would encourage anyone learning to be a change agent to foster processes that allow individuals to learn to be more effective, and the group to learn to be more effective together.

 Several years ago, a group of students at Meredith College began a Breast Cancer Awareness Campaign. This has grown each year with new students continuing the legacy. Now the campaign sponsors an Awareness Week, raises money, and generates new support.

THE SOCIAL CHANGE MODEL IN ACTION

Several members of the ensemble who created the Social Change Model went on to use the model as they advised student groups and taught leadership courses. Through group reflections as well as individual journals, the students in these groups and courses (referred to here as the SCM students) were able to examine what the model feels like in action. The following sections of the chapter describe the experiences of students from these groups to provide examples of how the model can be used to maximize effectiveness and foster growth and development in becoming a leader. The exhibits provided can be used to identify areas that the reader can contribute to a group and where new skills and knowledge can be learned from others.

Community/Societal Values

As anyone knows who has been part of a movement, a demonstration, a campaign, or a strike, struggles undertaken for the most limited and prosaic goals have a way of opening the most profound and lyrical sense of possibility in their participants. To experience even briefly a movement's solidarity, equality, reciprocity, morality, collective and individual empowerment, reconciliation of individual and group, is to have a foretaste of the peaceable kingdom. Once we have experienced solidarity, we can never forget it. It may be short-lived, but its heady sensations remain. It may be still largely a dream, but we have experienced that dream. It may seem impossible, but we have looked into the face of its possibilities.

Ronald Aronson

By this point, it should be clear that there are many levels of citizenship. On a small scale, one is a member of a family, organizations, classes, study groups, work teams, residence halls, houses, or apartments. Then, one is a campus community member, resident of a municipality, person from a state or province, citizen of a country, and member of a global population. People can assert their citizenship in a number of places, depending on where they wish to initiate social change. In fact, citizenship comes with responsibilities at all of these levels.

When the SCM students reflected on their overall experiences, Citizenship was sometimes the value they realized they had not been thinking about as much as the others. Some saw it in hindsight as reflected in their purposeful efforts to

 A group of students at Gwynedd Mercy College created their own newspaper recycling system on campus and worked with the local high school to have the newspaper delivered to the proper recycling system.

build partnerships with other campus groups or people in the local community. Others found that thinking about citizenship gave the group's purpose meaning at a different level. The change they were able to work on seemed small in the grand scheme of things, but thinking of the Citizenship value helped them to see how it contributed to a larger effort that citizens all over the world are working toward.

Group Values

> *If you have come to help me you are wasting your time.*
> *But if you have come because your liberation is bound up*
> *with mine, then let us work together.*
> ABORIGINAL ACTIVISTS GROUP, QUEENSLAND

As with all the C's, the group values are only truly learned from experience. It is quite useful for groups to talk about having a Common Purpose, being Collaborative, and welcoming Controversy with Civility. However, the only way for groups to learn to do these things is by doing them and reflecting on how they went.

Groups that intentionally reflect the individual values of the social change model in their group processes are even more effective. "When commitment emanates from Consciousness of Self and Congruence, it can help shape the group's Common Purpose, provide the energy for working Collaboratively, and create the goal-oriented perspective needed for handling Controversy with Civility" (HERI, 1996, p. 44). Exhibit 12.7 clarifies the group values.

EXHIBIT 12.6 Community/Societal Value and Becoming a Change Agent

Value	A Change Agent Should Understand	A Change Agent Should Have	A Change Agent Should Demonstrate
Citizenship	Community building Collaboration Social responsibility and larger social issues Personal and community values Rights and responsibilities Social justice/equality	A belief in one's personal ability to make a difference Patience with self and others Optimism and pragmatism Appreciation for diversity Interdependent thinking Ethic of care Tolerance for ambiguity Respect for self and others	An ability to work with others across difference Reflective thought/meaning making Self-motivation/determination Diplomacy Empathy Creativity Critical thinking Interpersonal communication Ability to challenge assumptions Advocacy

The SCM students described found that Common Purpose served to both motivate and clarify the direction the group was headed in. One student commented that "once I was clear on the purpose, then my motivation grew" (p. 145). One student group found it helpful to begin each meeting by restating the group's goal and planned outcome. On at least one occasion, this practice helped the group catch a fairly major discrepancy between the plans they discussed and what their overall goal was supposed to be.

Journaling about Collaboration, one student wrote:

> The collaborative piece was hard for me at first because I had a picture in my head that a 'good manager' was directive. However, the collaborative piece comes much more naturally to me and once I realized that being collaborative could be more effective than being directive, I was much happier. (HERI, 1996, p. 151)

Many of the SCM students were most struck by how differently they worked together when they continually reflected as a group about their process of dealing with Controversy with Civility. Students in one such group learned to approach controversy by asking for clarification rather than proof. They were more open with each other when they had an understanding that conflict was an expected part of the process. It helped them see that "disagreement would be *part* of the process and not an indicator that there was something *wrong* with the process" (p. 151).

EXHIBIT 12.7 Group Values and Becoming a Change Agent

Value	A Change Agent Should Understand	A Change Agent Should Have	A Change Agent Should Demonstrate
Collaboration	Intercultural awareness and competence Personal values and perspectives That multiple perspectives are both efficient and educational	Belief that working together can generate win-win solutions and can generate greater results through collaboration Belief in the importance of trust and openness Willingness to put personal agendas aside to create shared visions	Synergistic and cross-cultural communication skills Trust and trusting relationships Shared ownership toward a Common Purpose
Common Purpose	How change occurs The role of mission, vision, and core values How groups function Personal core values	Commitment (to the group, the vision, and social responsibility) Visionary approach Inclusive attitude	An ability to identify goals Decision-making skills Creative thinking An ability to work with others and collaborate
Controversy with Civility	Attitudes, biases, and values Various communication styles Difference in viewpoints is inevitable and contributes to the leadership process	Civility and commitment Inclusive attitude Patience Purpose	Active listening skills Communication skills Engagement in dialogue An ability to mediate and negotiate

Consider the RHA example in the opening quotation of this chapter. The members (advocates) of the group collaborated not only with their student constituents (stakeholders) but also administrators (stakeholders) through committee work and meetings. In the event controversy arose over something, such as a mandated fee increase, all members knew it was not out of malice but rather because of common purpose to create the best possible environment for campus students. How did their shared understanding of each other help the collaborators work together to develop solutions without fear of the other not being genuine?

Individual Values

> *I am only one, but still I am one. I cannot do everything, but still I can do something. And because I cannot do everything, I will not refuse to do the something that I can do.*
> EDWARD EVERETT HALE

While classroom or workshop exercises aimed at exploring values and personal style are useful for creating the self-awareness upon which congruence and commitment are based, nothing truly improves the individual values of the Social Change Model like actually doing leadership with others. Heifetz (1994) said, "Values are shaped and refined by rubbing against real problems, and people interpret their problems according to the values they hold" (pp. 22–23). As noted in Exhibit 12.8, putting the individual values of Consciousness of Self, Congruence, and Commitment to the test through action with others, and reflecting on how it went is the most powerful way to learn to do them.

The SCM students found that awareness of values was a more important part of Consciousness of Self than they had anticipated it would be. In their reflection journals, they described how useful it was for each person to be aware of how his or her values and personal style were influencing interactions with others. Individual differences in lifestyle also emerged as an issue "only as the process went on did we realize that conflicting priorities caused us to work at different levels at different times" (HERI, 1996, p. 151). Referring to the "mindfulness" aspect of Consciousness of Self, at least one individual found that he was able to monitor his own emotional state during group interactions as he became, "aware of the ways in which my own frustration . . . was affecting other people" (p. 151).

The students found that other group members helped them learn about their own congruence, "not only were we honest about our beliefs but members challenged one another on how honest we were being" (HERI, 1996, p. 151). Some members were able to identify moments when they were not congruent and considered the reasons for it: "I chose not to say some things I felt important but that seemed OK at the time— maybe I valued harmony more than honesty" (p. 151).

Reflecting together, the students found that commitment manifested itself most when everyone came to meetings well prepared, having done all of their assigned independent tasks. One group discussion revealed that many students valued the group's commitment to the Social Change Model's leadership process as much as commitment to the task itself, "our commitment to the process of stopping every now and then to recap helped us through some would-be difficult moments" (HERI, 1996, p. 151).

 Return to the student in the Residence Hall Association whose quotation appeared at the beginning of this chapter. How did this student's own interests and values affect his commitment? In the groups you are involved with, how do members share with each other what their interests, values, or commitments are? How might this help foster members' Consciousness of Self, Congruence, and Commitment?

WHAT TO DO NEXT?

Social change agents can utilize any number of avenues to achieve their aspirations for making a difference. First, change agents should find or organize groups with purposes that align with their own commitments. Second, they should participate in goal-setting activities with those groups. This can help them identify projects within the organizations that interest them.

EXHIBIT 12.8 Individual Values and Becoming a Change Agent

Value	A Change Agent Should Understand	A Change Agent Should Have	A Change Agent Should Demonstrate
Consciousness of Self	Values of self and others How change happens Personal strengths and weaknesses	Self-confidence Openness to feedback Readiness for change Commitment to positive social change	Ability to reflect Meaning-making skills Ability to give and receive feedback Active listening skills
Congruence	Personal values That values are relative to an individual	Commitment to self-evaluation Respect for values different from one's own	Consistent action with personal values Ability to work toward a shared purpose in a group
Commitment	One's personal values and passion The Goals or target of a group That change is needed	Self-awareness of personal values Congruence with values and actions Passion Internal motivation Engaged attitude Discipline Energy to move motivation from "should" to "want"	Follow-through on commitments Engagement and involvement Devotion of time and energy Willful action

Third, if the change agent is in a position of power or authority, he or she should divide up responsibilities and delegate tasks to group members. By identifying the skills and knowledge needed for addressing the problem along with identifying who in the group possesses those skills, change agents can use individual strengths for the collective good (HERI, 1996). Another possible avenue for change agents to explore is what additional skills or knowledge must be acquired by members of the group working for a change (HERI).

GOING FORTH TO MAKE CHANGE

The most important part of being a change agent is connecting to an issue that matters. That is the one part of taking on leadership for social change that cannot be learned from a textbook. An educational program at St. Norbert College (Langdon & Mathias, 2001) was able to help students tap into an issue that mattered to them. Through this program, college students used the SCM to implement an SCM-based leadership development program for area high school students. The program included an opportunity to design a change intervention. One group of American Indian high school students decided to design their change intervention around cultural education. They were frustrated and angry at the ignorant questions and remarks about American Indians they heard from their White peers. The students "developed a plan to

I want to talk about responsibility, that's what I always want to talk about. I think an education imposes a responsibility on you, that is, you are responsible for the knowledge you have. You are responsible for examining its implications and for acting on it in the world. If one takes a course, for example on women writers, and has a sense that American women writers have shared a strong concern about the ways in which society as a whole has excluded certain groups or has ignored the suffering of others, then you have learned something. In other words, that body of knowledge has made you sensitive to those issues. If you walk out of that classroom without acting on those issues, then you are being irresponsible. If you see the society continuing to exclude or to ignore or to cause suffering in its own members and you do nothing to change it, then you are being irresponsible. And that does not mean getting on a soap box if you are not an orator, it does not mean organizing mass rallies if you are not an organizer; it means finding a way, your way, to make a difference and to act on the knowledge you have. It means finding a way to promote some kind of change. If you are not responsible for your knowledge, then what on earth have we been educating you for?

Annette Kolodny (as cited by Sundberg, 2004).

teach kindergartners about Native American traditions so when they became high school students themselves, they would be better educated. With a deeply personal experience of racism, and an expectation and belief they could change this, these students were able to develop a meaningful plan for change (p. 142). The high school staff observed a noticeable shift in all the student participants in the SCM program: "The transition from participant to change agent takes an active role in changing a situation for the common good" (p. 142).

Having a focus on social change means looking for things that need and deserve attention and by focusing energy on them better experiences are created for other people. In the words of Robert F. Kennedy (1966),

> It is from numberless diverse acts of courage and belief
> . . . that human history is thus shaped. Each time a
> [person] stands up for an ideal, or acts to improve the
> lot of others, or strikes out against injustice, he sends
> forth a tiny ripple of hope, and crossing each other
> from a million different centers of energy and daring,
> those ripples build a current which can sweep down the
> mightiest walls of oppression and resistance.

DISCUSSION QUESTIONS

1. Can you think of a type of power you may have demonstrated in the past that is not mentioned in this chapter?

2. What are some responsibilities you have to people who are still developing a sense of self-efficacy for leadership?

JOURNAL PROBES

On Becoming

Preeminent psychologist Carl Rogers (1961) said that people are always in a process of *becoming*. The first two journal probes are intended to help you reflect on how you see yourself becoming a leader for social change.

1. In what ways are you becoming more effective at being a change agent?

2. Can you remember a time when you thought about your role as a change agent differently than you do now? How is your current approach different from your approach then?

Learning Through Experience

The ensemble that created the Social Change Model believed the best way to learn to do leadership was through experience and reflection. This involves challenging yourself to have new experiences that test your ability and awareness **and** to spend time thinking about what you have learned from that experience. The remaining journal probes are designed to maximize learning through experience by guiding your reflective journal writing through Kolb's (1981) four processes of experiential learning.

1. **Concrete Experience.** Describe a specific situation when you were a change agent. What happened? What details stand out to you? Describe briefly the situation, what you did and how you felt.

2. **Reflective Observation.** Why did this situation have the outcome it did? What caused the situation to happen in the first place? What responses from yourself and others worked in this situation? Why was that effective? What did not work? Why?

3. **Abstract Conceptualization.** What lessons can you draw from this specific experience that could apply more generally? Given both your reflections and the information in this chapter, what would you do if a similar situation presented itself? What general guidelines would you create for handling future situations like this?

4. **Active Experimentation.** What opportunities might you seek out that would give you the chance to apply what you have learned here? How might you test the lessons or guidelines you created in #3 to see if they work?

APPLYING THE CASE STUDIES

Go back to Chapter Three for more contexts on each of these case studies. Apply the material covered in Chapter Twelve to these cases.

Zoom In: Starving for Attention

In this case, Taylor has become involved in an organization that is challenging the university to pay its service workers a wage that better reflects the cost of living in the area. In addition to suggesting the group meet with campus workers who are affected by low wages, Taylor suggested the organization plan a hunger strike as a backup plan, in case the university administration ignores their message.

After weeks of not making headway with the administration, Taylor proposes they move forward with the hunger strike. He and several students provide the rest of the group with more detailed plans. The plans include:

+ Information on university procedures regarding reserving space and other regulations to insure the organization is not violating any campus policies

+ Handouts to provide information about the issues to passersby and a statement of support for them to sign if they choose

+ A list of community members with medical expertise who are willing to be on-site to ensure the safety of the fasting students

+ Names of members of the local labor union who have already agreed to voice their support of the fast

Although most agree that Taylor has done a good job of addressing many of their concerns, some group members are still against the fast. Some feel it would create a campuswide debate over the appropriateness of the organization's actions, thereby distracting attention from the issue of wages for campus workers. Some group members just admit they are afraid of the consequences of fasting to the point of a hunger strike.

The group begins to consider other ways to bring more attention to their cause in order to pressure the administration to act. Several fresh ideas are raised by new group members, including the idea of a teach-in about the living wage issue. These new members talk about the advantages of press coverage, the opportunity to have panels of employees sharing their real-life stories, and bringing more faculty and graduate students to their cause by enlisting them in the teach-in.

As the meeting adjourns, the group members agree to remain committed to working for change and plan to weigh the pros and cons of a hunger strike along with looking further into other ideas that more members would be comfortable with. Although some are disappointed not to be taking immediate, dramatic action, they all know their common purpose remains strong and the group will continue with plans to take action of some kind in the near future.

Think About It

+ Think about Taylor's leadership throughout this entire case study. How would you characterize his leadership? How do his actions fit with your definition of leadership? Of a change agent? Was Taylor an extraordinary student, or was he an ordinary student with extraordinary passion and commitment for this cause?

+ How do you see these three levels of the Social Change Model, individual, group and community, being addressed throughout the case study? How do they interact with one another?

+ How does the Social Change Model address or explain the administration's philosophies and behaviors throughout this case study?

+ If you were a member of this group, what next steps would you support?

Zoom In: Clear Haziness

In this case, you are the photography editor of the campus paper, *The Weekly*, where a tradition of hazing new members of the photography staff has been uncovered. As the title of this case study suggests, there is some clear hazing behavior among the photography staff of *The Weekly*. However, as the title also suggests, hazing on college campuses often involves a lot of gray areas. It is sometimes masked by justifications of culture, tradition, and pride. Sometimes the very students being hazed claim to support the organization's process of assimilating members. Yet, hazing victimizes students and has the potential to put them in danger. As a socially responsible leader who is seeking to become a change agent, your role in intragroup leadership is critical. You can help an organization define its values, mission, and vision.

Based on how this chapter presents how to become a change agent, how might the photography editor truly be a change agent in this situation? How could the process of change agentry be realized in the dilemma with *The Weekly's* photographers? You could make the decision to engage this change issue and be a change agent or ignore it. How might either course of action impact *The Weekly*, the students on your campus, and other organizations on campus?

References

Aronson, R. (1995). *After Marxism.* New York: Guilford.

Bandura, A. (1995). *Self-efficacy in changing societies.* New York: Cambridge University Press.

Conner, D. R. (1992). *Managing at the speed of change: How resilient managers succeed and prosper where others fail.* New York: Villard.

Denzine, G. (1999). Personal and collective efficacy: Essential components of college students' leadership development. *Concepts & Connections, 8*(1), 1–5.

French, J., & Raven, B. (1959). The bases of social power. In D. Cartwright (Ed.), *Studies in social power* (pp. 150–167). Ann Arbor: University of Michigan Press.

Higher Education Research Institute [HERI]. (1996). *A social change model of leadership development* (Version III). Los Angeles: University of California Los Angeles, Higher Education Research Institute.

Kennedy, R. F. (1966, June). Day of affirmation speech. University of Cape Town, South Africa. Accessed on April 22, 2007, at http://www.rfkmemorial.org/lifevision/dayofaffirmation/.

Kolb, D. A. (1981). Learning styles and disciplinary differences. In A. W. Chickering & Associates (Eds.), *The modern American college: Responding to the new realities of diverse students and a changing society* (pp. 232–255). San Francisco: Jossey Bass.

Komives, S. R., Lucas, N., & McMahon, T. R. (2007). *Exploring leadership: For college students who want to make a difference* (2nd ed.). San Francisco: Jossey Bass.

Komives, S. R., Owen, J. E., Longerbeam, S., Mainella, F. C., & Osteen, L. (2005). Developing a leadership identity: A grounded theory. *Journal of College Student Development.46*, 593–611.

Kotter, J. (1996) *Leading change*. Boston: Harvard Business School Press.

Langdon, E. A., & Mathias, N. B. (2001). Designing experiential training sessions for the social change model of leadership development. In C. L. Outcalt, S. K. Faris, & K. N. McMahon (Eds.), *Developing non-hierarchical leadership on campus: Case studies and best practices in higher education* (pp. 139–147). Westport, CT: Greenwood.

Martin, S. B. (2001). The peer-to-peer context. In C. L. Outcalt, S. K. Faris, & K. N. McMahon (Eds.), *Developing non-hierarchical leadership on campus: Case studies and best practices in higher education* (pp. 99–108). Westport, CT: Greenwood.

Osteen, L. K. (2003). *Virtual rollercoasters: A grounded theory of undergraduate change agent development*. Unpublished doctoral dissertation. College Park: University of Maryland.

Pearlmutter, S. (1999). Leadership for change: The role of self-efficacy. *Concepts & Connections, 8*(1), 6–8.

Rogers, C. R. (1961). *On becoming a person: A therapist's view of psychotherapy*. Boston: Houghton Mifflin.

Senge, P.M. (1990). *The fifth discipline: The art and practice of the learning organization*. New York: Currency Doubleday.

Sundberg, D. (2004, August 30). Unions and responsibility. *Samizdat, 1*(2), 1.

EPILOGUE

Susan R. Komives and Wendy Wagner

> *This process of the good life is not, I am convinced, a life*
> *for the faint-hearted. It involves the stretching and grow-*
> *ing of becoming more and more of one's potentialities. It*
> *involves the courage to be. It means launching oneself fully*
> *into the stream of life.*
> CARL ROGERS

Convinced that college students want their lives to make a difference in the world, the Social Change Model of Leadership Development (SCM) provides a framework for engaging in life in ways that matter. Ensemble member and co-principal investigator of the project, Helen Astin (1996), shared a reflection from a group of University of California, Irvine students who implemented a social change project using the Seven C's of this model. She reported:

> Among their many observations about the model and its underlying values, one is of particular interest. They decided to add one more C to the list: *courage*. Their

> reasoning was, as one student stated, "You can see the need to change something but it takes courage to do it." They also felt that the power of the group inspired courage among them and helped them persist in achieving their common purpose. (p. 10)

She went on to reflect, "Too often, courage is characterized as a trait exclusive to heroes—people who are glamorized for their individual and essentially solitary efforts to rise above common achievements or to rescue the rest of us." She encourages students to "embrace another view of courage, a view that honors the power of individuals coming together to work for change, and yes, the bravery required to do this collaborative work" (p. 10).

The ensemble members, editors, and authors of this book applaud that you not only have the courage to make a difference with your life, but that above it all you *are* the difference. In implementing the values of the Social Change Model of Leadership Development, you live the commitments of this model through your very being.

Reference

Astin, H. S. (1996, July/August). Leadership for social change. *About Campus*, 4–10.

FURTHER READINGS

SOCIAL CHANGE MODEL OF LEADERSHIP DEVELOPMENT

Astin, A. W., & Astin, H. S. (2000). *Leadership reconsidered: Engaging higher education in social change.* Battle Creek, MI: W. K. Kellogg Foundation.

Astin, H. S. (1996, July/August). Leadership for social change. *About Campus*, 4–10.

Bonus-Hammarth, M. (1996). Developing social change agents: Leadership development for the '90s and beyond. *Concepts & Connections*, 4(2), 1, 3–4.

Higher Education Research Institute. (1996). *A social change model of leadership development* (Version III). Los Angeles: University of California Los Angeles Higher Education Research Institute.

Kezar, A. J., Carducci, R., & Contreras-McGavin, M. (2006). *Rethinking the "L" word in higher education: The revolution in research on leadership.* ASHE Higher Education Report (Vol. 31, no. 6). San Francisco: Jossey-Bass.

Komives, S. R. (2007). The social change model: A decade of practice and progress. *NASPA Leadership Exchange.* 5 (2), 23.

Komives, S. R., Dugan, J., Owen, J. E., Slack, C., & Wagner, W. (Eds.). (2006). *Handbook for student leadership programs*. College Park, MD: National Clearinghouse for Leadership Programs.

Komives, S. R., Lucas, N., & McMahon, T. (2007). *Exploring leadership: For college students who want to make a difference* (2nd ed.). San Francisco: Jossey Bass.

Outcault, C. L., Faris, S. K., & McMahon, K. N. (Eds.). (2001). *Developing non-hierarchical leadership on campus: Case studies and best practices in higher education*. Westport, CT: Greenwood.

Outcalt, C. L., Faris, S. K., McMahon, K. N., Tahtakran, P. M., & Noll, C. B. (2001). A leadership approach for the new millennium: A case study of UCLA's Bruin Leaders Project. *NASPA Journal, 38*(2), 178–188.

Roberts, D. R. (2007). *Deeper learning in leadership: Helping college students find the potential within*. San Francisco: Jossey-Bass.

Seemiller, C. (2006). Impacting social change through service learning in an introductory course. *Journal of Leadership Education, 5*(2), 41–49.

St. Norbert College. (1996). *Citizens of change: The application guidebook*. College Park, MD: National Clearinghouse for Leadership Programs.

Wagner, W. (2006). The social change model of leadership: A brief overview. *Concepts & Connections, 15*(1), 9.

RESEARCH ON THE SOCIAL CHANGE MODEL FOR LEADERSHIP DEVELOPMENT

Dugan, J. P. (2006a). Explorations using the social change model: Leadership development among college men and women. *Journal of College Student Development, 47*, 217–225.

Dugan, J. P. (2006b). Involvement and leadership: A descriptive analysis of socially responsible leadership. *Journal of College Student Development, 47*, 335–343.

Dugan, J. P. (2008). Exploring relationships between fraternity and sorority membership and socially responsible leadership. *Oracle: Journal of the Association of Fraternity Advisors, 3*(2), 16–25.

Dugan, J. P., Garland, J., Jacoby, B., & Gasiorski, A. (2008). Understanding commuter student self-efficacy for leadership: A within-group analysis. *NASPA Journal, 45*, 282–310.

Dugan, J. P., Gehrke, S. J., Komives, S. R., & Martinez, M. (2007). Student programmers and leadership development: Select findings from the Multi-Institutional Study of Leadership. *Campus Activities Programming, 40*(1), 46–49.

Dugan, J. P., & Komives, S. R. (2007). *Developing leadership capacity in college students: Findings from a national study.* College Park, MD: National Clearinghouse for Leadership Programs.

Dugan, J. P., Komives, S. R., & Segar, T. (2008). College student capacity for socially responsible leadership: Understanding norms and influences of race, gender, and sexual orientation. *NASPA Journal, 45*, 475–500.

Ricketts, K. G., Bruce, J. A., & Ewing, J. C. (2008). How today's undergraduate students see themselves social responsible leaders. *Journal of Leadership Education, 7*(1), 24–42.

Tyree, T. M. (1998). Designing an instrument to measure the socially responsible leadership using the social change model of leadership development. *Dissertation Abstracts International, 59* (06), 1945. (AAT 9836493)

Concepts & Connections (a publication of the National Clearinghouse for Leadership Programs: available at www.nclp.umd.edu) featured the Multi-Institutional Study of Leadership (MSL) in its 2006–2007 volume.

Vol. 15 (1) MSL methods, MSL descriptive findings, the Social Change Model

Vol. 15 (2) Identity-based MSL findings (e.g., gender, sexual orientation, race)

Vol. 15 (3) Training and Curricular Findings

Vol. 15 (4) Co-curricular findings (e.g., service, mentoring, involvement, discussions of sociopolitical issues)

CREDITS

p. 134, Common Causes of Resistance: Original Copyright © Davies-Black Publishing, 1998. Copyright © 2005, Kenneth E. Hultman. Reprinted with permission of the author.

pp. 210–211, list from Johnson and Johnson: David W. Johnson & Frank P. Johnson, *Joining Together Theory and Group Skills*, 9/e. Published by Allyn and Bacon/Merrell Education, Boston, MA. Copyright © 2006 by Pearson Education.

p. 220, Be Willing to Understand: Reprinted with the permission of Simon & Schuster, Inc. from *The Magic of Conflict: Turning a Life of Work into a Work of Art* by Thomas F. Crum. Copyright © 1987 by Thomas Crum.

p. 250, list from Johnson and Johnson: David W. Johnson & Frank P. Johnson, *Joining Together Theory and Group Skills*, 9/e. Published by Allyn and Bacon/Merrell Education, Boston, MA. Copyright © 2006 by Pearson Education. Adapted by permission of the publisher.

pp. 369–370, list from Gerber: *Leadership the Eleanor Roosevelt Way* by Robin Gerber, copyright © 2002 by Robin Gerber. Used by permission of Portfolio, an imprint of Penguin Group (USA) Inc.

pp. 414–415, Differing Frames of References: From *Managing at the Speed of Change* by Daryl R. Conner, copyright ©1993 by O. D. Resources, Inc. Used by permission of Villard Books, a division of Random House, Inc.

INDEX